Advance Praise for ***Get the H***

"Erin has a brilliant way of explaining, step-by-step, how to radically shift your finances for the better."

—Peter Mallouk, President, Creative Planning

"Erin understands that wealth is about so much more than money. It is about creating, living, and leaving a legacy of love and happiness."

—W. Brett Wilson, Father, Entrepreneur, and Philanthropist

"With a welcomed irreverence and absolutely no judgment, Erin shows us all of the nuanced, messy, and dysfunctional ways we stumble and fall into debt. But then! Then she shows us how to get up and stand tall before we kick, claw, and fight our way out of it. It's you against your debt. Read this book if you're ready for your gloves to come off."

—Jesse Mecham, Founder of You Need A Budget (YNAB)

"Weaving personal stories, random hilarity, and brilliant insights, Erin Skye Kelly has given you everything you need to change your life. The framework presented in this book provides easy, hilarious, and specific step-by-step instructions for you to take action immediately, reclaim your power, and free yourself from the financial stress that holds you down. This is the funniest, most practical, most readable, and relatable book about money that I've ever read."

—Dr. Jeremy Goldberg, Author, *It'll be Okay And You Will Be Too*

"As soon as I began reading Erin's book, I immediately felt calmed by her personal understanding and experience of debt. Her book highlights and offers practical solutions to some of the biggest challenges that come up around money and debt. I loved Erin's brilliant and fierce sense of humor combined with her endless encouragement that shined through on each and every page. I felt hopeful and guided in the fullest way. I couldn't recommend this book more for anyone that is struggling to get out of debt."e

—Silvy Khoucasian, Relationship Coach

"Erin Skye Kelly is the greatest thing that ever happened to my potential as I didn't even know the path to get where I am today.... She helped me shape that path. Not only did she speak unlimited possibility into me, she also has constantly celebrated my wins and challenged me to always go to my edge."

—Mark Groves, Human Connection Specialist
and Founder of Create the Love

GET the HELL OUT OF DEBT

The Proven 3-Phase Method That Will Radically Shift Your Relationship to Money

ERIN SKYE KELLY

A POST HILL PRESS BOOK
ISBN: 978-1-64293-955-2
ISBN (eBook): 978-1-64293-956-9

Get the Hell Out of Debt:
The Proven 3-Phase Method That Will Radically Shift Your Relationship to Money

Cover art by Cody Corcoran

Post Hill Press
New York • Nashville
posthillpress.com

Published in the United States of America
1 2 3 4 5 6 7 8 9 10

Dedication

This book is dedicated to Jidi.

I was a teenager when I told my grandfather I was thinking of becoming a broadcaster. He paused, and then pointedly said, "*That's nice kiddo, but you are a girl and one day you will be fat, middle-aged, and ugly, and no one will want you on TV.*"

Now this sounds rather harsh, and yes, it smarted.

But it was my boorish Lebanese grandfather's 1990-ish way of saying, "*If you want to have a career you must not leave its success up to someone else's decision-making.*"

So, I started investing in real estate and businesses on the side, and plunged into my first long-term relationship—with debt.

It would not have mattered in the end what I had done with my life or how well I'd done it. It would not have mattered to my grandfather that I ended up failing spectacularly, if only he'd lived to see it. It would not have mattered that I worked tirelessly to recover. It would not matter that eventually I would abandon this idea of needing a backup plan and learn to commit myself fully to accomplish more than my teenage self ever dreamed of.

His eyes always lit up when I entered the room. He was unfussed about whether people liked him or agreed with his decisions. He was simultaneously horribly inappropriate and remarkably progressive. He loved me with his whole heart, and I felt it every day.

My wish for you, dear reader, is that you always have someone whose eyes light up when you enter the room. And if you don't, know that I am excited you are here, for the journey you are taking, and I believe in you, even during those times you are finding it hard to believe in yourself. The fact that you are here makes my eyes light up.

I miss you, Jidi. And in spite of how far we still have to go, you would not believe the kinds of awesome things women get to do now.

Author's Note

Pre-2020, you'd be hard-pressed to find a financial expert who didn't give conservative advice about having three to six months of expenses in a savings account for emergencies.

And then the pandemic hit to test that.

Having substantial savings is definitely helpful in pandemic times. But as you likely figured out, six months of expenses wouldn't have been enough.

One of the most frustrating things about pandemic life is how average humans were financially shamed for not having six months of savings on hand, and yet businesses that did not have cash on hand are now getting massive forgivable loans and corporate bailouts. The government has convinced us that millions of hard-working people are actually lazy in order to take the focus off the few hundred people who are truly greedy.

The whole system is a mess. And if you look closely at how it is designed, you can quickly see that if you carry consumer debt and you feel trapped in the cycle of minimum payments and maxed out accounts, you are right where the system wants you to be.

I want you to create your own personal economy so you are less at the mercy of what is happening around you and more in control of the flow of money in and out of your life.

When we carry consumer debt, we are in a position of weakness. Debt causes us to stay too long in relationships we ought to leave. Debt causes us to stay too long in jobs we hate. Debt requires us to often put up with toxic environments: physically, emotionally, mentally, and spiritually. Debt is a trap. And debt causes us to make decisions against our better judgement because being broke is expensive.

Imagine for a moment you have just become an adult and you have the opportunity to earn income. You first need to buy safety equipment in order to do this work. You could earn $1000 doing this work, but the equipment you need is either high quality and very expensive or poor quality and affordable.

The high-quality equipment is $2500 but it will last you for ten years.

The cheap equipment will keep you safe, but it only lasts one year and it costs $800.

When you are starting out, you do not have enough money to buy the expensive equipment, so you buy the cheap equipment, thinking you'll save up for the expensive equipment in time. But because you have other costs to keep you alive, you just never quite get around to it.

After ten years, the cheap equipment has cost you $8000.

The higher quality equipment would have cost you $2500.

These numbers are speculative, but they illustrate my point: being broke is very expensive, and there are systems in place to keep you there because *someone* is profiting off you buying $800 equipment every year for ten years.

Getting ahead is crucial to long-term happiness and freedom, and I know this from personal experience.

Years ago, before the #metoo movement, I landed a job I wanted so badly. I was the co-host of a talk radio program and had big visions for that show, what we could accomplish, who we could interview, and how we could impact the airwaves for the better. But the problem was: not everyone on the team shared this vision. I worked with this…man. I was going to say "gentleman," but that is not an adequate description.

He was a thirty-something petulant toddler at his best, and a megalomaniac-certifiable narcissist the rest of the time, and he felt impossible to work with.

Less than a year before this job, I had won an award for my writing on "Creating a Compelling Corporate Culture," so it wasn't like I didn't have the skills to work with difficult people. But there is a massive difference between working with a challenging coworker and trying to book a guest for the talk show while he pretends to masturbate when you are on the phone and then squirts your hands and keyboard with hand sanitizer to mimic ejaculate while you are carefully and calmly giving instructions to the guest on how to connect with the technical producer at the scheduled interview time.

sigh

It was emotionally and mentally *exhausting*.

The day of the Last Straw was a day like most others. There wasn't anything really earth-shattering that happened, but I think it's why it's called the last straw. On its own, it is weightless and overlookable. But when you realize you are carrying around a haybale of misogynistic bullshit, you can't ignore the heft of it anymore. I was on the phone booking us a guest for later that day—a psychologist, of all people. And while I was giving her instructions on how to connect with our technical producer for her timeslot later that morning, he started mocking me in a high-pitched voice—the one that men sometimes use when they want to mimic women in a condescending way. And halfway through my call with that psychologist, I simply put down the receiver, grabbed my bag, and walked out.

I drove home and called the program director, letting him know that I would not be back, and I'd had enough. We agreed to a meeting the next day, and in the meantime, he took my coworker *out for beers* to discuss.

A few weeks later someone from corporate HR flew in to have a meeting about his constant and relentless nonsense and they offered me a monetary settlement. They were offering me money if I would sign a document that stated I would never ever talk about the series of events that happened in that workplace.

Here's the deal, friend: I never asked them for a cent. I wasn't looking for money, I was looking to protect my own mental health and get the hell out of that workplace. But the minute they offered money to gag me, I was furious.

(I will never understand this practice. A person gets mistreated or abused, then is offered compensation, but only on another condition of abuse: forced silence.)

When I walked away and said, "No thank you, my freedom is more important," the HR fella said, "Ms. Kelly, do not do anything to disparage the company."

I had to gently remind him that it was not *me* who disparaged the company, it was my coworker.

Oh, and spoiler alert: that coworker kept his job for another two years.

As you'll learn in the chapters of this book, I am not a prude and I can take a joke. I do, however, know the difference between accidentally crossing the line and being someone who takes sick delight in manipulating, controlling, shocking, and gaslighting others.

But let me tell you why this story matters. Leaving suddenly and losing that income hurt significantly, but if this had happened to me when I was in the thick of my financial struggles, I would not have had the ability to walk away from that nightmare job. I would have been too worried about how I was going to pay for my housing or my kids' medical needs. I would have had to endure two more years of listening to that windbag drone on while cutting off listeners who called in and turning off my microphone if I tried to interject. I would have had to sit through his jokes about pedophilia for another two years.

And if I would have taken that stupid hush money, I would have had to wrestle with my own integrity by staying silent while the men back at the office continued to pat him on the back.

I realized I was free when I could walk out and not fear the financial repercussions. For a moment, I considered suing them and donating any proceeds, but then I realized that by taking care of myself, I had already won.

The system is afraid of financially free women. When women are financially free, they are more likely to use their voices. They are more likely to be advocates for change. Financially fierce women are more powerful, better equipped, and more independent. And the system of greed and power will shift dramatically if the majority of people are no longer chained to the system.

Maybe your last straw was a phone call from a collector.

Maybe your last straw was your twenty-third rejection letter from a prospective employer.

Maybe your last straw was having a declined card at the checkout counter.

It doesn't matter what the last straw is, the compounded weight of it can break you, or it can transform you.

If you've picked up this book, you know we are at a crucial time in history. The decisions you make today will determine how quickly you recover. If you are privileged, you might have lots of decisions available to you. If you are not so fortunate, it is likely going to be a slog. I can't offer you a quick fix, but I can offer you some insights that have helped other people create their own personal freedoms *in spite of their circumstances,* and in Covid times, perhaps that is all you have to work with.

Maybe you grew up in a home where money was not discussed. Perhaps it wasn't considered polite. Perhaps there was simply no access. Maybe you did receive that education, but you battled a health crisis or an addiction that wiped out your plans. Here's the best news: you are here now, and we can start today.

I wish I could tell you I have all the answers to fix the systemic issues that are making it so difficult to get ahead, but I don't. I only have a little bit of wisdom to offer you based on how I've changed my own life and how I've impacted others to do the same and while I had not lived through a pandemic prior to this, here's what I know about financial emergencies:

1. Our primary focus in a true emergency is focusing on not going into *more* debt. Often what happens when people are excited to pay off debt is that they start putting all their income toward debt payoff, but then they create more debt in order to survive and pay bills. What this does is keep us credit dependent. If you are experiencing

a financial emergency, it's imperative that you start to move away from using credit day-to-day, even if that means you are delaying paying down debt. What we have to do is get off the system that makes getting into debt and being broke the easiest financial choice.

2. If you are receiving any sort of stimulus money and you have lost your job or you think there's a possibility you might lose your job, your primary focus is stockpiling cash to prepare for any upcoming financial challenges. It is not the time to be making major purchases. When I say "stockpiling" cash, I am referring to padding up an emergency fund that will get you through the crisis. When life settles down and you have certainty around a steady stream of income, that's when you can resume paying down debt, making major purchases, or whatever it was you were intending to do with the money.
3. If the money you receive is taxable and income taxes have not been withheld, you must put the equivalent tax amount away in preparation for it to go to the government at tax time. If you can't prepay that tax, put that equivalent away where you won't see it and do your very best not to use it, otherwise you are just kicking your emergency further down the road where it will compound. Of course, if you need to use it for a true immediate emergency like medication or whatnot, do so, but just consider a plan to then pay the taxes in the future so you aren't caught off-guard when the tax bill comes. The important thing to remember is when you owe the government money and you struggle to pay it, they can simply come take it. I have had this happen and it's humiliating. It doesn't matter what gets deposited into your account, if you owe the government, every penny goes to pay them first, even if your cupboards are bare.

You'll learn all of the steps in much more detail in the pages to come.

If Covid has taught us anything, it's to learn the difference between what is *urgent* and what is *important*.

People who focused on what was urgent were out hoarding toilet paper, panic-buying, watching the headlines, and arguing with strangers on the internet.

People who focused on what was important were checking in with family and friends to ensure they had enough toilet paper, staying indoors for the most part, and dropping off groceries on grandma and grandpa's doorstep. They were watching their kids play in the backyard and sending positive, encouraging messages to strangers on the frontlines.

Financially, what this translates to is lack or abundance.

When we are living in urgency, we are making short-term, survival-based decisions. If this is where you are today, that's okay. I'll show you throughout this book how to transition this lack-based thinking into a longer-term financial strategy as we go. But urgency requires a credit card. It's "buy now and pay later." It feels like there is never enough. It feels like there is always an emergency on the horizon. It's very difficult to plan long-term because you are worried about how you are going to make it until next payday. Life can feel segmented or compartmentalized: my relationship sucks, my kids are misbehaving, I'm broke, my health isn't where I want it....

When everything feels urgent, it means we are moving from crisis to crisis, and it's very difficult to visualize a future where we feel both secure *and* free.

When we are living in importance, we are making longer-term, joy-based decisions. It means that sometimes we make sacrifices for comfort today so that our children are better off, or so that our future selves are more comfortable. It means we set our own financial goals, and we understand that while we can't control the market or the economy, we can make consistently healthy financial choices to make progress toward a goal, even if it seems like the goal is a long way off. It means we don't live in an all-or-nothing mentality, and we understand that even by making a little progress toward our financial goals today, we can see big future gains tomorrow. We understand that we can't rely on a credit card to build a healthy financial future. When we live by what is important, although we don't take on other people's emergencies as our own crises, we can help people from a position of abundance while still having enough for ourselves. It's a holistic view of life, one that incorporates your overall physical, relational, spiritual, emotional, and mental wellness.

As with anything, the story you tell yourself about who you are and what is happening in your life right now has greater impact on the future than the circumstances you find yourself in today. We all have a tremendous opportunity right now to use this Great Pause for good. Ten years from now you can look back on the pandemic as the thing that destroyed you or the time in your life you transformed your finances for the better. Let's imagine it is ten years in the future and you are looking back at your younger self (you've hardly aged a day in ten years, darling!) holding this book. You are absolutely living the life you imagined, and you are truly happy.

What decisions is future you proud that pandemic you made?

What decisions does future you regret making during the pandemic?

When you are ninety years old and telling your great grandchildren about how you lived through pandemic times, what stories are you proud to tell them that they can carry through their own lives?

We are at such a precious time in history. Some people will remember this as the worst time in their lives. It's like you've been handed a terrible plot, a not-so-great setting, a bunch of possibly insane political characters, a global health crisis, and a very scary and silent villain named Covid. But the very fortunate part of it all is that you have also been handed a pen. You get to write the next chapter of your life and make it mean whatever you want it to mean.

Disclaimer

The information provided in this book is for information and educational purposes only and does not constitute legal or financial advice for your unique circumstances. It is always advisable to contact a financial professional to determine what may be best for your individual needs. The publisher and the author do not make any guarantee or other promise as to any results that may be obtained from using the content of this book. You must never make any investment decision without first consulting with your own financial advisor and conducting your own research and due diligence. Things change quickly and what is printed here may not be current, so your own research is always encouraged. To the maximum extent permitted by law, the publisher and the author disclaim any and all liability in the event any information, commentary, analysis, opinions, advice, and/or recommendations contained in this book prove to be inaccurate, incomplete, or unreliable, or result in any investment or other losses. Content contained or made available through this book is not intended to and does not constitute legal or financial advice. The publisher and the author are providing this book and its contents on an "as-is" basis. Your use of the information in this book is at your own risk.

Further Study

If you find you want to do this work in a community for added support, check out www.getthehelloutofdebt.com

The online program has helped thousands of people pay off millions of dollars in consumer debt. Once you register, you can log on to your personal and private portal to watch videos on demand and even join occasional live calls with the author. Your exclusive online access will also give you entrance to a private social media group.

There are three ways to access the group coaching for *Get the Hell Out of Debt*.

1. You can sign up and pay the registration fee and be granted instant access.
2. You can register for the pay-what-you-can option if the registration fee is out of your reach today.
3. You can apply for complete sponsorship. One of the most beautiful parts of this community is often people who become debt-free turn around and sponsor new people into the program by paying for someone else. It's not an expectation if you've been sponsored that you must turn around and pay for someone else. It's truly a gift from a graduate who has a changed life and wants to pay it forward. We match every sponsorship, so one sponsorship provides financial

education for two people. We can't guarantee sponsorship, but you can scroll down to the bottom of www.GettheHellOutofDebt.com and apply. We will let you know ASAP if we have matched you with a sponsor.

You can also follow the author on social media @erinskyekelly and on Instagram @getthehelloutofdebt.

To book Erin to speak at your event, your bookclub, or for your podcast, head to www.erinskyekelly.com.

If you want to order bulk books for your organization go to bulkbooks.com.

Erin loves to check in on your progress and cheer you on during your journey to debt freedom, so if you are posting on social media, use the hashtag #GetTheHellOutofDebt.

Table of Contents

PHASE THREE

Introduction

GET THE HELL OUT OF DEBT

My phone was lighting up.

I had turned the ringer off for weeks and only answered it if I recognized the number on the call display.

"Hello?"

It was a client. They wanted to meet across town to discuss some business. We made arrangements to meet later that day, and I got dressed in my fanciest jeans and my least-scuffed boots and threw my bag on the passenger seat. I timed the meeting for the middle of the day so I could get away with not buying lunch or dinner. It was too late for coffee, so I could say I was trying to drink more water, and I could still buy the client a beverage on the remaining balance of a gift card I had.

I turned the ignition and began to cry.

Empty.

There was no fuel in the tank.

My bank account was overdrawn. I had no cash. My credit was maxed out. Even the piggy bank had been raided. There was no way I was going to get to that meeting across town on these fumes. I went inside, called the client, and made up a story about diarrhea, which somehow seemed less embarrassing than saying, "I'm on the verge of bankruptcy and I cannot afford to even do a transaction that would land me your business."

The shame told me that no one would want to do business with a big dumb failure like me anyway.

I shut the world out for a few hours, and as the darkness of the night took over, so did the darkness of the emotional weight of the debt.

I spent a lot of time trying to figure out how I got myself into this position. I was doing everything right! I had a near perfect credit score and I owned lots of assets! How could I possibly be so broke?

Chapter One

BEFORE YOU BEGIN

There are a few things you need to do in order to make this a successful journey.

If you are totally committed to paying off your consumer debt and living debt-free, then you absolutely will not start doing any fancy financing right now. *You will not consolidate.* You will not cash out any investments to pay off your debt. You pinkie swear that you will read the book and take action as required, and then re-read the book as necessary.

If you are ever tempted to solve your financial stress with a quick math solution, you are just kicking your problem further down the sidewalk. Most people, after consolidating their debt, end up in more debt in the long run because they did not learn to actually master their money. Most people who struggle financially and then win the lottery end up back in a financial struggle because they did not learn to actually master their money. Most people who cash out investments to pay off debt never actually rebuild wealth because they did not learn to actually master their money. The point of this book, the point of getting the hell out of debt, the point of changing your life and your mindset and your habits, is so that you can master your money.

But first, you have to master yourself.

This book is divided into three phases.

1) Phase One

   This is the planning and preparation phase where you will get yourself financially organized and get absolute certainty about the situation you are in and the patterns you've created that got you here.

2) Phase Two

   This is the part where you actually pay off your consumer debt. I consider consumer debt to be:

   - unsecured lines of credit
   - secured lines of credit
   - credit cards
   - bills you are behind on
   - overdue income taxes
   - overdue property taxes
   - second or third mortgages
   - vehicle loans
   - personal loans to family, friends, or other human beings

   If you have a lot of consumer debt, you are welcome to put your first mortgage/primary mortgage in Phase Three. If you have rental properties that you want to pay off, those will also go in Phase Three. The reason is this: if we use all our cash flow to pay off all the things now, we are delaying your investing and your wealth-building for too long. We need to get you out of high-interest consumer debt *quickly* so that we can free up that cash for wealth-building and planning for retirement. What I've seen time and again is once debt is paid off completely, typically in two years or less, then we can use some of the freed-up cash flow to hammer that mortgage down in half the time it would have taken you otherwise.

3) Phase Three
Once you've paid off all your consumer debt (yay you!) then you absolutely *must* keep going. If you quit here, you are highly likely to end up right back in debt. If you want to experience true financial freedom, you'll continue right through Phase Three and use the money you are currently paying toward debt each month to invest in order to build your wealth.

Becoming debt free, if followed Phase by Phase, will likely take you six months to two years.

I know this because of something called Total Debt Servicing. There is a formula that most lenders use to determine how much debt you "qualify" for. If you've maxed that out, you likely have half your income tied up in debt. Isn't that absurd?

If we add up all the consumer debt you have (all the debts listed in Phase Two) and that equals 50 percent of your gross annual income, this process will likely take you eighteen months to complete—If you are focused.

If you are less focused, it can take you two years or more, and if you are hyper-focused, it may only take a few months.

Allow me to help you visualize this. If you have a total household income of $80,000/year and you have $40,000 in consumer debt, you are looking at approximately eighteen months until you are in Phase Three. If you have $20,000 in consumer debt, you might be done in six to twelve months. If you have $60,000 or more in consumer debt, it might take you two or more years. This is all a guideline, but most people have at maximum 50 percent of their gross annual income as debt, which is why I predict it will take you less than two years if you want debt freedom badly enough.

There are some things along the way that can alter this course. If you lose your job, if you experience a pregnancy or childbirth, if you experience an illness or a new disability, if you experience tragedy in your life, etc.

These things tend to prolong your journey to becoming debt-free. If you get a raise, if you take on some part-time income earning experiences, if you downsize or right-size your life, these things can speed up your debt freedom date.

For optimal success, read the book through once and make any notes in the margins that you want. Mess this book up with a highlighter or Post-its or your tears. Then go back and create your debt-free custom plan by doing the phases in the proper order in this book. Do not start Phase Two until you complete Phase One. Do not try and do Phase Three at the same time as the first two phases.

I learned all of this the hard way. When I finally added up all my debts (liabilities), I discovered I was $2.1 million dollars in debt. I know, I know. That's an asinine amount of debt. And the worst part is I tried a few times to take some quick ways out: consolidation, moving-this-over-here-to-pay-that, refinancing, all the things you've either likely tried or been tempted to try too. But the only thing that worked is what I've laid out in this book, in the order I've laid it out.

It is *imperative* you do the phases in order. I am giving you the combination to a safe, and inside is so much money that you can be financially free for life. If I just wrote those numbers down randomly, the safe would not open when you tried it. That's what will happen if you jump around. But if I write those numbers down in order, and you enter the combination of those numbers in order, you will unlock the life-changing financial freedom that helped me and thousands of other people pay off millions of dollars in consumer debt.

Chapter Two

HOW TO MAXIMIZE YOUR MONEY SUCCESS

There are ten Success Principles you'll need to commit to.

1) PRETEND YOU KNOW NOTHING.

   Every time you tell yourself, "I know this already," you close your mind to learning. I want you to approach this work without any bias or assumptions. Sometimes we learn things, but we don't actually *know* them because we haven't put the knowledge into action. This program is very much about action-taking. You're going to have to start thinking new things, then taking new action, which will reinforce the things you are thinking. So, to start off, let's pretend you know zero things and do all the things with money that you wish you would have done way back before you started building destructive habits.

2) NO "SHOULD"-ING.

   The language in this book is not appropriate for everyone. If you are sensitive to words that might make your great-grandma blush, then this is not the right learning tool for you. But if you are a little salty, you can say whatever you want around me.

You can say motherf*ckingshittits and I won't flinch. But if you say, "You should know better" or, "You should read this" or, "I shouldn't have taken out that credit card"—*now I am steaming mad*. Anytime you "should," you judge. If you are going to get the results you want, you must be kind to yourself. Promise me you won't "should" yourself and you won't "should" all over anyone else. When you join our social media community, it's the only word you can't say there.

When you "should" on people, you are inferring superiority, and that limits both their potential and yours. Let's give each other the maximum potential to succeed, deal? I'm cheering for you!

3) FEEL YOUR FEELINGS FULLY.

Money is a form of energy and deeply connected to your emotional state. If you try to avoid any feelings throughout this process, you will limit your progress. Feelings are information. Honor them. Somewhere along the way, you may have been taught not to express your feelings. I was raised to be a "good girl," and that meant not making other people feel uncomfortable when I had big emotions.

So, in order to keep other people comfortable, I used to try to cut off parts of me that were in pain. Here's what I learned about my own pain: because I was avoiding it and trying not to feel it, I was ignoring some very helpful information that my pain was trying to get me to notice. And when I ignored it, it showed up louder—in the form of debt. When I meet people who are in debt, I don't see them as people who suck at adding and subtracting numbers. I see them as people who probably have unexpressed pain.

My pain showed up as resentment, and then eventually as vindictiveness. My vindictiveness was not violent, it was more like, "Aha! *Karma will get you.*" I thought I was enlightened because I didn't act on vindictiveness. But hoping that "karma" would take care of it *is* vindictiveness.

Any time we have resentment, it means there is unexpressed anger. The only way to get rid of that resentment is to express it in a healthy way. Healthy means you express your anger in a way that does not impose on other people. Yes, it is absolutely vital to choose your response in a moment of upset. But what I've seen over and over is people (especially nice ones like you) can choose a calm response on the outside, but yet are often truly seething on the inside. I want that emotion expressed when it's appropriate to do so.

Maybe you start budgeting and you get frustrated and you realize you wish you had learned this when you were younger. Well, go on and stomp your feet and have a good cry, but then carry on with the work. Maybe your spouse blows the budget and piles a bunch of unnecessary expenses on the credit card. Then go have a good run, or go on a long solo drive on a country road and say all the things that need saying to an invisible passenger. Get those feelings outside your body so that you have more room inside for healing and peace.

If you are stuffing down your feelings, you will have a harder time reaching your financial goals because everything you want is on the other side of that resentment. Avoiding the emotion does not bring transformation. Moving through the emotion brings transformation. Feel all the things.

4) BUT DO NOT LET YOUR EMOTIONS DICTATE YOUR BEHAVIORS!

Feelings are information, not an excuse to self-sabotage. You don't want your feelings to run the show. You can't get where you want to go if you let your exhaustion, stress, anger, or frustration rule your life. You can feel your feelings and act appropriately anyway. You can feel your feelings and do a budget. You can feel your feelings and pay off your debt. Obviously, we want you to be in the best possible emotional state when you do this work. Ideally, you'll sit down for a few minutes a day to take care of your money when you feel great. But even if you're not feeling good, it is absolutely *not* an excuse to *not* take care of your money. Repeat after me: I feel my feelings, but I do not let my emotions dictate my behaviors.

5) APPROACH EVERYTHING WITH GRACE.
This is not going to go perfectly. You are human. That makes you beautiful and messy and raw and imperfect. Having an attitude of curiosity from the beginning will serve you well. "I wonder what obstacles I will encounter during this process!" is a better setup for success than "I have set up a perfect system that will get me debt-free in exactly 322 days." This work brings up emotions. This work brings up our shortcomings. This work points out to us where we have let ourselves and other people down. This work shows us where we have failed to keep our promises to ourselves and others. But this work also brings us to the other side where we can live a life of confidence and integrity with our word and a powerful opportunity to extend grace to others.

6) BE WILLING TO GET UNCOMFORTABLE.
How you have been living until now has likely been stressful! But because it is what you are used to, it is highly likely you are also oddly comfortable here. You'll get better, different financial results once you do things outside of your comfort zone. The more open you are, the faster you will get the hell out of debt. This means you are going to have some uncomfortable conversations. You are going to have to do things that aren't fun, and you are going to have to say no sometimes to things that are.

You have a choice here: you can chase fun and stay comfortable, *or* you can get results. When you are faced with the thing you *want* to do versus the thing you *must* do, just remember that the people who have graduated this program almost consistently chose the thing they *must* do that wasn't comfortable or fun. I find swearing helps.

7) STAY IN YOUR OWN LANE.

If you are a helper, a fixer, or a rescuer, you are going to have a heck of a time knowing what is your stuff and what is not your stuff. A lot of your work in this program will be around taking responsibility for your choices and leaving the rest. Take care of yourself, and avoid solving other people's problems. Do not get distracted! Let others make mistakes. Screwing up is totally acceptable here, and it's how many of us learn! If you find yourself comparing your progress or your financial circumstances to others, try and identify where this is coming from or if it serves you. If you discover that following certain friends on social media makes you feel resentful, you can temporarily snooze their posts for a month and see if that lessens the urge to compare. Try and work on celebrating their successes instead of comparing yourself. Invest time in your own hobbies or spend time reading about or doing things that you are passionate about (choose things that don't derail your financial progress, please!) but carve out this year to work on you. Focus on cleaning up your own financial house, and pay no mind to how well other people appear to be doing.

8) WHAT YOU RESIST PERSISTS.

Psychologist Carl Jung said that what you resist not only persists but grows in size! If you avoid doing any of the phases of the program, you are simply kicking your problem further down the road. Leave time each week to do the things that you must do—

even if you don't want to do them—in order to have the life you want. Surrender to the work. Sometimes we want our lives to be different, but we can't expect change from just our hopes and dreams. We must lean in and take action, particularly if we are resisting the thing(s) we know we need to do only because we don't want to feel uncomfortable. When we avoid dealing with debt, it grows. Some of the work in this book will feel tiny or insignificant. It can be tempting to want to fix everything in one fell swoop, but that does not build the muscles we need to build or carry wealth. You don't wander into a gym for the first time in your life and curl the seventy-five-pound dumbbell without doing some serious damage. You work your way to a fit, strong physique. It's important to do even the little things that are easy to do but also easy not to do. If you want debt to go away, you have to push past your resistance to change and do all the steps along the way, even the seemingly small insignificant ones, in order to have massive results.

9) SHOW UP.

Show up for yourself in spite of how you feel. Show up to do your work, whether or not you want to, even if you don't fully understand it, and even if your friends think it's dumb. Show up for you because you said you would. Show up for you because you are someone who keeps promises to yourself. And show up because you are committed to your results, not your excuses.

Often when we work toward a goal, we have an idea in our head that it "should" go a certain way. (There's that swear word again.) When we let ourselves down, we can feel the need to quit or start over. This is self-sabotage. Instead, if we show up for ourselves (regardless of our progress) and keep showing up until we have our desired results, we practice self-support.

10) MAINTAIN AN IMPECCABLE STANDARD OF SELF-CARE. This term self-care has somehow come to mean that we deserve to spoil ourselves. Civil rights activist, writer, and feminist Audre Lorde said "caring for myself is not self-indulgence, it is self-preservation, and that is an act of political warfare." Lorde's idea of self-care came about as a survival strategy for humans who have been marginalized and therefore have an extraordinary and unfathomable amount of stress. Somehow, we've taken the term #selfcare and made it mean "treat yourself," yet again undermining and diminishing the very real challenges—particularly financially—that many face because of the historical uneven distribution of power.

You have *got* to take care of yourself. This work is emotionally and mentally taxing at times, and you have to keep yourself regulated. Sometimes it's both a marathon and a sprint, and I cannot help you if you do not take care of you. You'll first do this work for you, to radically and responsibly change your personal financial situation, but then I hope it compels you to take up a greater cause to help others.

If you are really open to my unsolicited advice on how to live your life, I need you to spend thirty minutes a day doing some sort of movement or exercise, and ten minutes a day focusing on your money. I also need you to drink your water. In a perfect world, you would wake up early-ish, move your beautiful and miraculous body however it is able for half an hour, sit at your computer for ten minutes to do your money work, and drink a glass of water while you do. This alone will start to transform your days and your life.

But if you have no idea even how to take care of yourself, you can start by creating a list of daily non-negotiables. These are things that you commit to doing *for you* before you follow through on any commitments to anyone else. Yeah. I see you. I know you are super amazing at following through on commitments to other people, and you often put other people's needs before your own. But if you consistently commit to finishing things you say you're going to do, you will build incredible confidence.

I received a social media tag from reader Sara Y who said, "Today is a pretty big day for me. It is day 100 of me doing my 11 daily habits. Every. Single. Day. 100 days in a row, no matter if I wasn't feeling well or had other commitments - these action items came first. Thank you Erin Skye Kelly for inspiring me to do this."

You know what you can accomplish when you start honoring your promises to yourself? Damn near anything.

PHASE ONE

Chapter Three

THE TWO TOOLS

THE ONLY TWO TOOLS YOU NEED TO MASTER TO GET THE HELL OUT OF DEBT AND BUILD WEALTH

Tool Number One: Your Net Worth

The first tool you need is a way to consistently calculate your personal net worth. This has nothing to do with your actual worth. I say that because there was a very dark period of time when my debt was so overwhelming that I could barely breathe. I realized mathematically that I was worth more dead than alive. That sat with me in the worst way for a very long time.

While the collectors were calling and while I was trying to figure out how to put food on the table, I carried deep secretive shame that made it very difficult to function. I felt like a Grade A Loser. (If you know how we grade our eggs in Canada, you'd know this is the highest form of loser you could be.)

I could not figure out how I could be so stupid. I "should'ed" all over myself. I should have known better. I should not have trusted that business associate. I should have saved more. I should have had better legal advice. I should have asked for help sooner. I should have seen it coming. I was covered in "should."

In order to change the trajectory of this story, and ultimately my life, I had to take full responsibility for everything. This meant that even though some things that happened to me were not technically my fault, I found a way to take ownership of it all so I could move on. Ultimately, I alone am responsible for my own results in life. If I want awesome results, I have to make them happen. If I want to be happy in spite of any and all pain I've experienced, I have to choose happiness. When I stopped making this giant festering pile of debt about anyone else except me, I started to conquer it.

Here's what's true: your past is not an indicator of your future. The trouble with debt is it becomes a constant reminder of decisions we made in the past that we are currently paying for. Debt can certainly feel heavy in the present, which makes it difficult to believe life could ever feel light and free again. But as you restore the integrity of your word, as you make good on these debts, dollar by dollar your confidence will build, and you'll soon feel the weight starting to lift.

NET WORTH

The simplest way to calculate your net worth is by taking everything you own and imagine you are paying off what you owe; the amount of money left over is your net worth.

The more in-depth way to look at it is: Assets (what you own) - Liabilities (what you owe) = Net Worth.

The mastery way to determine your net worth involves slightly different definitions of assets and liabilities. We'll get to that in a later chapter.

For now, it's absolutely crucial to fully understand this concept if you want to comprehend what is happening with your finances at any given moment. Plus, when you become a regular at updating your net worth, you start building a strong relationship with your money.

Think of it like this: if you want a healthy, strong relationship with your spouse, you don't just pay attention to them on your anniversary. You check in with them often to see how they are doing.

When you are mastering your money, at *minimum* you will need to update your net worth once a month. But the people I have worked with who have been the most successful have updated at least once a week. They sit down on Sundays, when they are planning out their week anyway, and they spend a few minutes updating their assets and liabilities.

How you choose to track these assets and liabilities is up to you. You can do it in a ledger, a notebook, a journal, a bujo, a spreadsheet, an app, a calendar—whatever you prefer. I prefer a spreadsheet to start; you are welcome to use mine at www.financialtransformation.ca.

In one column, list all your assets, and beside them, the total value.

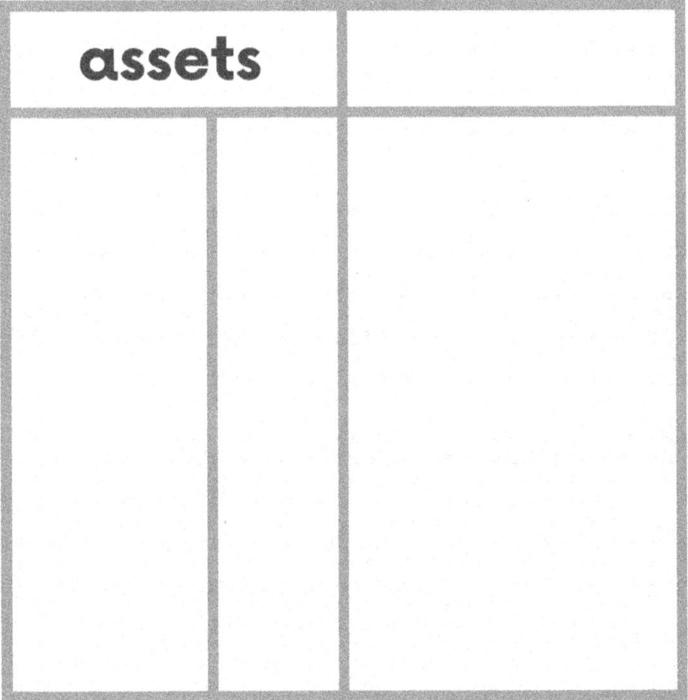

You might not have all of these things listed below, and you do not need them all. They vary based on where you live and what decisions you've made with your money. Your job is not to obtain all the assets listed here; your job is simply to list the assets you already have.

An example of some things your bank might consider to be assets include:

Tax-Free Savings Account (TFSA) (CDN)

A tax-free savings account is an account available in Canada that provides tax benefits for saving. Investment income or the interest you earn in a TFSA is not taxed in most cases, even when withdrawn. Add each investment to your net worth spreadsheet so you can track their growth.

Roth IRA (USA)

Like its Canadian cousin, the Tax-Free Savings Account, a Roth IRA offers tax-free growth and tax-free withdrawals in retirement. There is a limit per year as to what you can contribute, so it's important to know how much room you have left if you've been contributing. But the number you put in the net worth spreadsheet is the current value of the actual investment you hold.

ISA Individual Savings Account (UK)

This is the United Kingdom's version of the tax-free growth plans. You contribute money to it today, and if it grows, you don't pay tax on the new money. The number you add to the net worth spreadsheet is today's current value of the investments you hold.

Registered Retirement Savings Plan (RRSP) (CDN)

This is a Canadian tax deferral plan that allows you to contribute to retirement by not paying tax on the contributed moola today, but then being taxed when you withdraw it at retirement, the philosophy being that you will likely then be in a lower tax bracket.

401(k) (USA)

A 401(k) is an American tax-deferred savings plan that allows employees to contribute to their retirement using pre-tax dollars. You'll use the current number contributed to update your net worth, not the future value.

Royalties

Royalties are ongoing payments to owners or creators of things like intellectual property, copyrights, patents, and trademarks. Did you know the royalties from "Stand By Me" (Ben E. King) have earned over twenty-seven million dollars? So, if the royalties that you look upon should tumble and fall, and the net worth should crumble to the sea, I won't cry, I won't cry, no I won't shed a tear, just as long as you always update me. If you receive royalties on an ongoing basis, you'll put that number in your budget under "income" (coming up!) but otherwise, if you keep this money in an account or investment, that's the number you'll update.

Dividends

This is a sum of money paid regularly from investments. If you use the income from dividends to live, we update those in the budget. But if your dividends get reinvested in the asset, then you put the total value of the asset today in the net worth.

Vehicle/Trailer/Machine on Wheels

You don't put the money you paid for the vehicle as the net worth value (wahhh wahhhhhhh) but rather, you put the current street value today. So, if you were to hock this trailer online, the number someone would pay for it is the number you use. There are a number of sites you can look up the value (Kelley Blue Book, for example), but use conservative estimates wherever possible.

Real Estate

Whether you have rental properties or you own your primary residence, you only include the real estate to which you have a title. To determine what value to use, use the lower of a recent comparative market analysis (if your realtor gives you one) or the city-assessed value, *minus* any realtor fees you would incur if you were selling today. If you don't know what the realtor commissions and fees are, you can subtract $20,000 for now until you know. For instance, if the city-assessed value of your home is $305,000, you would put $285,000 as the value. If you have a next-door neighbor whose home sold for $300,000, then put $280,000 as the value of your home *even if you watch HGTV and you think your decorating skills are better.* Be conservative with your numbers, no matter what. Your home technically is not worth any of those numbers. Truthfully, your home is only worth what someone will pay for it, and equity is an imaginary number until someone else has the keys to your home.

Foreign Currency/Precious Metals

Use the current value in your currency (minus any fees to exchange) as the number. Your net worth should be calculated in one currency to keep it easy to understand. If you have items of value in other currencies, use a conservative number in your currency cell on your net worth spreadsheet to determine the value.

Stocks

If you own individual stocks that are outside of a registered plan, you will put today's current value of your shares for your net worth calculation. Because most people hold their stocks in one brokerage account, it can be helpful to simply record the total value of the brokerage account where all the shares are held as one number in the net worth spreadsheet. A brokerage is the financial institution you choose to use to purchase shares.

A Quick Note About Registered Accounts

It's worth noting that people often think their registered account *is* the investment. They'll say, "I have a TFSA," and I will ask, "What is it invested in?" and they will look at me like I have asked them to tell me the full legal names of the Spice Girls...something vaguely familiar they remember reading once but didn't think had any real bearing on their quality of life so they didn't retain it. When you set up your ISA/Roth IRA/TFSA/etc., you are not setting up the investment. You are setting up the structure that you are investing *in.*

A registered account is simply an investment account that is given tax-deferred or tax-free growth status by the government.

Let's say you set up a registered account at a financial institution and they hand you an orange bucket called the Tax-Free Growth Bucket. You have lots of options. You can put stocks in this orange bucket. You can put a mutual fund (a group of stocks that are traded on the stock market that are pooled together and managed by a "fund manager") in this orange bucket, you can put an Exchange Traded Fund or ETF (these also hold assets like stocks, but this fund itself is traded on the stock market) in this bucket. The money you put in this bucket is money you will have already paid tax on (your "after tax dollars") but when your investment grows, there is no additional tax owing to the government. The government taxes you at your marginal tax rate before you invest in something you want to keep in this orange bucket. Taxes are fdofdjdfjlfejlfjlfejfaejifajfelfjl.

Oh gawd. I just bored myself typing that and fell asleep on my keyboard. Anyway, taxes are boring but necessary to understand when it comes to your money.

Now, let's say you set up a registered account at a financial institution and they hand you a purple bucket called the Tax-Deferred Bucket. Again, you have lots of options. You can put stocks and mutual funds and ETFs and all kinds of investments in your purple bucket. But this time, the government isn't going to take any money before you put it in the bucket. Instead, they will wait until you are older and your face is withered like a raisin. Then, as you dip your hand in the bucket to pay for your BENGAY, the government will dip their hand in too and tax your investments based on your marginal tax rate at that time.

We want to truly save these investments for retirement. Think of your Tax-Free Growth money as old age adventure money. It's for going on a safari or a cruise, or replacing that hip you stressed when you took that burlesque class for seniors.

Think of your Tax-Deferred Bucket as your old age steady income. These are not designed for lump-sum withdrawals on a whim. These are excellent for planning ahead for what is needed for regular income while maximizing tax savings.

But when an unexpected issue comes up in retirement, we don't want to be forced to withdraw $1.30 or beyond for every $1.00 of Rogaine we need. We'll use the Tax-Deferred money we've invested to give us a steady income for living, and we'll use the Tax-Free Growth money we've invested to give us a life.

The TFSA and the RSP (and the Roth IRA/401(k)) are all just buckets that hold the investments to determine how they are taxed. Again, they are not necessarily investments themselves. If you have any investments at all, your homework is to learn what investments you have and how they work. Oh, and *do not cash any of them in to pay off debt,* please. Only in very rare circumstances, like Armageddon, when an asteroid threatens to collide with Earth and Billy Bob Thornton determines that the only way to survive is if Bruce Willis drills a hole into the surface of the asteroid and detonates a nuclear bomb and Aerosmith makes a theme song for it…*only then*, if the world is truly ending for you, do I recommend you cash out those investments. We're going to leave all investments for now. Worst-case scenario, we might hold off on doing active (new) investing, but we need to finish doing all the preliminary work in Phase One before you know what the right decision for you will be.

So, let's calculate your net worth.

It might look something like this:

assets		
savings account	$704.34	
retirement fund	$6120.72	
total assets	$6825.06	

Savings Account $704.34
Retirement Fund $6120.72

When we add it all up, we see that the total value of your assets is $6825.06

Liabilities

An example of some things your bank might consider to be liabilities include:

- Credit Cards (put the total outstanding balance in the liability section).
- Bank Loans (put the total outstanding balance in the liability section).

- Family or Personal Loans (put the total outstanding balance in the liability section).
- Lines of Credit (total amount to pay off, including any penalties for early payment).

Yes, you read that right. Some loans have a discharge fee (it's just as gross as it sounds) that you have to pay if you plan on paying off the loan.

- Student Loans (total amount to pay off, if they actually let you do this! Some won't).
- Vehicle Loans (total amount to pay off, not the monthly payment).
- CRA/IRS/ATO/HMRC Payments or Back Taxes (total amount to pay off, not the installment payment).
- Outstanding Total Mortgage Balance, including penalties and discharge fee (not just the monthly payment).

assets		liabilities	
savings account	$704.34		
retirement fund	$6120.72		
total assets	$6825.06		

I don't have to explain what those are because if you are here, you know damn well what liabilities are and how they work. But the number you will use for all these things is the total big-ass number that represents all the debt and interest you've accumulated, plus any fees.

(Important distinction: we aren't going to put in the monthly payments. Those go in the budget, the second tool you will master in order to master your finances, coming up!)

assets		liabilities	
savings account	$704.34	credit card	$3576.12
retirement fund	$6120.72	line of credit	$2052.87
total assets	$6825.06	total liabilities	$5628.99

It might look something like this:

Credit Card Balance $3576.12
Line of Credit $2052.87

When we add it all up, we see that the total value of your liabilities is $5628.99

When we subtract your liabilities from your assets…voila! Net worth. In this case, the net worth is $1196.07

($6825.06 - $5628.99 = $1196.07)

Know that your net worth will fluctuate. That's why it is important to update your net worth regularly.

Listen, I'm not asking you to sit in front of your computer for hours a day, obsessing over all the details and changes as they happen. I want you to live your dang life.

But I do want you to be in the numbers until you are *familiar* with your numbers. I want you to know them in the way that you know when your best friend wants to leave a party because they pull a subtle face at you from across the room. I want you to have comfort and ease with your numbers. But that comes from first getting acquainted with them, and then getting intimate.

In the beginning, this exercise can take quite a while, especially if you haven't done it before. You might have to search up logins and reset passwords and monkey around on the internet for a while. Once you have figured out where to regularly find all your information, it can be easiest to set up bookmarked tabs in your browser to open with one click and have everything accessible at a glance. Then, as you update your net worth, you can close each tab and be done.

When done weekly or monthly, most people find this process takes less than ten minutes and brings so much peace of mind. When done annually, most people find this process to be a giant clusterf*ck of goat herding and it brings so much mental chaos.

Once you have your initial net worth compiled, you just make note of the date and the number of your net worth. As long as your net worth is increasing month over month, at least by $1, you are headed in the right direction.

While paying down debt, it is *critical* to focus on *increasing the total net worth*, not just paying down the debt. When we focus on our debt, we can actually experience negative emotions, which pose a challenge when you are trying to overcome obstacles. When we focus on our net worth, we can see *past* the obstacle, which is crucial for overcoming it. Training our brain to focus on the net worth number is also helpful for the wealth-building years once your consumer debt is paid off, as you will use this same process to create financial freedom; you will be buying assets and watching your net worth increase each month.

For now, it's very important to note that your net worth might be negative. This means that when you add up all your assets, and subtract your liabilities, you might realize you're still very, very broke. You still, however, would be very, very sexy. And very, very smart. And very, very funny. Your gross worth is still valuable and awesome, even if your net worth feels a bit gut-punchy. It's all okay. Ideally, you'll see that sucker go up by at least a buck a month. Provided you are doing the work properly, you'll be able to squeeze more dollars into your liability pay-down, which makes your net worth go up even faster. The more dollars you allocate to paying off those liabilities, the faster you get the hell out of debt.

> "Remember, buying something is not the problem.
> The problem comes when we believe, for that moment,
> that the object we're buying is going to make us happy."
>
> — Celso Cukierkorn

Allissa says: "So far, my specific results have been:

"1. I have more than doubled my income.
"2. I have paid 3/4 of my life-crushing consumer debt.
"3. I started my own thriving company.
"4. I've asked for three raises and got them.
"5. I have learned to be more open with my feelings, wants, and needs, resulting in closer relationships.
"6. I have learned to love myself and know that I am worthy of being loved by others. I think this one made the biggest impact on my life because it drove away all the self-sabotaging thoughts and behaviors I once had."

Chapter Four

THE SECOND MASTER TOOL

AS A REMINDER, THERE ARE ONLY TWO TOOLS YOU NEED TO MASTER YOUR MONEY. YOUR NET WORTH WAS TOOL NUMBER ONE, AND TOOL NUMBER TWO IS YOUR BUDGET.

BUDGET

Listen. If there was a list of the sexiest words in the English language, "budget" would be right up there with "lugubrious" or "curd" or "execrable." I've taught budgeting courses in the past called "50 Shades of Budgeting" to try and make it hotter. But even though the word isn't exciting and the act of doing it isn't even appealing to most people, once it's done you feel like you are curled up in the arms of the one you love, post-budgetous.

I don't care what you call the budget. It can be called a cash flow plan. An abundance plan. Angela, who took the Get the Hell Out of Debt course a couple years ago, called hers the "Sunshine List." Whatever you have to do to describe the way you want to feel about doing the budget is fine by me. I just need you to do it.

I'm going to show you a few basic ways to manage cash, and your job is to make a whole yucky mess of it until you figure out what works for you. If you are the kind of person who hates getting your hands dirty, this is going to require you to roll up your sleeves and be okay with a perfectly imperfect financial challenge. In my experience, every single person who got into debt did it without a working budget. "Working" meaning a budget where the expenses are less than the income and a choir spontaneously sings "Ode to Joy" when you open it. That might seem impossible if you had to rely on credit through extreme financial hardship, or maybe you budgeted while putting yourself through school and realized there was no way in heck you could maintain studies while working three jobs. I get it if you had to consciously make a choice to enter debt-land. Hey, there's no judgment here. But if you are here to argue with me that you think budgeting is stupid, then I will make you the Parade Marshal of the "Debt Is Awesome Parade." You can wave at people in your shiny suit, sitting atop a convertible as you wonder how you'll pay for it, all through a gritted smile.

(I'll give you my old parade sash. That used to be me.)

So, let's make a working budget, shall we?

A WORKING BUDGET IS A CONSTANT WORK IN PROGRESS.

When I first budgeted, I was making a budget based on assumptions, and then I was horribly frustrated when things didn't happen exactly according to the budget. I would abandon the budget and go "eff it" and try again weeks down the line, until I eventually quit altogether. Obviously, I did not get out of debt during those times! I eventually learned that when I do next month's budget, it is a guideline, and my job is to try and keep everything within the goal posts. It doesn't have to be a shut-out. If the final score at the end of the month is 11-4 for Erin, I still win the game. So even if I go over on a category or two, I can adjust and make up for it, and still win the month. It also helps me play better defense next month if I don't just quit, or worse, grab my Visa, rack it up, and score against myself.

(I would still like to apologize to my Grade Six floor hockey team and Mrs. Jones for that embarrassing shot on my own team. I would like to point out, however, it was the only point I ever scored in any sports at all in elementary school. So. We all start somewhere.)

I needed to get used to reconciling my budget frequently to keep gentle tabs on myself. The first time I went to budget, it was a tissue-inducing, snot-filled sob-fest that lasted three hours, followed by a walk outdoors to calm down and then another forty-five minutes of the odd tear just rolling down my cheek. If this was a movie scene, my first budget montage soundtrack would've been Boyz II Men's "It's So Hard to Say Goodbye to Yesterday."

A WORKING BUDGET IS NOT PERFECT.

This is the part most of us have to let go of. If you struggle with criticism or get down on yourself when you muck-up at paint night, if you care what people think while you are going through this process or are highly judgmental of others and their money habits, you are going to have a *hell of a time* with this.

You are going to have to quickly let go of two things:

Your expectations of yourself
Your expectations of others

I want you to trade your high expectations for high standards. There is a subtle distinction between expectations and standards, but it makes all the difference when it comes to your success and happiness.

When you have a high expectation, you are putting your beliefs about how things "should" be on yourself and others. Having an expectation means that you will likely feel frustration and judgement. It doesn't leave enough room for you and the people you love to be human. So even if you consider yourself financially knowledgeable and are still in debt, it is *very important* to your success today that you approach this book as if everything in it is new information.

As I mentioned earlier, what we *know* is not as important to eliminating debt as what we *do*. I am often approached by people who have heard a few of the things I say but haven't done the course completely. They'll be like, "I was doing ______________________ and it didn't work," and I'll ask, "Well did you do ______________________ first?" They'll say, "No, no, I already *know* that," and I'll respond, "Yes, but did you do it?" And when they say "No," I can't help them.

I can't help you unless you actually do all the things. I don't care what you know, to be honest. I care about what results you get. You cannot get results unless you take appropriate action to get you across the debt-free finish line.

If you instead simply *raise your standards*, you'll be happier. What this does is bring the focus back onto you and the things you will allow or not allow in your life. This is a boundary. We talk a *lot* about boundaries in this book because if you are reading this book and you carry a lot of consumer debt, it is almost certain that you have terrible boundaries. I don't just mean with your money. I mean with your family, in your workplace, everywhere. You are very likely to be putting other people's needs and emotions in front of your own. Gosh, it looks so harsh all typed out. Read that again, but in a gentle voice, like if you were talking to adorable kids, because I want you to know you learned this from childhood. You were taught to be a nice girl or a good boy or a well-behaved person, and you were doing it to make someone happy. When it comes to your finances, you carried over this desire to be likeable somehow or other. It's okay if you need a minute to process this.

It's not a pretty thing to become aware of. If this paragraph hit you like a ton of bricks, it can be helpful to stop and journal for a moment. I find that a trigger, while painful, is always an opportunity for my own growth when I am ready.

(A lot of what we do here is going to feel like repetition. You're going to hear the same themes come up again and again, and when you notice that happening, what you are witnessing is your personal transformation in action. And if you are like me, when you take on a new goal you want to hurry up and do something. So, you might have skipped ahead to the "to-do" parts and missed out on the "to-think" parts, and it's my job to make sure you don't miss the importance of changing your thinking while you change your behaviors. Repetition is the key to commanding your finances, so you'll see a few themes pop up time and again.)

Just get a scrap piece of paper and, stream-of-consciousness style, just start writing whatever comes up for you. I tell you to do it on a scrap piece because often what comes up brings out a lot of resentment, and you'll want to throw that piece of paper away so that you don't carry that energy with you. But getting through the emotional gunk will be important. Most of us feel emotions and then try to distract ourselves from them. We'll eat. Drink. Scroll. Do anything to avoid feeling the feels. But there is *information there*. Feelings are information. It's crucial for the next few months of your life, as you go through the *Get the Hell Out of Debt* process, that you feel your feelings fully. Otherwise, this will feel like a diet, and then you'll hit your ideal number and binge yourself right back up to where you started.

A standard is *the level of quality of life you are willing to accept for yourself.* Raising that standard to be "I will live a debt-free and financially abundant life" will allow you to make hard decisions today so that you can protect your future. Raise your standards. Drop your expectations.

A WORKING BUDGET ALMOST NEVER ENDS UP AT THE END OF A MONTH LIKE YOU ANTICIPATED IT WOULD AT THE BEGINNING.

What you are doing with your budget is gazing into a crystal ball and trying to pre-make decisions so that you don't emotionally make decisions. Remember this? Repeat after me:

My emotions do not dictate my behaviors.
My emotions do not dictate my behaviors.
My emotions do not dictate my behaviors.

You are going to make a plan for every single penny that hits your account before it arrives. I don't know if you have ever let your emotions run the show, but I have. When I was in my early twenties, I dated this guy who was Level Ten Handsome and very charming, and I thought he was the Greatest Man on the Planet for a while. We were supposed to spend some time together one particular weekend, but then I didn't hear from him. When he finally called, he didn't mention the date he ghosted me on. Eventually, I asked, "What did you do on the weekend?" and he mentioned that he went skiing. Just like that. Casually. Had forgotten all about me. It hurt so much. I started to notice other patterns that I had been blind to. Red flags that only looked yellow and orange in the sunset depending on the weather patterns. I felt like maybe I should break up with him, but I didn't have a solid plan. It was easy to justify his behavior in the moment. "Oh well, he just forgot about me one time. We all make mistakes."

But it didn't feel like a mistake. Especially when there was no apology, and soon he was twisting it around to blame me in some weird way. But if I was feeling good about him in the moment, I was overlooking major future disaster cues, and if I was feeling bad about him in the moment, I was avoiding a tough conversation I needed to have, and instead numbing my feelings with a blender drink called a Frozen Chicago.

I am ashamed to tell you I let this behavior continue for far too long. Much later, I ended up in the same elevator as him accidentally, and everyone in the elevator I'm *certain* could hear my heart pounding. This guy could activate my emotions with one glance.

If I let my emotions decide moment-to-moment how to make decisions, I would have had a ten year on-again-off-again relationship with that turkey.

I eventually escaped both the relationship and his charm by creating a solid plan, in spite of how I felt. I turned off my phone ringer. I instructed my roommate to delete his answering machine messages (!!!) if she got to them before I did, and if I heard his voice by accident—his sweet, gorgeous, sexy voice—I immediately would put on my shoes and go for a walk. Every time I felt like drinking a Frozen Chicago, I would instead first drink a tall glass of blended ice water. And I made sure for sixty days I would not end up anywhere he might be.

I had to decide ahead of time how I would respond in the moment *in spite of how I felt.* And that's what you have to do with the budget. You decide where every penny will be spent and then you act according to plan, even if you are in your room sniffing his sweatshirt for traces of his cologne. Hypothetically.

When things are stressful and you are feeling financially overwhelmed, you look at the plan and follow the plan. And sometimes, partway through the month, you realize things are not going to plan. You end up in an elevator with Handsome Turkey Face. And because your goal is to become debt-free and master your money and not end up with an STI, you do not make out with him in the elevator or anywhere ever again. You have something else to focus on: freedom. So, if you run into an issue where not as much money comes in every month or an expense is higher than you anticipated, you adjust those things as you go. You do not decide "screw it, this did not go according to plan" and undo all the things you worked for.

Come at every month with a plan and a simple curiosity: *I wonder what interesting financial adventures I will experience this month and how they will challenge me to be resourceful.* When your goal is having the month come out as close to plan as possible you are more likely to succeed. We do all that we can do in a day, and we let the rest go.

A WORKING BUDGET IS THE BEST TOOL TO KEEP YOU CALM AND FOCUSED ON YOUR JOURNEY OUT OF DEBT.

During the 2020 pandemic, I did a podcast with Jade, who graduated from the Get the Hell Out of Debt program a year before. She had just delivered a baby, she and her partner had a massive drop in income, and I wondered if she was stressed. She said she was absolutely not and that she was in a "state of calm." She was budgeting more frequently, and by going into her numbers and her budget every day, she was leaning into her fears. Looking at it more frequently helped her fully see where things were coming and things were going, so she could make adjustments long before it was too late.

A budget also acts like an emotional anchor. When you are feeling stressed, you can just head to the budget and have a look and make some tweaks. You've got a safe space to go. It certainly doesn't feel safe when you are starting, but imagine that you'd been budgeting for the last ten years of your life and you had it mastered now. Would you love to look at the budget today if you'd been working with it over the last ten years? Of course you would! Think of all the things you freaked out over financially that you could have prepared for, had you been mastering your budget. You budget so that you can take care of yourself financially, but also so that you can take care of yourself emotionally.

A WORKING BUDGET IS THE SAME TOOL YOU'LL USE TO BUILD WEALTH AND BECOME FINANCIALLY FREE.

I used to believe that I didn't need a budget because I didn't *have* any money to budget. But when I decided to just see what happened if I tried, I discovered that I actually could make rapid financial progress if I was consistent at budgeting. The techniques I will teach you about budgeting are the same techniques I use for investing and retirement planning. Getting in the habit now of managing your finances is important if you want to take advantage of wealth-building once you are debt-free. Think of yourself as an air traffic controller. Your job is to direct the money, and the budget allows you to have the dollars safely land and take off where you need them to go. You'll do the same when you are debt-free. Instead of directing the dollars to pay off a credit card, though, you will be directing them to your investments and your retirement accounts.

A WORKING BUDGET IS MORE LIKELY TO GET YOU LAID.

Just kidding. I wanted to see if you're still paying attention. But when you feel more confident about money, you'll feel more confident in general, and I can't see how that can hurt.

A WORKING BUDGET CAN BE PER MONTH, PER WEEK, PER PAYCHECK...YOU DECIDE.

You'll hear me talk about budgets as though they are meant to be monthly, but if that doesn't make sense for you and you get paid bi-weekly? Then budget bi-weekly! A budget is essentially a plan for the next batch of money you expect, so please make a budget fit *your* life instead of trying to fit your life into a budget. You can customize and adapt this budgeting information to the schedule that makes the most sense to you.

A WORKING BUDGET PLANS FOR THE MONEY YOU DO NOT YET HAVE BUT THAT YOU ANTICIPATE.

For the most part, you can anticipate the money you are likely to receive. This is more difficult for you if you are self-employed, but if you really pay attention to your receivables, you can at least see what is in the pipeline. That way you'll know how much more marketing or sales you'll need to increase your business. You are going to budget the dollars you do not have yet. You don't look at what is already in your account. You look at what is coming and budget that. Usually by the time the dollars hit the bank account, they are already owed to something. So those dollars need to get reconciled against the budget you already set out. *Pinky swear you will reconcile.* It's crucial. Reconciling is basically the grown-up way to "check your work."

A WORKING BUDGET NEEDS TO BE ADJUSTED THROUGH THE MONTH TO ACCOUNT FOR THE DIFFERENCE BETWEEN WHAT YOU ANTICIPATED AND WHAT ACTUALLY HAPPENED.

In case you slipped up on the way to the grocery store and some tacos from your favorite drive-thru accidentally fell into your mouth, you will need to make some adjustments. When you start the budget, you are looking at a clean slate and anticipating all the expenses you think will happen. But on account of you being human, there will definitely be some slips, some muck-ups, and (gasp!) even some self-sabotages. There are definitely money gurus who will tell you to automate all the things so you do not have to look at your money every day because that is boring. This is true. Money can be boring. Debt is dramatic. But because we have been living like broke drama queens, the *exact* thing we need for a while is boring. Predictable. Consistency. When you've been out of debt for a few months and you start to build wealth in Phase Three, you could automate some aspects of your wealth-building. But for now, I want you to *manually* look at your moola every day and adjust.

When you sip your morning coffee and log into your device, do a quick check of the account and the budget, and see what kind of damage (if any) you did the day before. Then check if you have any expected expenses today, and make sure you are still on track for the month and that you'll have enough money to cover everything. You are trying to squeeze out every dollar from the budget you can for a while. So, paying attention to it for five to ten minutes a day gives you a better outcome than herding cats at the end of the month.

Or not checking at all.

Listen, it's true that some people don't need to spend five to ten minutes checking their money every day. It's also true that some people cannot drink one tequila shot without then getting totally rip-roaring drunk and dancing on the speaker at Yucatan's Bar and Grill while other people can enjoy a sipping tequila. (Seriously? You sip it? That seems like a marketing ploy to me.) Some people can eat cheeseburgers and pizzas and still weigh 105 pounds while other people dare to put a pat of butter on their broccoli and the next day their pants don't button.

As for you? If you picked up this book for the reason it was intended, you *need* to check in with your money every day, at least until you don't. You will know when that time comes because suddenly your money metabolism will feel like it is working *for* you, not against you. You'll see the tequila shots on the table and you won't be compelled to smash seven of them into your guacamole hole. Most importantly, you'll have a healthy relationship with money. But if you are anything like me, you'll want to nurture that relationship for life. Checking in with your money will be a daily positive habit, like kissing your gorgeous spouse goodbye before they leave for work, no matter how many dirty socks they might have left on the floor.

When you identify as "I am someone who simply chooses to quickly check in with my money every day," you can come at it from an empowered perspective.

A WORKING BUDGET IS THE START OF YOUR MUCH NEEDED BOUNDARY WORK.

We're going to talk a *lot* about boundaries in this book, and your budget is the representation of your financial boundaries. If you tell me you have no budget, I hear "I have no boundaries." If you tell me you hate budgeting, I hear "I hate boundaries." If you tell me you don't need a budget, I hear "I don't need boundaries." And in all of those scenarios, you are setting yourself up for emotional, mental, and financial failure, so let's think of your budget as your financial hopes and dreams on paper, and let's protect them with a boundary that shields them from unhealthy and toxic decisions that can derail your life.

A WORKING BUDGET IS SIMPLY THE ORGANIZATION OF INCOME AND EXPENSES.

All you are doing is tracking the amount of money that comes in every month, and the amount that goes out. If the tooth fairy leaves you five dollars under your pillow, that is income. Your government benefit that gets deposited automatically into your account? That's income. When you get overtime pay or commissions, that is *income*.

Every penny that comes into your life gets tracked and counted as income.

When you pay the electricity bill, that's an expense. When you get a haircut and you pay and tip the barber or hairstylist, that's an expense. When you have to pay school fees, that's an expense. When your rip-off bank takes their $10.95 a month for the account maintenance fee, that's an expense.

Your job is to be the boss of all the dollars in and all the dollars out, and boss them around like a naughty dominatrix. They answer to *you*. In all seriousness, part of the reason you are in this situation is likely because you've been very submissive with your money. You've been letting money run your life instead of you running your life and telling your money what to do. So, roll up your sleeves, put on those shiny black PVC gloves, and be the boss of your life.

A WORKING BUDGET WORKS BEST WHEN IT IS KEPT SIMPLE. In the beginning, I much prefer you do things with pen and paper. Mostly because you are better able to retain the numbers when you write them down, and because over my years of teaching this, I've seen this as one of the defining success strategies. People who are quick to find an app or spreadsheet are often looking for a quick fix for the painful budget. I want it to hurt. I want it to hurt *sooooo* good.

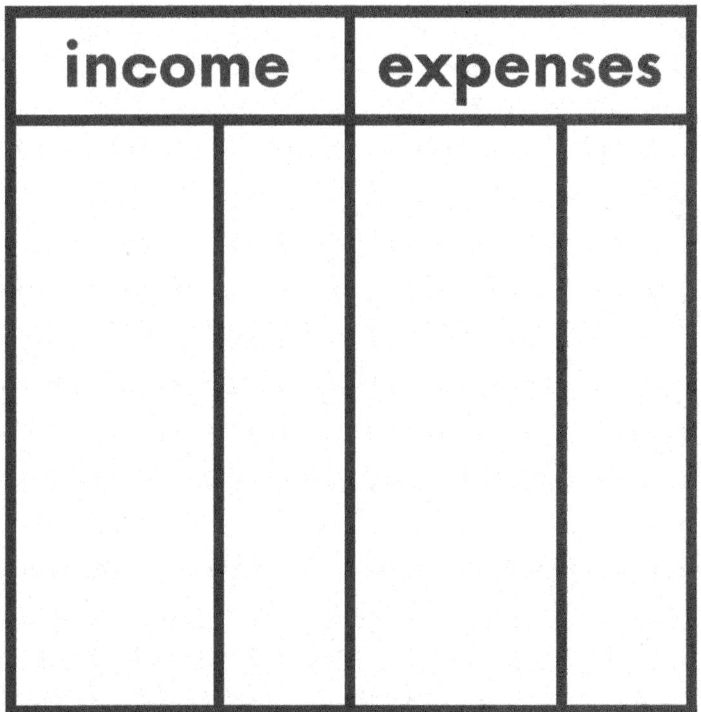

Keep the budget as simple as possible. I only want you to track two and a half things:

- The expected income coming in
- The fixed expenses (the ones that stay the same every month)
- The variable expenses (the ones that adjust, like groceries or utilities)

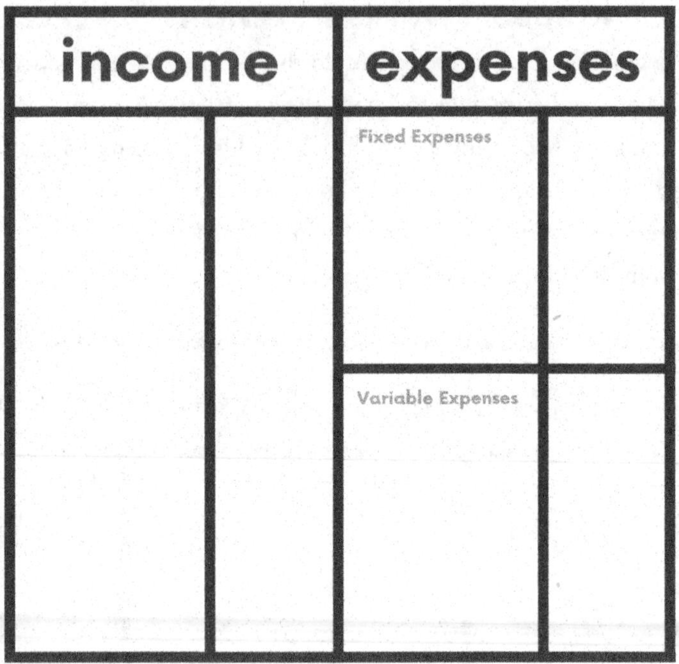

THE WORKING BUDGET WORKS BEST WHEN IT IS MANUAL, NOT AUTOMATIC.

There are lots of great apps on the market for budgeting. But when I was trying to automate everything in the beginning (of my failed attempts at budgeting), what I was actually looking for was an external solution to my internal chaos.

Usually when people automate something, they become unconscious. They stop paying attention. I was one of those people. In order to rewire my money habits, I first had to spend three months with a notebook and pen in my bag, tracking everything and crossing things out and saying lots of swear words before I even knew which end was up. I eventually started tracking my budget on a spreadsheet because I found most budget apps link to your bank account and only tell you where your money *went.* Past tense. I want to be in control of where it *goes*, so I now use a spreadsheet to first tell my money what I want it to do, and then I follow up to see if it listened. I've learned so much about my personal money habits by listening and being intentional with my spending.

But it started with a notebook and pen.

LET'S DO THIS.

In order to start, you need a scrap piece of paper. You can even use a white space in this book if you can find a nearby pen. You're just going to start by writing down all the things you think you will earn in the month ahead. You can check this against your bank account for months past if you need a general idea.

income		expenses	
• salary • commissions • bonuses • side job • government benefits • any rebate thingies • all the dolla dolla bills that come in	$ amount goes here	• housing costs • groceries • transportation • childcare • phone and internet bills • insurance • contributions to retirement • all the dolla dolla bills that go out	$ amount goes here

So, you can start just like that. Two columns. If you like to color code things, you can make the Income column green, like money or growth. You could make the Expenses column red, like danger or raging PMS.

Then, if you want to get extra fancy-like, you can divide the Expenses column into two parts: the set expenses, which are the dollar amounts that don't fluctuate each month, and the variable expenses, which are not always the same.

income		expenses	
• salary • commissions • bonuses • side job • government benefits • any rebate thingies • all the dolla dolla bills that come in	$ amount goes here	Fixed Expenses SET AMOUNTS or expenses that do not fluctuate each month	$ amount goes here
		Variable Expenses AMOUNTS THAT CHANGE or expenses that are kind of sneaky buggers that can mess up your budget if you don't pay attention	$ amount goes here

If you have enough money coming in every month and everything is working, then it's okay if you want to have the fixed expenses come out of your account automatically with an auto-debit (even though you are still tracking them manually). If money is really tight and the timing of the cashflow is off, I want you to contact the companies that receive those fixed expenses.

First, decide if you need them or if you can get rid of the expense while you get the hell out of debt. Then I want you to make sure the automatic payment, if you have one, lines up with a time when there is enough money in the account.

If you have variable expenses, however, I prefer these to be paid manually. For example, the cell phone company does not get your bank account number to pull the money out every month. *You* are the boss of your money. You'll get that bill every month and pay it (on time, if possible!) when you get the money, based on the flow of cash in and out of your life that month. And definitely remove all automatic payments from credit cards, until we get those under control.

But this is where I want you to be certain that you are absolutely committed to paying off your debt.

If you take your bills off automatic withdrawals, and you forget about them, you will fall behind and have an even bigger hole to dig yourself out of.

Commit. Be certain. Pay attention. And set yourself up to succeed.

Here's what happens for you if you *are* totally committed. Let's say you forget to reset one little button on your phone while you were traveling or hotspotting or just being alive, and you rack up a massive charge with your mobile phone company that they expect you to pay.

You can make partial payments online through the bank when it is convenient for you. So, if the bill comes to $350 and you expected it to be $50, you can make the $50 payment. Then you move your buns to find the additional money by selling things, increasing your income, or reducing other expenses. If you put $75 on this week, and another $125 next week and then $100 by the last week, you are all caught up by the next billing cycle.

But if you aren't caught up because you can't quite gather enough to make the full payment, you do as much as you can. This is a lot better than what might've happened if they tried to take $350 out of your account when the bill was due. That payment could have bounced, leading to fees from both the bank *and* the cell phone company, and you'd still be $300 behind on the next bill too.

When you start out with your budget, you are *actively* managing the income, the fixed expenses and the variable expenses. But once you master budgeting, you'll only have to worry about managing the variable expenses. (And when you are out of debt, you'll be focused on managing your variable expenses, plus the money that you HAD been paying to creditors that now goes into your investing and wealth-building. That is sure a fun transition!)

So, the only way to get out of this debt mess is to:

1) Increase income
2) Decrease expenses
3) A combo of increasing income and decreasing expenses

Okay, well, that's still only two things, but I think it sounds fancier that way.

If you are serious about becoming debt-free and you want to make it happen as fast as humanly possible, I have to be honest with you: it is *going to require* some lifestyle changes. If you are serious about changing your life, then these lifestyle changes will be temporary. If you are only half-assing this process, then you're likely going to feel more frustrated in the long term because you will be constantly trading short-term relief for long-term pain.

Listen. I want to be sitting on the beach in Bora Bora one day, and I want you to come up to me with a big floppy hat and oversized sunglasses and an obnoxiously large blended drink in your hand, and say "*Dahling*, thank you for the book. I traded a few pedicures back then for all this!" And then I want you to gesture (with your pinky up) at the over-the-water bungalow you are staying in for the next eight weeks that you paid for…in cash.

I want you to consider the big picture. Short-term pain for long-term gain. I'm not being the Ultimate Fun Destroyer™ and telling you that you have to cut everything from your budget except for oxygen. Heck, every day while I was paying off debt, I still had a tall-five-pump-non-fat-no-water chai tea latte. But I didn't drink a drop of booze. I didn't buy new clothes for fun. I didn't get pedicures or go on fun vacations. I had to consistently battle temptation like I was the Rebel Alliance trying to finally overtake and defeat the Galactic Empire. (Admittedly, I have never even seen one single Star War, but I hear that is a thing.)

I want you to choose the luxury item or the frivolous spend that is most important to you and keep it in the budget. If you don't have something designated to be your frivolous spend, it's kind of like going on one of those 600 calorie diets. (Oh gawd. You can tell I was raised in the '80s and '90s, can't you?) They don't last a long time because you start off all zealous and keyed up, but at some point you smell fresh-baked bread and you're a goner.

If you restrict without fully choosing, you might find you have an unhealthy preoccupation with money and spending. You might also swing wildly between restriction and binge-spending, depending on your personality. Lastly, you might start to live in a lack mentality, which can have negative emotional effects.

Spend on the thing that is super important to you. It can help you stay sane during the process of reducing expenses and tightening up the budget. Then I want you to get ruthless with all the other expenses. I want you to cut them like chocolate-covered octopus in a *Top Chef* High-Stakes QuickFire Challenge. I want you to get rid of every expense that is not crucial to your survival and get absolutely serious about being financially free.

Zero-based Budgeting:

You're going to make the budget balance to *zero*. Cero. Null. Nulla. Số không. *Nothing*.

I think because we have this understanding that we should "spend less than we make," there is a misconception that you need to have a bunch of money in your account every month. But most people who dabbled in debt will be relieved to know that you can actually spend all the money in your account every month and still be wealthy. You'll eventually be spending some of it on investments instead of online purchases. You truly need to let every cent live its life purpose, but you have to tell it what its life purpose is. If you increase your income by $200, you have to find a place for that $200 to go before Amazon does. Think of all the businesses that are competing for those 200 dollars. You need to take care of your dollars before someone else convinces you they'll do a better job of it.

The best part about Zero-based Budgeting is that it requires impeccable execution because you have no buffer. You can adjust as you go, and you *will* reconcile. (You pinky-swore!) But if you leave money in the account thinking you have a buffer of $550 left to spend for the end of the month, guess what you are likely to waste? Yup. $550.

Once you've configured a budget for the month ahead, look at the previous couple of months to see how you actually spend your money. Some of us (including me) can delude ourselves into thinking we have better money habits than we do. Your past is not an indication of your future if you are willing to change. Just because you've always struggled with money doesn't mean you always will. We can get locked into old patterns because of our beliefs about who we are, but you can interrupt this pattern and chart a new trajectory right now, my friend.

So, if you are seriously looking at driving on a new highway, it is absolutely imperative that you glance in that rearview mirror now and then. You can't drive the entire way to your destination by looking in the rearview the whole time. You'll crash. Or if you live near me in Canada, you'll hit a moose. You've got to focus by looking out the windshield, far enough down the road that you can anticipate any challenge and you can watch the road signs. But every now and then, you have to take a *quick* look back.

Temptation is not a sin, but free cheese is always available in mousetraps. So, here's a bit of bonus homework for you to keep you on track.

Bonus Budget Tip: Unsubscribe + Organize

If you find you are often sucked in by big-box craft stores who send you a coupon for a ridiculously low price on one item that isn't in your budget, it might be time to hit the unsubscribe button.

Statistics tell us that it takes seventeen to twenty-two mentions of a product before we buy it. This means retailers are spamming the heck out of us to get our attention. Your inbox is likely littered with digital flyers. They can tell when you've opened their emails. They even often know if you've clicked any links in the emails they send. This allows them to segment their list between the *cha-chings!*, the people who are going to buy (you get more emails…surprise!), and the *deadbeats*, the people who aren't actively engaging with the emails.

If you are a deadbeat, definitely unsubscribe anyway. Every distraction takes up a lot of your mental space, so let's ensure we are focused on the results *we* want, and not the results our favorite department store wants.

Alternatively, if you love the coupons and newsletters that are cluttering up in your inbox, then create a new free email account called ErinSkyeKellyCoupons@gmail.com and use that to subscribe to the companies that are sending you the mousetrap cheese. Okay, not that one, it's taken. But you get the idea. Don't add that email to your phone emails, but simply log in to it now and then with intention instead of distraction. Also, turn off app notifications (honestly do this anyway!) for any apps you have that tempt you to spend with their adorable little dopamine hits to your brain.

The ones that get me are the food delivery services that pop up at 3:00 p.m. *How do you know I was thinking about carbs*, UberEats? Go to your notifications and disable them. Your future floppy hat and oversized sunglasses wearing Bora Bora self will thank you.

If you are self-employed or you have expenses to track for your employer, you can also set up an email account like marysmithsreceipts@gmail.com so that you simply have to take a photo of your receipts and email them there. There are lots of apps that do this, too, but this is a free option if you don't have the software, and you can access the receipts from anywhere you have internet access (or share the email address with your accountant).

> Cindy says: "Before Get the Hell Out of Debt I would spend and wouldn't give a flying f*ck how I was going to make it work. I always did somehow but I was always stressed too. Not anymore. I think about what I spend and how it fits into my budget, and the results are amazing!"

Chapter Five

WHAT TO DO IF YOU HAVE UNPREDICTABLE INCOME

BUDGETING ON A FLUCTUATING INCOME

First things first:

1. This sucks donkey balls. I know how difficult this is because you may have trouble anticipating what next month's income looks like. So, you're probably thinking, "*Erin!* This is all cute that you want me to *plan next month.* But I have no idea which clients are going to pay their bills *on time* or what commissions I will earn. So, this is impossible." I hear you.
2. It's no reason to quit. You know *half* of the equation. You likely know your expenses, so we've got something to work with at least. If you don't budget, we know you are never going to get there, so why not have a never-going-to-be-exactly-perfect budget? At least it will get you closer to your goal!
3. People who master budgeting on a fluctuating income are the richest people in the world. All of the wealthiest people on those silly worldwide billionaire lists are asset owners or business owners or investors. They have giant ups and downs. But they have learned

how to adapt to fluctuating income and make it work *for* them instead of being a victim to it. You likely do not have a ceiling on your income, whereas a salaried person does. You might even have unlimited income potential, depending on where you work, how efficiently you work, or how innovative you are. So, if I'm in your shoes, then I'm going to make the absolute most of this scenario and commit to doing my best every day, in spite of the challenges I will face.

If you have a fluctuating income and you do *not* budget, here is what you are up against:

a) You are more likely to end up in debt. We know that you are most likely to use sources of credit to make up the shortfalls on the months where your income is lower. The credit card companies certainly know that. And they want you to know that if *you* aren't there for you, they will be there for you. And what I'm saying is *please show up for you*!

b) You are more likely to experience stress about retirement. When you have a fluctuating income, you may have a hard time planning for the future because you are so worried about what money will be in your account next Friday. You're more worried about how you will feed the family this week. You are more worried about your next income cycle, so retirement is the last thing on your worry list.

c) You are more likely to "wing it" when it comes to financial decisions. Because you aren't planning ahead, you are often caught by the seat-of-your-pants spending plan, which means you're navigating your money without any real purpose and flow. That often results in your money decisions working against each other.

d) You are more likely to overspend in months when you have extra money. You've had months when things felt *tiiiiight*, so you are more likely to get a little too relaxed when the money comes in. Again, since you've been unable to plan for that income, it's difficult for you to manage because you live by the subconscious belief that you don't know when money like this is going to appear again. We've got to work at evening out the lows and the highs so that we aren't praying for a high to be able to live our lives.

BUDGET

A budget is only based on two things: *income* and *expenses*. So, let's keep it simple.

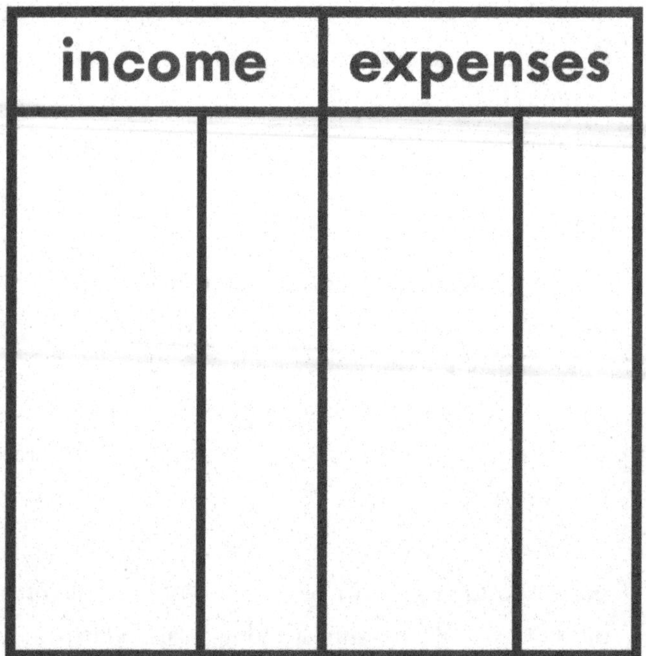

Now, we're going to do this before the month actually starts. It's important to remember that you're planning for the future to set yourself up for success.

You're going to start by assembling all the income you are expecting.

income		expenses	
Base Salary	$1000.00		
Government Benefits	$545.30		
Commissions	$300.00		
Other	$100.00		
TOTAL INCOME	$1945.30		

And now we are going to assemble all the expenses we are expecting, but this time we are going to list them in order of importance to survival. Prioritizing expenses will make it easier to figure out what to do when we run short on income.

income		expenses	
Base Salary	$1000.00	Housing	$500.00
		Utilities	$130.00
Government Benefits	$545.30	Transportation	$82.80
		Childcare	$500.00
		Groceries	$400.00
Commissions	$300.00	School Fees	$20.00
		Chai Lattes	$63.50
Other	$100.00	Fun Money	$50.00
		Debt Repayment	$350.00
TOTAL INCOME	$1945.30	TOTAL EXPENSES	$2096.30

This means we have a $151.00 deficit and a whole lot of swear words. So, all we can do is go as far as we can.

WHAT TO DO WHEN THERE ISN'T ENOUGH

Our priorities are always going to be the things that set us up to be able to earn income in the first place.

FOOD: When we nourish our bodies, we set ourselves up to be able to learn better, work better, function better, and support our immune system. Healthy food can be expensive, so it is important to shop wisely and plan ahead. If it makes more sense to have a few nights of ramen noodles in order to make the budget work, then you could choose that. If it makes more sense for you to cut something else out of the budget so you can afford organic avocados, then you could choose that.

SHELTER: You need a home base to feel safe and secure. Cultivating as much certainty for yourself as you embark on the debt-destroying process is critical to your success. You might discover your rent or mortgage situation is far too rich for your budget, and it might make sense for you to start considering, at least temporarily, whether you want to right-size your life. Your home can be a great place to start.

TRANSPORTATION: When I refer to transportation, I am talking about your ability to get to and from your place of employment. That might look like your feet. That might look like a bicycle. If you have kids who have to get to school, that might look like all of them crammed into a tiny car like clowns. It does not mean a car you can show off or use to impress people in traffic. When I talk about priorities, I truly mean what you need in order to make the most of where you are now financially, so that you can get even further in the future.

CHILDCARE: Quality childcare is important. In this scenario, I am referring to quality care for your children so you can earn income to get yourself out of debt. There is one crucial thing you must always consider with regards to this: the money you earn frequently has to add up to more than the cost of childcare.

For example, if you consistently earn $1400 per month, and your child-care costs are $1200 per month, that is a *lot* of hours to be away from your precious little people for $200 dollars net earnings. So, it's important to be conscious of the spending in this category and how it lines up with making your life better. If this was your scenario, it might make sense to work from home in some capacity, or to find something that increases your income substantially. Or, if it turns out parenting is not your jam and you need to work for your mental health more than for your financial needs, then be clear about that when making decisions.

In my own life, it became extremely important for me to be mindful of the influence the caretakers had over my children. If my kids were not spending forty hours a week with me, that meant they were spending a couple thousand hours a year under someone else's health, financial, relational, emotional, and moral influences, and this was one area for me where spending for higher quality care if necessary was more vital than a tall-five-pump-non-fat-no-water chai latte if it came down to it.

PEGGY'S BUDGET

income		expenses	
Base Salary	$1000.00	Housing	$500.00
		Utilities	$130.00
Government Benefits	$545.30	Transportation	$82.80
		Childcare	$500.00
		Groceries	$400.00
Commissions	$300.00	School Fees	$20.00
		Chai Lattes	$63.50
Other	$100.00	Fun Money	$50.00
		Debt Repayment	$350.00
TOTAL INCOME	$1945.30	TOTAL EXPENSES	$2096.30

To better visualize this, we will use an imaginary person, Peggy Chicken (she/her), as an example. This is how Peggy chose to prioritize her expenses. She decided that the most important things were housing and utilities, then transportation and childcare and groceries. At first, she felt groceries might be the most important thing, but then decided her resourcefulness around getting groceries could be taken into account. If things ever got too bad, she could use a program that gives people groceries and perhaps start freezing and canning things to make her feel less food-scarce.

So, given the situation above, Peggy has $1945.30 for income and $1612.80 for prioritized expenses. This means she only has $332.50 left to pay $483.50 in expenses. What can she do?

Here are the rules: Peggy gets to decide how to allocate that money based on her preference.

Fluctuating Income Budget Shortfall Strategy One: Proportional Payments

Peggy has $332.50 left. The outstanding expenses add up to $483.50. She can divide that amount between the four remaining items on her expense list.

So, for example, debt repayment ($350) equals 72 percent of the outstanding expenses ($483.50). Given that she only has $332.50 available, she will allocate 72 percent of $332.50 toward debt repayment. Meaning, she will end up making a $239.40 payment to her debt this month.

The school fees ($20) equate to 4 percent of $483.50. Because she only had $332.50 left to pay bills, she would give 4 percent of that to the school this month. That means she is paying the school $13.30 toward her $20 owing.

The chai lattes ($63.50) equate to 13 percent of $483.50. Because she only had $332.50 left to pay bills, she would spend only $43.23 on chai lattes this month. $43.23 is 13 percent of $332.50

Her fun money ($50) would equal 10.3 percent of $483.50. Because she only had $332.50 left to pay bills, she would only allocate 10.3 percent of that to fun money this month, which works out to $34.24 to blow on fun stuff.

When we add up these proportional payments, we get:

$239.40 towards debt
$13.30 for school fees
$43.23 for chai lattes
$34.24 for fun stuff

$330.17 (The number is approximate because of conservatively rounding percentage decimals.)

But you can see she made it work! She was able to at least make a partial payment to everything on her expenses list. This way she won't be carrying over the entire debt payment or falling too behind, or being delinquent with payments.

By the way, if you judged Peggy for having the chai lattes on her list, you just should'ed her, and I told you not to do that. You get to decide what financial integrity means to you, but remember that you do not get to put your opinions in other people's wallets.

This system does require a little math, but if you love math…first of all, who didn't hug you as a child?! (Kidding.) But secondly, here is the formula so you can play with your mechanical pencils alone in your room.

Equation for Percentage of Proportional Payments

Y=P%*X
Or Y/X = P%

You can fill these in based on what you remember from high school math, and if you have no clue what happened in high school math because you were busy reading love notes from Ricky S. like I was, then you can just google "how do I figure out the percent of something" and there are all kinds of online calculators that do the work for those of us who are only medium smart.

1. Find P percent of X
2. Find what percent of X is Y
3. Find X if P percent of it is Y

Here's a fun fact! If your eyes glazed over like donuts while you were reading that, I've just saved you some time because that very well might not be the system for you! Keep reading!

Fluctuating Income Budget Shortfall Strategy Two: The Theory of Least Social Repercussions

Peggy might decide that paying the school first will bring less emotional embarrassment, which might feel important to Peggy. She still has $332.50 left over, so she might choose to pay them first, and then that will leave her with $312.50 to pay the rest of the debts.

Or, if she's friendly with the school, she might ask them for a bit more time for her payment because communicating with her creditors is an important proactive step. Maybe she puts all the money she can toward her debt this month, and she will give up the chai and the fun money.

Basically, this strategy employs you choosing priorities and making *no* apologies. You must pay everyone eventually because you said you would. But *you* have to stay in control of the money.

Fluctuating Income Budget Shortfall Strategy Three: The Bum's Rush. The Elbow Grease Strategy. The Achiever.

When we were slow-moving, our third grade teacher used to say, "Hurry up or I'll give you the bum's rush," which I thought had to do with your booty. I always hurried up because I wanted no part of that. Turns out it was early 1900s slang for getting rid of an unwanted vagrant, which now seems horribly politically incorrect; however, in order to prevent yourself from becoming homeless, you might want to put a little rush on things, which is why you might want to employ this strategy.

Because Peggy budgeted ahead of time, she now has thirty days to make it to the end of the month. That means she is going to start *now* to make up the deficit because maybe some of the debt payment dates are looming faster than thirty days. Plus, there are a lot of things she doesn't have control over. She's learned she works best when she does as much work as she can up front. So, because she can pay down the deficit by selling stuff she doesn't need any more, she'll give up bingeing screens at night. Now, instead of watching three hours of Bailey Sarian's *Murder, Mystery and Makeup* videos on YouTube, she'll take photos of her clutter and post them on some kind of marketplace, like Craigslist or Kijiji, or prep for a garage sale. She is then going to work extra efficiently at her job because she gets paid on commission. So, she'll start on "pipeline generation" every morning first thing before she dives into the admin tasks of her day. Because her business doesn't generate instant sales, sometimes there is a lag between the day she acquires a potential customer and a sale. By being proactive and "filling her pipeline," she will increase the odds that her income will steadily increase in time. When she stops focusing on the pipeline or potential new sales, she typically sees an income drought sixty to ninety days in the future, and she wants to prevent that. Once she's done all the things she can to generate new business, she'll treat herself to a Bailey Sarian video. That woman is fire.

Peggy is also going to find creative ways to get some of her expenses covered.

She has friends that hate cooking, but she loves it. She's going to offer to make the meals if her friends buy the groceries, covering hers, too, and she'll deliver them in freezable containers. That would free up most of her grocery money. She's also going to look into sharing a commute with coworkers to save on fuel. She might even sell pre-bagged lunches to her coworkers who always comment on her amazing salads.

No matter what strategy you choose to help you cover your shortfall, you must do the best you can and then let it go.

At the end of the month, no matter what, Peggy needs to update her net worth spreadsheet just like you do.

Remember that we are looking for that net worth to increase by a dollar or more. If it does, things are moving in the right direction.

WHAT TO DO WHEN THERE IS EXCESS (YAY!)

Budgeting on a Fluctuating Income When Things Are Awesome

So just like before, every month you assemble the list of income you anticipate before it even starts.

(Now I am using "month" as a default, but if it is easier for you to budget per paycheck, then budget every two weeks or semi-monthly, or whatever makes the most sense for your life.)

income		expenses	
Base Salary	$1000.00		
Government Benefits	$545.30		
Commissions	$1300.00		
Other	$200.00		
TOTAL INCOME	$3045.30		

You can see that there is extra money coming in this month. In order to capture it and use it as a force for good, you will write it all down the minute you know it's coming and not after it lands in the bank account. And then you list the expenses you anticipate.

income		expenses	
Base Salary	$1000.00	Housing	$500.00
		Utilities	$130.00
Government Benefits	$545.30	Transportation	$82.80
		Childcare	$500.00
		Groceries	$400.00
Commissions	$1300.00	School Fees	$20.00
		Chai Lattes	$63.50
Other	$200.00	Fun Money	$50.00
		Debt Repayment	$350.00
		Plus $151 from last month	$151.00
TOTAL INCOME	$3045.30	TOTAL EXPENSES	$2247.30

Let's say Peggy didn't make up that shortfall from last month. Now we have to make sure it appears in this month's expenses, regardless of the income situation. We want to keep our financial integrity in check as much as possible, so we want to track all the expenses.

This month when she adds everything up, she is Carlton Dancing to the tune of a $798 surplus! Now, what do we do with this money?

You can choose your own adventure, poppet.

Fluctuating Income Budget Surplus Strategy One: The Float Strategy

You will put this money in a no-fee, high-interest savings account. We'll call this a float fund. When I was a (horrible) waitress and a (terrible) bartender, we would have a cash float of fifty dollars before every shift to allow us to make change for the first few customers. If we didn't have a float when we opened, and someone ordered a drink and didn't pay the exact total, we wouldn't be able to give them their change. We would be in trouble with the customer and lose business. So, your float is the thing that allows you to pay expenses until you have enough income coming in to cover expenses.

Your float doesn't need to be in low denominational cash. Your float can live in a high-interest, *no-fee* savings account and be untouched. Don't have any automatic withdrawals come out of that account. It's simply a place for storing the float. A digital cash register if you will. But don't touch that money unless you need it. (It's separate from your Quick and Dirty if you've read ahead, which is designated for emergencies.)

The float is there to cover shortfalls in your income for months where there just isn't enough pay. It needs to be liquid, which means that it can be accessed in a moment, but not a blink of an eye—more like you running slo-mo to the bank to the *Chariots of Fire* theme song. The float cannot be held in an investment and it needs to cost you nothing to access.

P.S. Your line of credit is not your float. That is your *bank's* wealth-building tool, and they thank you very much for your loyal patronage.

Fluctuating Income Budget Surplus Strategy Two: The Double-Budget-Deluxe Strategy

We have a look at the month after next and make a budget for that. If there is a chance it's going to be tight, you can either hang on to the money in your checking account for a month or prepay some of next month's expenses. I don't love giving people or companies money before they deliver the service I'm paying them for, but that's because I've been ripped off in the past. Then I suffered financially as a result, and it made it difficult for *me* to pay bills… oh gosh. Sounds like I should make a quick call to my therapist. That one runs deep. But there was definitely a season in my life where I didn't trust myself with money. I was so overwhelmed at the beginning when I had so many debts and expenses and I struggled to keep track of it all, that it was easier to overpay some bills while I knew I had the money.

That way, I let the credit-for-payment accumulate on my account so the following month the company wouldn't have to take a payment. This can be a great temporary solution if you feel like a hole is burning in your pocket when there is extra money sitting in your account. This way, you can be sure you take care of your obligations so that you can get back to annihilating your debt.

Fluctuating Income Budget Surplus Strategy Three: I'll Deal With It When I Deal With It

This scenario is for people who can handle a little drama and uncertainty. Maybe you are used to feeling broke all the time and you want to leave next month's worries to next month. What you'd do here is allocate the $798 to whatever upcoming phase you are working on in the program.

So, if you are in Phase One, that $798 goes directly into your Safe Zone Account to be put towards your Quick and Dirty Fund. (I'll explain this in a hot minute.) If you are in Phase Two, that $798 gets applied directly to whatever debt you are on. If you are in Phase Three, that $798 gets applied to whatever asset you are purchasing.

And then you budget ahead for next month, and so on.

Okay, friend, move in close. Real-talk time. We've been talking about budgets for pages and pages now. You might be tempted to angry-tweet me and say, "These examples of budgets are unrealistic! I have so many more expenses than this!" Yup. I get it. But this book is not called "All the Maths" or "The Most Practical and Realistic Budget You've Ever Seen!" It's your *job to work with your numbers and create your own custom budget. It's my job to help you understand the functionality of the budget. Don't get hung up on the fact that these samples are short and quick. If you have two hundred and twenty-two expenses, you have got to get those numbers under control, so save your 140-character rants and channel that energy into making sh*t happen!*

An important distinction: Your budget's job is to *increase* the net worth.

Let me say it one more time, in case you did that thing we humans do when our brains get overloaded and you are reading something and haven't yet realized you are skimming and not absorbing it.

The whole point of the budget is to *increase the net worth.*

If your net worth is being depleted to support the budget, you are going broke.

> Victoria says: "You've got me really observing myself and noticing little things that I do when it comes to spending money. For instance, I didn't have a hair tie at work yesterday and really needed one. Fast forward to this morning and I see it sitting on the coffee table and my very first thought was to stop what I was doing and order more of them. Instead of spending money unnecessarily, I can just make sure it is always on my wrist in the morning before I leave for work. I don't forget my earrings, so there's no excuse.
>
> "The modern convenience of being able to pick up your phone, click some boxes, and boom, whatever item you just had to have shows up at your house the next day, makes it way too easy to not even think about how it all adds up. There's a noticeable difference in my checking account since I've been practicing awareness and sticking to my budget. Thank you!"

Chapter Six

THE SAFE ZONE

I remember reading something about saving money, and thinking, "Yes! This is it! I'll start to save money!" like it was a brand-new idea that trumped sliced bread in the Greatest Things Department.

So, I started squirreling away money, and I had deposited about $141 in my Brand-new (*insert trumpet*) Designated Account for Saving Money. A couple weeks passed, and I ran into yet another cash flow problem when I got a bill for $139. I decided that I would use my squirreled-away savings to pay it, but when I went into the account, there was $131.05 in the account, not even enough to pay the bill!

The bank had taken their $9.95 account management fee, the money I had agreed to pay them to hold my money for me.

It occurred to me for the first time how absurd bank fees are. Let's say you went to the bathroom at a restaurant with a friend and said, "Here, hold my purse for me," and inside was fifty bucks. Then, after flushing and washing your hands, you reach for your bag. But first! Your friend reaches in and takes ten dollars before handing your purse back. A fee for holding your money.

If this happened, it's highly unlikely you would remain loyal to that friend. And yet, we trust our banks with our money all the time, especially if we've been with them since childhood.

I promise you I'm not wearing a tinfoil hat at the moment, but hear me out. *This is such a weird concept.* We are so loyal to our banks when, generally, they are not loyal to us. I mean sure, when you have a few million in the vault, they are very much, "Yes sir," "Here you go, madam," and "How can we help you ma'am?" But to the average consumer, they are not rolling out a red carpet. They don't even lend you money when you *need* money. They lend you money when you *don't need* money and hope that you will not ever be able to pay them back in full. The worst part is, when you give them your $9.95 account maintenance fee, do you know what they do with it? They lend it out or they leverage it to earn more money. So, they take your money to earn more money. Then, they turn around and charge you for that privilege.

Oh sure, sometimes they'll tell you they'll waive the account maintenance fee if you jump through a few flaming hoops. Like, if you keep a minimum balance of $5000 in your account, then they won't charge you the $9.95.

Let me just take you on a side tangent to show you how maddening this is, from a math perspective.

Scenario One:

You have $5000.

You choose to put it in your bank account to save the $9.95 monthly account fee, assuming they never raise the fees.

HAHAHAHAHAHAHAHAHAHAHAHAHAHA

...

Okay. Where was I?

Over ten years, you save $1194 in bank fees. That's a lot of money in fees. That's an all-inclusive trip to somewhere with sombreros and only moderate hurricanes! *But wait!* Don't pat yourself on the back yet, friend.

Scenario Two:

You have $5000.

You invest that $5000 in a conservative investment at 5 percent compounded monthly for ten years. You don't add another cent to it. You just put it in an investment, and at the end of ten years, you have $8235.05.

So, in scenario one, you have $5000 in ten years' time, but you have not paid out $1194 in bank fees. But in scenario two, you have $8235.05. Even after you pay your bank maintenance fees, you have $7041.05. You still come out $2041.05 ahead.

Please note: this is not an endorsement for paying bank fees, believe me! I want you to be aware of the bank's tricks and gimmicks. When the bank says, "We will waive the fees if you do XYZ," just know that whatever they've asked you to do always involves them making more and you making less.

Do you know what *they* earn on your bank fees each month by investing them? *Eleventy kasquajillion dollars.* Okay, I might have rounded up there. But you get the point. Whenever the banks want you to do something in order to save money, I want you to think critically about the math and the marketing around that.

And here is what I want you to *actually* do.

YOUR SAFE ZONE ACCOUNT

I want you to put the money in a no-fee bank account. Yes, they do exist. And if you are like, "Wait. This sounds too good to be true!" maybe it is. You'll have to read the fine print at the bank to know for sure. But if you can have a safe place to store cash as you work on radically transforming your finances, then absolutely do it.

Your no-fee account must not have a bunch of pre-requisites. If the bank says, "We will give you an account with no fees if you give us your mortgage, take out a credit card, and give us your next-born child," then you say, "No thank you, bank."

If the bank says, "We will give you a no-fee account, but you have to put ten thousand dollars in there," then you say, "No thank you, bank."

If the bank says, "We will give you a no-fee account so it won't cost you any money to deposit here, but if you transfer money, withdraw money, pay a bill, or think about the money in this account, we will charge you a small fee," then you say, "No thank you, bank, and also what part of *no-fees* didn't you understand?"

Wouldn't it be refreshing if next time you logged in to your bank, they said, "Hey, we are about to rip you off. We are raising your account fees by one dollar every month, which doesn't seem like much to you but increases our revenues by millions a year! And we are just going to do this without your permission because you signed something that said we could, so you better change banks in the next thirty days if you want to save this dollar."

You likely wouldn't bother changing banks, but holy heck, that would be refreshing to read. Instead, the banks are *masterful* at making you think they are doing you a big ol' favor by *letting* you access your own money.

My point is you can find an institution to open a no-fee account with. Oh, and don't use your current bank.

Here are my top reasons why this money needs to be at a different institution than your main bank:

1. I want the money to be easy to access but not easy to access, you know? I want you to have a little time delay to talk yourself out of blowing that money but enough time to access it to pay a plumber if your tenant flushes a lot of condoms down the toilet. (Not that I am bitter or anything.)
2. I want you to put your money in and keep it there. When you look a couple of months later, you should *still* have *that same amount of money* in there so you don't have that massive feeling of defeat I

experienced when I was struggling. Ideally, some institutions actually pay a small amount of interest on their deposit accounts, so you might even earn a little moola while the money is not being touched. Please know: *This is not the point of the account* (more on that later). The point of this account is: *do not lose money.*

3. I want you to get in the habit of building a money muscle. This muscle is going to be used once you graduate out of having consumer debt and start building wealth. You need to get used to seeing money in your account instead of living in overdraft. Or living in lack. Or whatever is happening for you that is causing you to be in this vicious cycle. We are going to start using *money* to buy things, not using credit to buy things. We are going to come at life from an empowered state, not a disempowered one. And that starts with this little no-fee account that we will call your "Safe Zone Account."
4. Having money at another institution gives you options if the government ever freezes your account. Yeah. I didn't think it would ever happen to me, either.

The argument I often hear about this money is: but this money could be *doing something* like earning interest. It's just sitting there, Erin. Shouldn't it be making me money?

No. Absolutely *not.* That is not its job. Do you want to know what this money's job is? To keep you away from your freaking credit card.

When you are debt-free, I have all kinds of amazing ways for your money to make money. Your money will be in an account earning compound interest, which is basically where your money has sex with more money, and together they make even more money. Like bunnies. It will multiply in glorious ways. But that is not *this* money's job. This money's job is not to procreate. This money's job is to stop you from being in the red again. This money's job is to keep you from using your fecking credit card.

This money is going to retrain your brain to handle emergencies instead of letting your access to credit be the thing that helps you through emergencies.

A little side note: when I owned my mortgage brokerage, I would hear from clients who went into the bank to sign their mortgage documents, and do you know what the kind people at the bank would do? They would give them a line of credit along with their mortgage. "For emergencies!" And the clients would be thrilled to have access to $40,000 when they first moved into their house in case they needed it. Do you know what actually became the fuggin' emergency?

The forty thousand plus dollars of new debt the client accumulated.

They almost never used the money for real emergencies. There were little perceived things like, "Our couch doesn't fit in the new living room, let's just use the line of credit and get something that will work." Or, "We could really use a new lawn mower now that our yard is bigger." Over time, these little tiny cuts added up to a big gaping debt wound. Instead of being resourceful and budgeting for these household expenses, clients would rely on credit, and suddenly their dream homes became a financial nightmare.

So, no, your money does not need to be "working for you" in this no-fee bank account. This is the bank account that protects you, like a debt condom. So, please, please, please do not flush it down the toilet.

> Wes says: "I had issues with my new bank card/PIN number. But I got it figured out! Deposited $515 in it now. First savings I have had in 22 years! Feels good. It's not huge but it's a bigger cushion than I have had in my lifetime!"

Chapter Seven

THE QUICK AND DIRTY FUND

Once the Safe Zone Account is opened, your next task is to start filling it with the equivalent of one paycheck.

This does not mean take your next paycheck, if you are lucky enough to have one, and put it in there. That would leave you no money for monthly expenses. This is going to require you to access your personal resourcefulness: a way to accumulate the equivalent of one paycheck.

This can typically be done by decluttering (and I say this with all the love in my heart) because usually we got into debt by cluttering. Debt itself is clutter.

In all my years teaching financial strategies, what I have discovered is this: rarely has a person gotten into consumer debt in one go. It was a series of mini go's. Little tiny things that added up. Groceries. Maybe some beer. Clothing. Sporting events. Tickets to concerts. Fuel. Medicine. Birthday gifts. A plane ticket. Some household gadgets. Electronics. Knick-knacks.

One exercise I often have students in my debt-annihilation courses do is list all the things they spent money on that got them into debt. Yeah, okay: house, car, student loan. Those things aside. What else?

Most of the time they don't even know. A number of factors are at play when you are considering what you actually purchased to get into this rut in the first place. Maybe you didn't quite have enough money, so you put it on a credit card. Then you made a partial payment, which freed up room on the card. Then you bought something else. Then the bank decided you were such a good customer they raised the limit on the card. Then you put something else on the card. It's a cycle, see? It becomes such a normal part of our spending pattern that it can be hard to identify how it all specifically happened.

I don't need to know you personally to know that when you got your first credit card, you *did not* say to yourself, "I cannot wait to rack this up and make my life miserable later!"

So, no shame, friend. The entire system is designed to get you into this place. You were just human-ing along, living your life. Many vendors *only* accept credit cards as a method of payment, and if you didn't have a backup plan for how you were going to function without credit cards, it's highly likely you slipped into this debt unintentionally. Maybe you were seduced by points or the idea of "free" trips. All of it is okay because it led you here, and you can make changes starting now. I don't mean starting next Monday. Or starting on the first of the month. I mean starting right now. Doing as much as you can today and doing as much as you can tomorrow.

So, here's the point of the Quick and Dirty Fund. It's your new credit card—except it's *real money* that you already have. It's cash that is going to live in the Safe Zone Account that you opened up, the one with no fees, and you are going to do your darndest not to touch it.

In order for this to be successful, you have to do three things.

1. You have to, as quickly as possible, go through your home and sell everything you are not using to generate the equivalent of one paycheck. This is sometimes embarrassing and always humbling.

The point of this exercise is to generate a safety net without interrupting your already tight cash flow situation. It's also to help you become aware of what things actually cost.

Even when we think we got a great deal on the brand-new smart TV, we quickly learn what the true value of an item is when we sell it for much less than its sticker price.

I remember when I saved up $400 to buy a brand-new Palm Pilot. It had a little stylus, and I had to learn to write a whole new fancy alphabet so my Palm Pilot could take notes. And then, years later when it was time to bin the thing, my five-year-old found it and curiously asked what it was. I explained it was like a phone that could take notes and showed him the stylus that was stuck in the side. His eyes opened wide and he said, "*Wow*. This must have been before they invented pencils."

Do you know what that Palm Pilot was worth? Nothing. Nada. Zip. Zilch. Nothing. Especially to a five-year-old. When I recovered myself from my financial shipwreck, I learned that I definitely do not value owning the newest, flashiest piece of tech on the planet, but I do value money in my bank account.

If you *are* someone who needs all the new tech, then cool. Just be aware of its true cost (to your budget, your net worth, and your long-term financial and emotional well-being); you'll have to make more conservative choices in other areas.

2. The second thing you have to do, in order for the Quick and Dirty Fund to be successful, is sell everything you're not using as quickly as possible.

Busted. I know I just said that in the paragraphs above, but most people skim over that and immediately get overwhelmed thinking about everything they have to declutter. Don't think too much. Just do. If you are hanging on to stuff because you think you might need it one day, you are likely stuck in lack thinking.

Abundant thinking says, "Hey, I trust that if I need something, I will be resourceful enough to borrow it, buy it on discount, afford it easily, whatever." The "trust in yourself" and the "resourcefulness" is key to the wealth-building stages after you get the hell out of debt, so you might as well practice it now.

Set a deadline to have the quick-and-dirty equivalent of one paycheck in your (no-fee) Safe Zone Account in the next forty-eight hours. Yes, I said *forty-eight hours*.

There is this principle called Parkinson's Law. To paraphrase, it states that the amount of time something takes is the amount of time you give it. For example, when you went to school and your teacher said, "This assignment is due Friday," you didn't plan out the assignment to work on it a bit each day, refining and perfecting it as you went. You likely distracted yourself with other things and then slapped that assignment together before the deadline. If your teacher gave you a month to do the assignment, it would take you a month. I'm telling you forty-eight hours because I want you to put this book down for a very short period of time, list your stuff on a buy-and-sell website of some kind, and get rid of it. Go at your life like Joanna and Clea just rolled up with a bunch of boxes and you have to make instant decisions before *The Home Edit* rolls the credits.

You are definitely not going to rake in millions here. This is going to be a humbling experience in consumerism. And I'm telling you right now, straight up, that you have more to sell than you realize you do. If you take this assignment seriously and do this work immediately, I can tell you with almost absolute certainty that you will succeed. If you procrastinate on this part, the journey will take you longer and be more frustrating. I don't exactly know why that is, but I do know that in my many years of teaching this, the people who got out of debt fastest were always the ones who came flying out of the gates.

There is so much more work ahead, so cross this one off the to-do list now. And if you do not think you can do this in forty-eight hours, I encourage you to watch the online course videos in the Get the Hell Out of Debt portal where I gave this assignment. You'll see all the participants' mouths drop open with impossibility, and then in the *very next video*, recorded a couple of days later, you'll see them cheering with victory that they did the thing they thought they could not do. This is not a suggestion, my friend. This is a must.

3. The third thing you have to do in order for the Quick and Dirty Fund to be successful is not complain. Not even once. One of the other factors that will determine the success you have in this program is the energy you put behind it, so I'm challenging you to challenge yourself not to whine, complain, grumble, distract, b*tch, whimper, or feel sorry for yourself. You are about to deal with weird online strangers, so you are going to need all the positive energy you can muster.

And on that note: let's talk about safe selling online, shall we?

In an ideal world, you are selling no-contact, meaning you are not meeting up with people to do the transaction. This is my preferred method, partly because I'm an introvert and making small talk sucks the life out of my soul. But in all seriousness, it's mostly because of safety.

This depends greatly on the value of the item you are transacting. It definitely is not worth your while driving across town to transact a one-dollar item. It's not worth the time or the money or the hassle. So, if the item is small in value, I will simply use the bin or tub system, which is putting a plastic bin out on my doorstep, putting the item in the bin, and giving the purchaser the ability to drop by any time and pick the item out of the bin and leave the money under the doormat. Or they can mobile or email transfer/Venmo the money or use PayPal. I'm not picky.

Yes, the items can be stolen. Yes, the money can be stolen. But I do this from a place of abundance, not fear. If an item gets stolen, well, that's what happens. I don't make it mean anything. I don't take it personally. And if I absolutely cannot afford to lose five or ten bucks, then I either don't sell the item or I don't use the bin system for it. I love the bin system as an introvert because it's efficient, there's no on-site haggling, and I'm not wasting my time driving anywhere or waiting for someone to show up.

I also never use my real name online. The app I use to sell items online allows you to create a name, so I have a separate email address and a whole pretend name online for selling items. I only use it for good, not evil. It's a way to protect myself and create emotional distance from the seller so that I don't get offended when they offer me less money than I was hoping to fetch. I never give out my cell phone number, and I only communicate through the app. At first, I was worried that using a fake name lacked integrity, but then I decided that my family's safety and well-being matter more than whether some stranger buys used skis from Erin Skye Kelly or MichelleSells2024.

If you live in an apartment building, you can get your building manager to change your buzzer code to your fake name (why is your real name on there, anyway?) and you can have people buzz you when they arrive. Then you can meet them outside or wherever your building cameras are.

Ideally, you can use the bin system at a public place like an office that might allow you to do this.

For larger value items, a bin system might not work, and you might have to meet the person to do the transaction. In the area where I live, the police allow you to do buy-and-sell transactions in front of the police stations. You could choose a public place to transact, but make sure there are cameras nearby.

Worst case, you could have a proper, old-fashioned garage sale, but know that these are a heck-ton of work for even less financial payoff than online selling.

Here are some quick tips for selling your items:

1. Never let people into your home to view or test an item. Come up with a different innovative way to sell, if that's the case.
2. Make sure someone you know and love is aware when you are meeting a stranger. (Basically, the same rules for Tinder!)
3. Be prepared to meet some interesting people, but absolutely do not meet them if you get a little wiggle in your tummy that makes you nervous. Listen to your gut. You do not need to apologize for feeling uncomfortable. You don't need a reason not to sell to someone. You can just say, "No thank you, I don't think this is going to work," and block or delete the correspondence. You can take responsibility for your safety and not their emotions.

4. Do your research to learn the best-selling platforms in your area. Different communities have different tendencies for apps and communication, and what might work on the east coast might not on the west coast.

I realize all of this sounds scarier than it seems. I want you to know I've only had two bad online selling challenges in nine years on the app I used. Once, a pair of ice skates were stolen from the bin in front of my house. The person arrived and the skates were not in the bin, and they were mad at me. When I realized they were stolen, I apologized. The person was still not happy. Well, internet stranger, I'm not exactly Walmart and I can't offer you any other alternatives.

The other bad situation was someone asked way too many questions once about an item, and I realized they were trying to figure out if I was single. So gross. So, I just blocked them and hid all my listings for a while.

When you want something bad enough, you'll figure out a way to make it happen. When you don't want something badly, you'll find an excuse not to do it.

Other things you can do to fill your Quick and Dirty:

1. Flip items. You can find items you are familiar with that are on discount through garage sales or in the *free* section of your online buy-and-sell. You can pick those items up, polish them off, take well-lit photos of them, and upload them for a profit. This month, a woman in Phase 2 made $900 selling items she picked up for free. It was a bit of a pain storing the items in her garage, cleaning them, and messaging people online; however, it paid off half of her credit card, and she was able to do all the work while her toddlers watched their daily viewing of *Frozen*. She joked that she knows all the words to that movie already, and it was the perfect theme for her to "Let it Go."
2. Take your bottles to the depot if you get refunds for deposits in your area. Have a yard sale. Open yourself up to any and all oppor-

tunities that work for you, your values, your family, and your time. Find a buddy who is also getting the hell out of debt and brainstorm together. The only rules around this are: it must be legal, and it must not take unfair advantage of another human.

3. Offer your expertise or services by creating income. Many years ago, this fantastic woman named Chelsea was focused on paying down her debt. She was working in admin at a financial services company, but she had experience in the beauty industry. One of the services she began providing for her friends was box-dying their hair for twenty dollars. It saved them money; they didn't have to go to a salon, they simply showed up at her house on a Friday night with the box of dye, and she would apply it while they socialized, making sure she got all the hard-to-see parts of the hairline that makes a home dye job so horrendous. She climbed her way out of debt twenty dollars at a time using her expertise.

On that note, I want to point out that many of the people who pick up this book or take the Get the Hell Out of Debt course work in finances. There is a stigma attached to working as a realtor, mortgage broker, accountant, bank teller, bank manager, investment advisor, bookkeeper, or insurance expert and being in debt. If that is you, please do not feel guilt or shame. These are the emotions that *keep* us in debt. If we are embarrassed, we are less likely to seek help. I'm not saying you need to make a TikTok or Reels video of you dancing and pointing out your liabilities to the beat of a song. But I am suggesting that you open yourself up to a new way of handling your finances so you can live in alignment with the products you offer the masses in order to truly help and serve your customers. Some of the greatest financial transformations that I've been a part of have been with people who are in the industry. I won't out you, I promise. I'm here to celebrate your progress and your debt freedom on the day you make it happen.

QUICK AND DIRTY RECAP

This is why it is affectionately called the Quick and Dirty Fund. Your job is to fill it up as quickly as you can, and you're going to have to get your hands dirty. Work is going to be involved.

I held a live seminar and I was explaining how the Quick and Dirty Fund is going to require a little bit of *grind.* It involves working a few extra hours a day to make happen. Yes, you can contribute ten minutes a day, but then it will take you forever to make progress, so it is best to just roll up your sleeves and put in two solid days of hard work and get to it. It might take someone a week to see your ad anyway, so get your stuff up online as soon as you can. And then go back to monitoring your money for ten minutes a day.

People in this seminar were taking furious notes, but a radiant woman in the second row listened intently with her hands holding one of those gorgeous designer handbags in her lap, as if she was trying to decide whether to stay or bolt for the door. She had eyelash extensions and gel nails and just the right amount of Botox and filler so that you could barely tell she'd had work done. When I asked if anyone had any questions, she raised her hand, almost timidly. She spoke with a beautiful calm tone, and said, "I really dislike the term and the energy around the word 'grind.' I am trying to live my life in harmony both with Mother Earth and my Creator. I will not spend my precious life here on earth doing any grinding. What *other* advice do you have for me?"

I have no judgment for those choices, as I myself have injected my forehead with Botox in order to look less weary ($700). I have laid on an uncomfortable padded table for two and a half hours to have little tiny bits of horsehair glued painstakingly onto the insufficient eyelashes my Creator gave me ($220). And I have had unchippable toxic paint applied to my fingernails and toenails and then sealed in with ultraviolet lights ($90). So I, too, fully understand how asking someone to sell their clutter on a buy-and-sell app or website might be...unbecoming.

But let's just imagine for a moment that you are floating out to Mother Nature's bountiful sea in a little boat, and there is a leak in your canoe. Water is coming in, and your boat is sinking deeper and deeper into the water. Let me ask you this, as you sail further and further away from the shore:

Would you be lying back in the canoe in harmony, enjoying the last few minutes of your precious life, or would you be f*cking *grinding it out* to bail the water out of the canoe so that you can patch the leak in the boat and survive?

Good. Let's continue.

Your Quick and Dirty Fund is:

- *Not* for paying bills. It is for all the surprises we haven't accounted for yet.
- Going to be held in your no-fee Safe Zone Account.
- The equivalent of one paycheck.
- For emergencies. Real, true emergencies that you would have otherwise relied on credit for.

Given that most emergencies happen when we are between paychecks and that most people live paycheck to paycheck, we want to have one paycheck's worth of cash in the Quick and Dirty Fund. If you get paid a larger amount once a month, this is going to be trickier for you. If you get paid weekly, this might be easier. All of this is simply a guideline. But what we need to do is have the equivalent of one paycheck in there to tide you over until the next paycheck. It takes a wee bit of the worry away.

Most times when your paycheck hits the account (if you are a typical person), there is an hour of glory. And then the bills come, and *sad trombone* you are back to feeling broke.

What we are doing with this fund is bridging the gap between paychecks. Now, if you already have savings of some kind and you consider them to be your emergency fund, then you can combine them with your Quick and Dirty. If you are at risk of losing your job in the near future, you might want a couple more paychecks socked away in the Quick and Dirty.

But once we have the Quick and Dirty funded, we *back slowly away from the account* and leave it. In a perfect world, you will not need this money, ever. But because we live in a messy, imperfect but equally as beautiful human world, you likely will need it. We are going to plan for you not to, but there is no shame if you suddenly do. That's what it is here for. We're going to keep it out of sight for now because it can be tempting to spend this money. Once we have your budget mastered, we will more clearly be able to see how to best plan for emergencies. But right now, we need something. So, the equivalent of one check in your no-fee Safe Zone Account is the something we need to get started.

Once you are out of debt, we will load this account up with more moola and do some amazing things with it.

Oh, and one other little thing before we move on:

You can make this decision on the fly if you want, but I would not personally track my Quick and Dirty Fund on the net worth spreadsheet. Not in the beginning, anyway, because this account is likely to be used. If I have $1600 in there, and then I need some of it to fix my car, that number will fluctuate too rapidly.

However, if you are someone who truly wants to feel better about your net worth situation and want this to build your self-esteem as well, then go ahead and add it to the asset column. This is not truly an asset, however. It's simply emergency money that hasn't been spent yet.

More on assets later. But I totally get if you have been feeling defeated by your finances lately and you want a "win" to feel good about. So, go on and pump your own tires. Just don't be hard on yourself if you get a real-life flat tire and you have to deflate this account to pay for it.

> Malinda says "I just e-transferred into my quick and dirty account and I'm happy to say I have 86% of what I need to get the full amount in there! What an incredible and humbling experience this has been! My kids are even excited to come up with some new ways to contribute! The plan is to take some bottles in and sell some more things we have listed. Humbled and excited... all at once!"

GIVE THOSE CREDIT CARDS A BREAK

I want you to Ross and Rachel the credit cards, the lines of credit, the overdraft, and anything else you've been using for a while. I'm not going to come at you with giant scissors and tell you to cut up your cards, though. Frankly, that is what I had to do for myself. It became too difficult for me to pay off a card while there were still things being put on the card. It felt like trying to brush my teeth while I was eating Oreos. I felt like I was *doing* something but I wasn't getting results, you know?

So, you're going to put the credit cards on a break for a while. This *does not* mean, Ross, that you can sleep with the girl from the copier place.

We're going to take a true breather and decide if we can get healthy enough to get back together with credit cards one day or whether we instead date Joey. (Side note: Joey definitely treated Rachel better than Ross did. Also, Joey is less manipulative and whiny.)

But, hey. I know what it's like to have "history" with a credit card. After you recover, you only remember the good times, and you end up back together.

Here's what happened to me when I decided to take credit cards back. I applied for one, and even though I had been a beacon reject for years (no credit history), they approved me and sent a card in the mail. Do you know what the CVV code on the back was? 666. This proved to me that credit cards are the devil and I did not need them in my life.

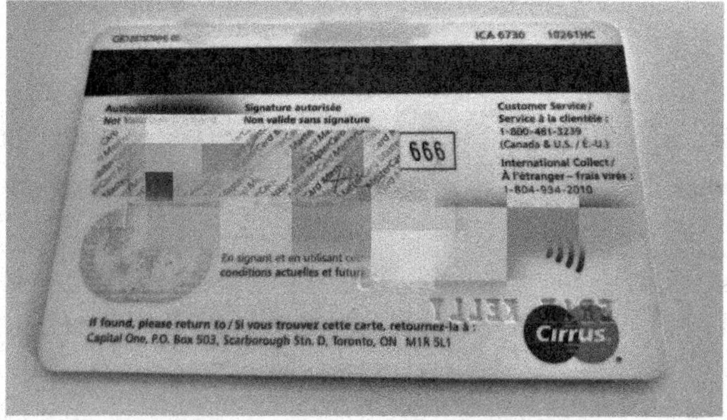

I'm not anti-credit card for everyone. I'm anti-credit card for me. And maybe you decide that you do not, in fact, want to live an on-again-off-again life with Ross. Or maybe you love the drama. Your decision.

For the purposes of getting the hell out of debt, I want you to go on a credit card detox for at least ninety days, but ideally for the duration of however long it takes you to complete the program. Every time a participant has used credit cards, even somewhat responsibly, it has set them back in the program by months. These are the most common reasons why:

1. When you spend money that is in your bank account today, you feel the pain today. When you spend money that you don't have to pay back for a couple of weeks, you do not feel pain today so you are more likely to spend more than you budgeted for.
2. The term "available balance" is psychologically more appealing and reassuring than "this-is-how-far-in-the-hole-you-are-already." I've even seen some lenders term "available balance" as "left to spend," which is kind of cheering you on. "You're almost there! At your max limit! Keep going! You can do it!"
3. It is so much more difficult to manage cash flow when you aren't controlling the flow. When you have all your bills coming off your card automatically, you are less likely to pay attention to how those bills might be inflating. Like when your cell phone service increases your bill by twenty-five dollars per month, you might just ignore it because the transaction is going through anyway. But when it's a bill you intentionally sit down to pay, you can make a five-minute phone call and save yourself $300 per year because you catch it. There are certainly going to be things I want you to automate down the road, especially the wealth-building stuff. I want there to be a slow, boring baseline of wealth-building automation in your life. But when it comes to getting the hell out of debt, I want you to fight with all-hands-on-deck until every leak in the boat is secured. When you pay a bill manually, you typically are sent a bill, and you have usually thirty days to pay. This makes budgeting a dream.

When you pay automatically, you sometimes get the notification the *same day* that it is coming out of the account, and if the notification is higher than you were expecting, it's out of your account before you can take action. Then you are left reacting instead of being proactive.

4. You can get suckered in by points. First, I want to point out that I have yet to meet a wealthy person who credits their financial freedom to all the free gifts or non-blackout flights they obtained. They became wealthy because of money management. There are lots of gurus out there who will teach all kinds of tricks to maximize credit card points, and when you are out of debt and want to study this stuff for fun, go right ahead. What I want you to master first is money and your own psychology.
5. It's far too easy during a moment of frustration to say, "Eff it" and just rack the thing back up. I'm telling you to put down the loaded gun, raise your hands in the air, and walk to safety until we can get you some proper training.

Side note: I just texted my Manhunk, "Was it okay that Ross slept with the copier woman?" No context. Just that sentence from a show that aired over twenty years ago, and he knew exactly what I was talking about.

Hahaha

Before you I thought Ross was right

Since you I think he shouldn't have

Why

I'm watching a movie with the kids so if I mistype on such a serious question you have to have grace with me!

But I just figured if you're broken up, you're broken up. Game over. He can't be blamed.

But if it's really your person, you don't go messing with someone the next night or whatever.

He replied, "Hahaha, before you I thought Ross was right. Since you, I think he shouldn't have."

I fished further. "Why?"

Manhunk: "I'm watching a movie with the kids so if I mistype on such a serious question you have to have grace with me!"

(I did not intend it to be a serious question; I was mostly just goofing around. But he might have felt the way some spouses do when being suckered into a conversation—that it is a *trap*. Much like you might feel when you are on the phone with the credit card company.)

Manhunk: "But I just figured if you're broken up, you're broken up. Game over. He can't be blamed. But if it's really your person, you don't go messing with someone the next night or whatever."

Awwwwwwww.

Here is my serious, non-baited question for you. What kind of relationship do you *want* to have with money? Do you want to have a relationship that grows and that is built on respect? Or do you want the ups and downs and the drama and the terms and conditions that a credit card relationship has?

I just got a text from Manhunk while I was typing that.

Makes sense

That was very articulate.

Haha I doubt that!

Did I just start a fight and have no clue I did, as guys sometimes do?

Hahahaha omg no

Hahahahaha ok

But I can't wait to tell you how funny that was

I'm just writing a paragraph about it. Fill you in shortly.

"Did I just start a fight and have no clue I did, as guys sometimes do?"

"Hahahahaha omg no but I can't wait to tell you how funny that was. I'm just writing a paragraph about it. Fill you in shortly."

Whoops. I shouldn't have left him "on read" there.

So, what are you going to use if you can't use credit cards? You'll need to plan for an alternative.

I use a Visa debit or Mastercard debit as much as possible. These are fairly new in some countries, and not all institutions have ones that work well. Essentially, they are debit cards that work on the credit card systems and offer many of the same perks as credit cards, just usually without the points; however, when you are spending less using debit or cash instead of credit, then you can afford to buy your own damn perks.

In 2020, a study by Fundera said that the average cash transaction is twenty-two dollars and the average card transaction is $112. *Ummmmmmmm.*

Let's just pause for a minute and have a moment of silence for all the dead dollars we lost.

There are also prepaid Visas and Mastercards offered by some institutions. I'm not talking about those Visa gift cards. I'm talking about a reloadable credit card offered by a bank that you put money on like a bill payment, and then you have access to that money once it appears on the card. There is usually an annual fee for these cards, but it's a handful of dollars versus the fees that "real" credit cards have, and definitely much less than the interest you pay for keeping a balance. If your bank offers this, it can be an alternative to credit while you sort out all your dollars and your spending patterns. You would simply put an amount on the card that you would need for things that require credit cards (a downtown parking garage, for example). And all your other spending would be debit or cash.

It's important to note that Visa debit and Mastercard debit cards do not report to the credit bureaus, so they do nothing to help you build credit. If having a good credit score is important to you, then you will not want to use a credit alternative; however, if getting the hell out of debt is important to you, then you might consider not trying to impress the credit bureaus for the season of your life when you are getting your finances in order.

Here's two truths that we forget to consider:

It's entirely possible to be wealthy and have a bad or no credit score. It's entirely possible to be broke and have an excellent credit score.

In fact, you might be one of those people or know those people. Your credit score is an indication of your ability to manage payments on debt, not manage money.

If you plan on going back into debt in the next couple of years, you'll want to keep a small payment on your credit card that you pay off every month. You can have the minimum payment either scheduled to come out of your checking account, or you can make sure you mark it in the calendar so that you pay the balance off each month.

If you plan on conquering your debt and want to throw your credit cards in a blender because you swear you're like Taylor Swift and you are never, ever, ever getting back together, then go ahead and chop those suckers up. Call the credit card company and get all spicy with the retention department as they convince you to stay by telling you closing your card will make your score drop.

Most people fall somewhere in between extremes, which is why I think a healthy break for a period of time can give you the perspective you need.

The argument I hear most often for keeping credit cards is: but we pay our balance off in full every month…can we keep our credit cards?

The glaring problem I've encountered by people who struggle with consumer debt *and* pay their cards in full every month is: you are always living life one month behind.

Yes, you rack up the card (thinking you also rack up the "free" points), but then you truly are waiting and needing that paycheck to come in so you can make your payment. And if, for some reason, that paycheck is delayed, or you don't get one that month because of job loss or transition, then whammo! You are now in debt.

There *are* ways to do a "put everything on a credit card and pay it off" strategy, but you likely would not have picked up this book if that strategy was working for you. So, I invite you to look at all those different strategies once you have mastered *this* book, this strategy, and your own psychology so that you can best determine if that is a game you want to play.

* * *

At the end of last year there were 43.4 million active credit cards in Canada. The population of Canada is thirty-six million.

According to the American Bankers Association, there are 374 million open and active credit cards in the US, and the population, including babies who likely do not carry credit cards in their diapers, is 329 million.

So.

From a CBC news article:

> The executive director of Consolidated Credit Counseling Services of Canada, Inc. found it encouraging that Canadians are carrying fewer cards in their wallets, but said consumers are still struggling to manage the debt on the one card they have.
>
> "The findings from this report suggest that many Canadians are stretched very thin and that credit card debt is helping them to stay afloat," said Jeffrey Schwartz.

Derp. Very encouraging, Jeff.

Do you want to know what is messed up? Often, when it comes to department store cards, over a third of the department store's profits are not from the things they sell but the method by which they sell them. They profit from a consumer's need to buy something right now and pay for it later. But they are the ones that convince you of that urgency.

I don't know how that makes you feel, but it sure as hell made me realize that the credit card companies are *not* in this to help me.

Tammy says: "I went on a date this weekend! He seems great! After discussing many other things, I asked him what his thoughts are on consumer debt. I told him that I don't use credit cards and I'll be debt free in April. We laughed about the ridiculous "points" and "rewards" that banks offer. He laughed; he has no consumer debt and pays everything with debit. It felt awkward to talk about money at first, but then felt GREAT because as it turns out...this is important to me! Who knew?!?"

Chapter Eight

LOVE AND MONEY

MONEY AND RELATIONSHIPS

BUDGETING FOR SINGLES

One of the biggest complaints I hear from singles is, "This is so hard to do all on my own!" If you are single, you might think that "if only" you were coupled up, you could have extra income to help with the cash flow. But do you know what also comes with that extra income? Extra spending. An extra cake hole to feed. Maybe a sleep apnea machine. All the things you don't usually find out until you are shacked up together.

Some people in couple-dom would like to cut their partner loose to make the budget work. It can be extremely frustrating when you are celebrating making an additional payment on a debt and you discover your partner bought a round at the pub on the Visa. If you are single and you think that the answer to your problems is a mate, you are going to attract a mate with problems. (I'm not cursing you, I swear.) We tend to not attract the partners we want; we tend to attract the partners we are. We tend to attract the partners we need in order to learn some lessons. The best thing you can do for you, and your future partner if you want one, is be the best possible, most joy-filled, radiant-with-gratitude, financially literate version of yourself.

I have match-made many couples (true story!) and many broke people have joked with me that they want a wealthy partner. But I have yet to meet a millionaire who says, "Erin, do you know a kind, attractive, smart person with a ton of credit card and student loan debt who I can date? I'm looking to wipe out someone's bad habits with my lifetime of hard work."

If a Jonas brother falls in love with you, bonus. In the meantime, stay in your lane, do your own work, and make the most of your debt-free journey. Someone else is not going to fix this for you.

BUDGETING FOR COUPLES

This is only going to work if you agree that the relationship is more important than being right. When couples fight about money, it's not actually about money. Think about the last time you and bae fought about money. If you go deeper beyond the money, what were you actually fighting about?

Not feeling provided for?

Feeling fearful?

Feeling disrespected?

Feeling insecure?

Odds are it wasn't simply about the debt or the spending. It was something deep down that made you afraid.

ALL CHOICES ONLY COME DOWN TO TWO THINGS: LOVE AND FEAR

When we understand that we can respond with either love or fear, we can start to take responsibility for our challenges in money discussions.

Maybe your partner is angry with you because of your spending. When we look at this as a fear-based response, we see that they are possibly afraid of not having enough money to enjoy a comfortable life with you. They worry you don't care as much as they do about what that looks like.

Maybe you are angry with your partner because they spent money out at a restaurant with friends that wasn't in the budget. But it turns out you are feeling left out because maybe you and your partner haven't had a date night in a while. You do not feel chosen when your partner chooses to spend money out with others.

At the heart of all the money struggles are two people who both want to meet a need. We just have to get those two things aligned so you are working together toward a common goal of harmony.

Sometimes it helps to talk to your partner about what you want life to look like when you are debt-free. You might go further and identify what you want your lives to look like when you are financially free.

There's no "right" way to handle money as a couple. Some couples have everything completely separate. Some have joint everything. And some do a combination.

SEPARATE ACCOUNTS

Because we humans are coming together later in life now, some couples already have established bank accounts and utilities, so they prefer to just keep everything separate and divide up all the expenses. "You pay the electricity and cable, I'll pay the heat and water." This method works fine, provided both people have a good understanding and respect for what the other person pays.

But sometimes when finances are tight, we assume that we are carrying more of the load than our partner. We might begin to "scorekeep," which is looking for evidence that they are doing or paying less than we are. This allows us to act like a victim, and it's a disempowering position to be in. We want to make sure we consistently look at the things our partner *is* doing and express our gratitude for these things.

When this is your scenario, you must budget together and have access to all the numbers that affect both you and your partner. Where the funds to pay expenses come from is handled separately, but all the numbers need to be disclosed.

If, however, it is true that the load is unevenly distributed, that means it is time for an open, healthy, honest conversation about what you need to feel more secure. This includes explaining how you will show up in the partnership too; it's not about pointing out your partner's defects and expecting them to change.

If one of you is a better budgeter than the other, even if only by a small margin, that doesn't mean that one person has to take on the delight of budgeting all alone while the other person says, "You handle it, you are better at it than me." It's critical that you budget together in this situation. You can reconcile alone, meaning you can separately check your accounts against the budget you created together. But you have to share your findings and work together to master the common goal of becoming debt-free.

If only one of you has consumer debt and the other does not, you'll have to have a frank conversation about what the uncommunicated expectations are about the debt. If you are not legally married or in some kind of formal commitment, I highly encourage you not to pay off your partner's debt. This isn't intended to punish the partner that has the debt, it's to make sure everyone is cleaning up their own side of the street and to allow the partner with debt to truly master and change their money story.

If you are fantastic with money and your partner is not, your life's work might be biting your tongue when your partner has a eureka moment with money over something you've known all along (or worse, that you tried to teach them before). Your life will feel much happier if you are not your spouse's coach or teacher or mentor. Be your spouse's spouse. Their lover. Their teammate. Their biggest fan.

I debated whether to share this story because I certainly do not want to disparage anyone who is struggling financially. I hope it comes out the way it is intended, which is to help you understand the challenges of being in a partnership when there are very different income or debt scenarios.

I was debt-free and my partner was extremely debt-laden. He seemed to be actively paying down his debt, so I wasn't bothered, but a few months into the relationship when it was getting serious-ish, we had the Money

Conversation. Even though I was earning less than half the income than he was, he was struggling to make ends meet because of the extreme amount of consumer debt he was carrying. We talked about all the money things, and I decided that I would just start "helping." It's important to note that up until this time, I had also been paying for all the meals, travel, and dates on my tiny little income, so I had stopped working toward my own financial goals in order to give us a bit of quality of life.

"I *know*…I'm in the future also." - Mike Birbiglia

As I started to spend more time in his home, there were noticeable repairs that needed to be done. As a landlord, I know the future expense of not dealing with a repair as soon as it arises, so I hired a plumber to fix a $300 leak, and I justified that it saved him money to help him pay off his debt because his water bill went immediately down afterwards.

I also helped by making two payments on his credit card. They were not big payments, but each time I did it I was sick for a whole day afterwards. I thought it was the weirdest coincidence, you know?

This is really embarrassing to admit, but I also "helped" by never being hungry while I was at his house. I never wanted to be a financial burden to him, so I made sure to eat before arriving if I didn't have the money to order us both dinner and left when I was hungry so that I didn't deplete his groceries. Sometimes I brought food, but I didn't like the way that felt, so I just managed my hunger by not having any.

I arrived to spend the weekend there one rainy spring day, and there were giant buckets in the bedroom. The roof, which had needed repair for years, was leaking into the attic, and had made the ceiling so wet that it was drooping. There were two holes where active rainwater was coming directly into the master bedroom, with two buckets strategically placed under them.

My inner landlord was like, "Omg, there is probably mold in these walls; we are going to die," but he seemed so casual about it that I decided maybe I needed to just chill. "This happens every spring," he said nonchalantly. (I need to mention that he was ridiculously handsome, and it is amazing what you can get away with when you are ridiculously handsome.)

He changed the buckets before bed, and within minutes he was asleep. I, however, could not. Drip. Drip. Drip. I ran numbers in my head all night. The cost to repair the roof leak was three months of my income after taxes. Drip. Drip. Drip. I ran through all kinds of scenarios. What could I sell? What could I do to generate more income? Drip. Drip. Drip.

The next morning, he emptied the buckets. The rain really picked up through the day and by that evening it was quite literally pouring. There was a steady stream of water, so he replaced one bucket with a really large plastic garbage can. I was doing my best impression of someone who was not sleep-deprived and irritable AF. I made some jokes, saying, "It is just like camping!" but when I heard it outside my head, it felt ugly. I am not passive-aggressive, I'm not sarcastic, and I'm not rude to my partner. I value speaking the truth, but when it was disguised as a joke, I knew I was bordering on dangerous relationship territory. I also knew after the second night of not sleeping at all that I could not stay there again while the roof was leaking. So, I said I would pay for the roof.

I know, I know.

I was gathering up the funds as fast as I could. Now, I was not even sleeping even when I wasn't there. I was making payments to the contractor, who did exceptional work and was far too kind with my haphazard email money transfers.

And while the home was being fixed, the relationship itself was getting torn down.

Without realizing it, I was becoming deeply resentful.

For many months, I had avoided "score-keeping," but I do think it is important to glance up at the scoreboard at least once a quarter, you know? There is a huge difference between not keeping score and being totally taken advantage of. I didn't know where I was on that spectrum, but I knew everything was horribly out of balance. And at the core of the money issue was something I did not want to admit to myself.

Deep down, when I looked at why all of this was making me anxious, it was because I didn't feel safe. I didn't feel provided for.

Oh, I hate even seeing that typed out now. I was mad at myself. I'm a grown woman; why would I need someone to provide for me? Yet here I was: highly anxious, uncertain, and losing money every month because I was overspending *on the relationship*, trying to get the feeling that I wanted to *feel from the relationship*.

And when I look back on that season now, I see that he did nothing wrong.

He had entirely different standards for what he was willing to accept for his life than I did. He had entirely different priorities for his life than I did. He had entirely different ways of viewing and handling money than I did.

And it was working for him. He could sleep at night. He was happy.

When I'd be busting my ass to come up with funds to pay for my life plus his roof or his dinner and he was at home watching movies on the couch or sleeping soundly next to the waterfall in his bedroom while I was slowly becoming resentful, do you know who was at fault? *Me.*

He never asked me for a single penny. This was entirely me trying to fix or take care of someone else because of what *I* wanted.

I was pushing my expectations on to him. That is completely unfair. And when I realized this, I also realized one other thing: the only person I can change in this situation is me.

And we broke up.

Today, my money boundaries are much stronger. I don't think boundaries are ever perfect because messy, beautiful humans—and their boundaries—are works in progress. But I've learned that I will not be happy if I drain myself to fill someone else up.

You cannot expect that everyone you meet treats money and finances the same way you do, but you can set a high standard for your own relationship with money.

Interestingly, the break-up over the financial stress and the leaky ceiling was a gift of freedom for him too.

While your partner is paying off debt, you can make life easier with free date-night ideas or spend time investing for retirement, intended for you both to enjoy later in life. But they do not get a free pass by not contributing to your life. If your partner isn't bringing anything to the table or making your life better in some way, then it might not be a true partnership.

JOINT EVERYTHING

Some couples have joint accounts and joint assets, and it works great. Others have joint accounts, and it is disastrous. The key with all finance management in relationships is communicating, and we need to communicate often!

Hopefully you have a partner that shows up and is willing to do all the work with you. If not, you could try suggesting a Naked Budget Meeting. Attendance is usually pretty good at those, and it's difficult to fight when your jubblies are on display.

If you are nervous and brand-new to communicating about money with your partner, I encourage you to invite them to a conversation. It can be on a nature walk, or even sitting across from each other at a leisurely cafe. Try and do it outside the home where there will be less distractions like laundry and did-you-take-the-garbage-out-yets.

Here are the rules for communicating about money:

1. You have to listen fully and completely to each response until your partner is done. You will not interrupt or interject with your own thoughts or your own answers. When it is your turn, your partner must listen to you fully and completely as well. If your partner does interrupt you, you pause lovingly, wait for them to finish, and start again. You do none of this passive-aggressively. You do it because you know everyone deserves to be seen and heard, and being a perfect person is unsexy.
2. You take turns back and forth with each question. If you do not get through every question because the conversation is so good, that is extra awesome, and you finish again another day. If your partner

answers shortly and quickly, you can kindly question to see if they have more to share by saying, "Tell me more."

3. You are listening and observing with love. You do not get a say in whether your partner is right or wrong. They get to speak from their own experience. You get to speak from your own experience. You will not "should" on them, and they will not "should" on you. The point of all this is to learn. When we are in a relationship for any length of time, we tend to make assumptions about our people. We engage in this open dialogue to allow ourselves to release our partners from any shackles of their past we are holding them to so that they can be free to be the best version of themselves too.

Here are some questions to open the dialogue:

- How was money discussed in your home?
- What was your parents' relationship with money like?
- Describe your earliest memory with money, and how it impacted you.
- Were you given an allowance? What were the expectations for that money?
- How old were you when you first had your own bank account? What was that experience like?
- What did you do with the money you earned from your first few jobs?
- Is that similar to how you spend money now? Explain.
- How does your relationship with money differ from your siblings' relationship with money?
- How did you feel about money when you were younger?
- Describe your relationship to money today.
- What do you wish your eighteen-year-old self knew about money?
- What money decisions have you made that you are not proud of? Why?
- What money decisions have you made that you are proud of? Why?
- When we are debt-free, what is the first luxury purchase you want to make with cash?

- How do you want to spend your time in your seventies?
- How do you want to spend your time in your eighties?
- What is it about becoming debt-free that most excites you?
- Is there anything about becoming debt-free that makes you nervous?

It's critical to make money decisions together. If one of you has your foot on the brake and the other has the foot on the gas, it'll be that much more difficult to get where you want to go financially.

FINANCIAL ABUSE

I just need to address this little subject that is horrible to discuss but is often left out of conversations about the kinds of abuse that people can face behind closed doors. If there is one person in your home who is controlling all the money, and all the money decisions, I want you to carefully consider how this makes you feel. Financial abuse can be a subtle but powerful control tactic. If this is something you've agreed to and your relationship is by and large healthy, I still want you to take control of some of your own money for your own financial education. That way, you can also work with your partner to make sure you are both assisting in the common goal to become financially free.

Have a gander through the list below and see if any of it resonates or if you notice these subtle control tactics in any of your friends' relationships who might be unable to ask for help. Financial abuse often occurs in relationships where there is also physical, mental, or other forms of emotional abuse, but not always.

According to Sherri Gordon, bullying prevention advocate, victims of financial abuse may have a partner who:

- Forbids them from working or gaining employment.
- Sabotages their employment opportunities or their ability to work effectively.
- Decides how all the money is spent.
- Gives an allowance.

- Gives an allowance but demands favors to "earn" more money.
- Blocks access to bank accounts or investments.
- Blocks access to credit cards or any financial product.
- Racks up debt in their name or their partner's name.
- Racks up debt and doesn't tell their partner.
- Controls who they work for or controls how much they earn.
- Spends money how they want but doesn't allow partner to do the same.
- Requires their partner to work, even though they might not work, and forces them to hand over all the money or pay.
- Uses their assets for personal gain, and perhaps even without permission.
- Lies about bill payments.
- Lies about their own assets or liabilities or income.
- Asks their partner to lie about assets or liabilities or income.
- Harasses them at work by constantly calling, texting, or stopping by without consent.
- Drags out divorce proceedings with the simple goal of crippling their partner financially.
- Forces them to sign documents they don't understand.
- Withholds or avoids child support or payments for the wellbeing of children.
- Controls their spending.

If you resonate with this list, I need you to do two things. I need you to first recognize that *this is not your fault*. You've done nothing to deserve this treatment, and this is not true unconditional love. You may have a partner who is hurting, but that is also not your responsibility. This financial relationship you have will ruin you eventually. There is no happy ending for this behavior. There is no solution in this book that can help you. Only you can help you. And as scary as it might be, I need you to do a very brave thing, and call the domestic abuse hotline in your area. Right now, if it is safe to do so. Not when the next bad thing happens. Not when things get bad. Right now.

Oh. And one more thing.

You are loved.

Singles and Dating

This is one of my favorite stories.

Before she died, a mother said to her adult child, "Here is a watch that your grandfather gave me. It is almost two hundred years old. I want to give it to you, but first go to the jewelry store and tell them that you want to sell it and see how much they offer you."

He came back and said, "They offered $150 because it's so old."

The mother said, "Now, go to the pawn shop."

He came back and said, "The pawn shop offered ten dollars because it looks so worn."

The mother then asked the son to go to the museum and show them the watch.

He went to the museum, came back, and said, "The curator offered $500,000 for this very rare piece to be included in their precious antique collections."

The mom said, "I wanted to let you know that the right place values you in the right way. Don't find yourself in the wrong place and get angry if you are not valued. Those that know your value are those who appreciate you. Don't stay in a place where nobody sees your value."

When you're dating, it is very important to choose a partner who understands your value. Not the bullsh*t value you give yourself when you are feeling worthless. Your *true* value. The value I see in you. For the most part, dear reader, I am an absolute stranger, and I know you are worth so much and that you deserve to be treated in the highest regard.

I want to be clear that I absolutely do think you should date and marry someone you are in love with. Except if they are broke. (Kidding.)

(Sort of.)

I'm not saying you can't love a broke person. Love is love. I'm saying: do not marry them. Not today. Not while they are broke. You can be with them and support them emotionally and create all kinds of fun memories together. But anchoring your dreams to that sinking ship is a bad financial idea.

I look forward to hearing from the 2 percent of you who can prove me wrong. And I love love, so I truly want to hear how putting them through medical school was the best decision for you. But for the rest of you, the ones that are nodding your head in agreement or who feel resentment toward an ex because you bailed them out of credit card debt or took care of them while they sat on your couch and played Xbox even though they were capable of earning an income: I feel you, and I'm sending you extra love. Giving your partner the opportunity to clean up their mess is an invitation to growth. Taking care of your partner's mess is becoming their mother.

There's something super attractive about a person who has goals and goes after them. And if you ask my friends, they will dish that it's mega hot *even* if the person fails. They'd rather have their partner fall on their ass and skin their knee from riding a bike down Kicking Horse Mountain than stand beside a bike trying to look cool.

We want a partner who has bigger dreams than just the relationship. That's what makes the relationship sexy. It is what also contributes to polarity. The best kind of partner, financially speaking, is one who is generous yet wise.

When you come into a new relationship ready to "help" someone be a better person, you are setting yourself up for disaster. You're going to need some solid boundaries, friend. And you're going to need some discernment to ensure you can see what kind of financial mess you might be headed toward.

So how do you know if you are headed into date-disaster territory? Everyone puts on their best shirts, and they magic-eraser all their quirkiness away in the first few weeks of dating. How do you tell whether someone is good with money without actually asking them straight up?

Here are a few flaming orange flags. If these themes are coming up in your dating life, it might be okay for you to pass in order to take good care of your future self.

- If you give them a twenty for a ten-dollar item and they don't bring you the change, hard no.
- If you are expected to pay for you, plus their share of everything, in order for you to see each other, no thanks.
- If they do not show up for you with careful thought on important days, like your birthday or other holidays that are important to you, no thank you.
- If they expect you to spend outside of your comfort zone in order to hang out with them, mmmmm no.
- If they are totally comfortable with you putting things on credit without regard for your financial goals, kthanxbye.
- If money becomes a measure of scorekeeping in the relationship, then adios.
- If they are not open to discussing money in general terms (you don't need to know each other's incomes on the first date) but get uncomfortable talking about how you will split the check, or who will pick it up, and it becomes an issue, bye bae.
- If they are happy to spend your money on things that need to come out of their own budget like gas or groceries, then get the hell outta there.
- If they like to flaunt purchases or consumer items or they are flexin' on social media outside of what you see to be true in their real life, then nope.
- If their words do not match their actions, nay-nay.
- If their spending seems to be unaligned with their values, buhbye.
- If they talk about their financial circumstances not being their fault, laters baby.
- If they have parents that are unnecessarily making their financial decisions, see yaaaa.

By the same advice as above, if you do these things to another person or expect someone else to take care of you, no matter what your financial situation is, it might be best if you took time to clean up your side of the street first and then start dating.

There are even people who will offer to take care of you financially in exchange for favors. This is not dating, my love. This is an "arrangement."

When we first start dating, we create a checkbox system. For some of us, this is a real checkbox list that we text to our friends in order to find the perfect person, as if we could order them online with free shipping. Those checkboxes are important when we first look for love because they help us find the people we believe we might be compatible with. Plus, they help us eliminate people who are unaligned with our needs (like if I am sober, I would be incompatible with someone who is a heavy drinker, for instance).

But once we commit to a relationship, we must throw those checkboxes away and choose to love wholly and completely. If you are in an existing relationship with someone who has unaligned financial behaviors, you are going to have to find a way to work together. This is different from financial abuse, which eventually destroys you emotionally, mentally, financially, and often spiritually. (Any abusers have what we call a spiritual sickness, so their spirit is not well, and that darkness sets out to destroy yours, too, to gain control. That all sounds very Voldemort.)

The point is that real love is messy and it can be hard, but when we hold our committed partners to a checkbox system, we are setting them up to fail. We aren't paying attention to who they are. We are simply paying attention to *how they serve us*, and that is inherently flawed.

Standards vs Expectations

Remember how we talked about standards vs expectations earlier? Let's revisit that quickly because they are so intrinsically tied to your money story. Standards are the level of quality you live your life by. Standards increase your happiness.

Expectations are an assumption that other people need to live at your standard and that decreases our happiness. To get the hell out of debt for good, we have to raise our personal standards.

If you spend the next two years trying to get someone else to change, you'll be miserable. Simply set a higher standard for your own life, commit entirely to living there, and everything will improve, even if it is uncomfortable for a time.

Things we must never lower our standards on:

- Our boundaries
- Our worth
- Our financial goals
- Our quality of life and how we live
- Our goals and dreams
- Our health
- Our relationships

> Amanda says: "Amazing the little things that happen when you make a plan, practice gratitude, and do your best! Since we've started budgeting religiously, my husband's hours at work have been out of this world, we've been able to feed a family of five off of $159 for 15 days, we've caught up or made an immediate plan to catch up anything that was behind, he's had a promotion at work come to light, and we are somehow now managing to do totally great on a single income and making ourselves wonder how we couldn't manage to pay sh*t off before when we had two incomes. Ah life lessons. It's changing our relationship with each other too, we don't fight as much, we are both happier, more active, more engaged, more helpful… Gah! I had to share."

PHASE TWO

Chapter Nine

PHASE TWO

LET'S PAY OFF SOME DEBT, SHALL WE?

There are a number of strategies that various debt experts believe in, and truthfully, I don't give a flying squirrel which one you choose. I just want you to do the one that makes the most sense to you.

Highest Interest Rate

Some experts will tell you that you'll save more money by paying off the card with the highest interest rate first. The strategy is that you list your outstanding debts and their corresponding interest rates, and then you put them in the order of the largest interest rate to the smallest interest rate. Gail Vaz-Oxlade, Canadian TV host and author, is known for this method.

Smallest Balance

The strategy is that you list your debts and their corresponding outstanding balances according to the smallest amount owed to the largest amount owed, and you knock them out one by one. Dave Ramsey, American radio show host, author, and business dude, is famed for this method. What is brilliant about the psychology of this is that Dave knows that when you get a "win," you are more likely to use that positive momentum to keep going.

Highest Payment

This method requires you to put them in the order of the highest payment, and the theory is that as you work your way down the debt chain, you'll quickly hammer out the smaller payment debts because you'll be putting a lot of money toward them near the end.

Emotional Mastery Method

When I was up to my eyeballs in debt, I jokingly called this strategy the spicy method. Basically, the cards or the debt that peeved me off the most or made me super spicy were the ones I paid first. If I had a bad experience with the card or the company or just a negative emotional connection, I made those the priority. This is the method that worked for me because I was motivated daily. None of the math mattered to me, I just couldn't stand to owe another cent to certain people or companies and so they went to the top of the list so I could get them the hell out of my life.

All the experts agree that the government gets paid first if you are behind on taxes.

This is mostly because if you don't pay them, they can actually come take it. They just drop into your bank account and grab it from you. And when your accounts are frozen, it makes it damn hard to pay the other bills, or more urgently, eat to stay alive. Yes, you truly need to be considering taxes in your financial decisions. But the reality is: not everyone who falls behind in taxes is a reckless, avoidant, naughty taxpayer, even though that is how you will be made to feel.

If you do not voluntarily pay the amount you owe on time, the government can send a legal notice to a third party to collect your debt directly. This third party could be your bank, an employer for salary (wages, commissions, bonuses, reimbursement of expenses owed to an employer), amounts due to a contractor or subcontractor, rent or lease payments, loan payments, fees owed to a professional, annuity payments, interest payments, the air that you breathe, dividend payments, cash in a bank account, you get the idea. Basically, most things. The third party collects your money on behalf of the government via the government's demand and hands it over to the government because the government thinks you can't (or won't).

When you become debt-free, I'll have you put together an account for taxes, *even if* you are a salaried employee. You put a wee bit of money in that account if you are salaried, and you put a larger percentage in that account if you are self-employed. Then, if you don't need the money, you can invest it in a registered investment plan of some kind that will lower the amount of tax payable this year, and you will invest in your retirement. Many people bank on getting a tax refund to help them financially, but then they blow that money on an all-inclusive. I hear people say that their tax refund is a "forced savings" plan, but why not just save when you are able? Forced savings implies that saving is completely out of your control and has to be done at gunpoint, as though you cannot be trusted with your money and you have to rely on the government to help you. This is not the empowered money mindset we are going to transform in this book. So please don't wave the white flag yet. Let's first get down to business by paying off your debt.

MAKE A LIST

Have a look through the liabilities list you compiled when you did your net worth spreadsheet. When you've listed out all your debts, what is the order you would like to see them gone? The CRA/IRS/HMRC/ATO is going at the top of the list. Then what?

I don't actually care what the interest rates are. I don't actually care what the balances are. I know that the thing that pays these debts off is not math. It's determination. When you can identify the feelings you have around these debts, we'll have *emotional leverage* to get you to pay these suckers off faster.

When we are paying down debt, all experts with successful clients agree that you have to go at it aggressively. If you can focus for twelve months, you can see huge gains. But you have to want it like you want oxygen. If you are tempted by concert tickets and YOLO and fun experiences over the grit and grind, then it's going to take you longer. When you're facing a financial decision, I'll often have you put the numbers in the budget and net worth spreadsheet, so you can see how the decisions today affect your financial freedom tomorrow.

The challenge with all of this is: life is short. It can be tempting to say to yourself, "But if I die tomorrow, I don't want to have spent my last week on earth pinching pennies." Let me tell you that the odds of that are very low, and if you continue on this path, you will be in your nineties pinching pennies. You might even pass your financial burden down to your offspring, who then have to budget their own lives and make expensive care decisions for you.

I type all this to you with a giant lump in my throat as I remember Lynn.

Lynn was a beautiful mom who came to me in about 2014 with a lot of debt and a humble request for help as she was navigating a separation and divorce. One of the underlying scripts people have running through their heads is that small choices are inconsequential. I know this to be true of people who struggle with both weight loss and debt. I wanted to put my eyes on a group of people who would be open to sharing their experiences with both. I ended up teaching a year-long course with a couple phenomenal ladies and a dozen participants where I closely monitored the stories these women told themselves about who they were through what they believed. And I measured this against the results they got.

The ones that were successful had a massive shift in their thinking. The ones that struggled had a more difficult time navigating the stories they told themselves about who they were. More on that later. But for now, dear Lynn.

She overcame so much in our twelve months together. She shared her deepest, darkest demons with me, which had impacted her habits and behaviors. If you are wondering what heals both overeating and debt, it isn't judgement or shame.

One day in front of the group, we were talking about kids and daily routines. Lynn shared that her daughter woke up first and came to wake her up because she struggled to get out of bed in the morning. Her daughter wakes up, gets cereal or breakfast, watches cartoons, and waits quietly and patiently for her mom to get going, which sometimes took a few hours. Lynn had asked a question, something like, "What if I'm not a morning person?" and I took a deep breath and felt a searing pain in my gut.

The moment where I have to decide: How do I tell the truth in a loving, kind way without judgement or shame and still empower her to change?

I knew I could not let this slide. I tried to control both the tremble in my voice and the dryness in my mouth as I spoke.

"That girl deserves a mother whose eyes light up when she enters the room in the morning. That girl deserves a mother who says, 'Oh yay! You're awake! Let's nourish our bodies together and talk about the day ahead.' That girl deserves a mother who is ready to greet the day like a warrior, who has taken care of her own basic needs, so she can focus on being a present parent who is consciously raising her daughter to be a woman of character, not hoping the programs she's watching on television do it for her. That girl deserves to see her mother up and awake and going after her own dreams, so that she can be inspired to do it herself. I care less about how much debt you pay off and more about how you show up in the world, especially to this wonderful little girl who deserves you at your best."

The room was silent.

For a moment, I was worried I overstepped. But then the part of me that doesn't care what other people think kicked in, and I thought if Lynn is mad or leaves the program because I've offended her, then I'm okay with that. This debt will not get paid off with discipline, anyway. Debt gets paid off with love. Sometimes that love shows up as discipline, meaning some people choose to do hard things in the name of love and self-respect. Some people value fun, and making their debt pay-off process fun for them is a way of loving themselves. I cannot get Lynn to pay off anything if she is sleeping until noon and battling negative self-talk and emotionally abandoning the people she loves most. I know she wasn't doing that intentionally. Luckily, she wasn't dealing with a mental illness, but she had fallen into a pattern of making choices that were mentally unwell.

I know from my own parenting journey that the times I've been short or sharp with my kids, it had nothing to do with them. It was because I was stressed financially or tired or hadn't eaten a sandwich. Every time my kids needed me and I *had* taken care of myself, I was amused and entertained by their bids for connection, not treating them like an annoying distraction.

In the month that followed, Lynn swiftly changed her life for the better. In fact, she became debt-free on October 15th of that year. Ten and a half months. She *radiated* confidence and joy. She reported that her time with her kids was enjoyable. She was more present with them. Not perfect, mind you, because none of us are. But she was focused less on money stress and her separation and her struggles, and she was focused more on marveling at her children's growth and development. Spending time with friends. Laughing more. Being in control of her money instead of letting debt control her. She was making excellent progress with her boundaries, which was helping her conquer some of those inner demons that lurk within us all.

Then, two months later, she found a lump in her leg. After testing, she was diagnosed with advanced lymphoma, and she was to start chemotherapy. But on the weekend before she was to start treatment, she passed away. Suddenly. The worst unexpected ending life can offer.

It's true, we never know what life will bring us. Most of us do not know how many days or hours lie ahead. Maybe it would have been fun for Lynn to take out five credit cards that year and spoil her kids with trips to theme parks. But we didn't know. She didn't know.

Lynn's choice left her family debt-free before her death, which alleviates a lot more stress than a quick rollercoaster ride and some corn dogs ever could. I wish she had extra years to truly build a financially-free life for them all to enjoy together, but her final financial decisions were an act of love all the same.

Whether we are paying off debt, building a company, writing a book, making dinner. Whether the collectors are calling or your mom is sick in the hospital. Whether you've lost everything or won the lottery. You always have the option to show up in love.

Love is the greatest legacy we will ever leave.

> Tia says: "This has completely changed the way I live. I am more present with the people I love. I thought this was going to teach me money tips, but it turns out I had so much to learn about relationships and the way I had been previously showing up. I've paid off $62,000 in the last twelve months but for the last eleven, I've been the happiest I've ever been."

Chapter Ten

UNDERSTANDING DEBT BEHAVIOR

CLASSES OF EXPERIENCES

How you choose to view your life and the stories you tell yourself about who you are have a tremendous impact on the outcome and results of your life. If you decide, "I am not a morning person," you could be living that out in a way that is a detriment to your body, your finances, or the people you love. Sure, you might have a predilection to feeling energized in the morning or late in the evening, but you can absolutely train yourself to do anything you want to do.

You can change your physiology any time you want. Energy doesn't come from the foods you eat or how much sleep you had the night before. You can clearly set yourself up for success and make it easier on yourself by having great sleep hygiene, proper rest, and nourishing food and hydration. But it is also possible to have a terrible night's sleep, wake up a little groggy, slam on some Britney, and dance like your life depended on it, and instantly feel energized and better. It's going to be so much easier for you to have vitality when you nourish, hydrate, and take proper care of your body. But your health is not a destination. It's not a finite goal. You will be managing your health infinitely, so don't give up on a day because you aren't "feeling it."

It's that little space in between "feeling" and "doing" where we get caught. You know you'll feel better after dancing around and getting your heart rate up, but actually getting up and turning the music on is where we stop ourselves. In the beginning, training our minds comes not from the exercise itself but from getting your arse to start exercising in the first place. When we reach a place where we start looking forward to it, it's not much work. But training is often required to get us there.

With enough practice, the things that once felt hard become so much easier. Training for your first 5k run is greatly different from training for an IronMan triathlon. What once was difficult to do as you were learning to run a 5k is a nice, easy, fun warm-up for your IronMan training. This is how human growth works, friend!

The best way I can explain it is through one of the many life-changing things I have learned from Tony Robbins.

The following does not have a formal name, and I've adapted it in order to explain it when it comes to finances, but for now we'll refer to it as the Classes of Experiences.

If we were to take everything you do in a week financially and divide it into categories, we would come up with four classes.

CLASS ONE **things that feel good and are good for me**	**CLASS THREE** **things that feel good but are not good for me**
CLASS TWO **things that might not feel good but are good for me**	**CLASS FOUR** **things that do not feel good and are not good for me**

Let's start at Class Four and work backward.

It's important to note that you need to fill out *your own chart* as the examples I'll use below are generic. You will have your own unique life experiences, and what constitutes a Class Four experience for you might be a Class Three experience for someone else. You have to fill this chart out as authentically and honestly as you possibly can.

Class Four experiences are Things That Do Not Feel Good *and* Are Not Good For Me.

Financially speaking, this might be things like:

CLASS ONE **things that feel good and are good for me**	**CLASS THREE** **things that feel good but are not good for me**
CLASS TWO **things that might not feel good but are good for me**	**CLASS FOUR** **things that do not feel good and are not good for me** • when collection agents call • falling behind on taxes • fighting with my partner about money • opening credit card bills after I've overspent

These are things that if you did them repeatedly, they would destroy you financially. This is the place where you usually think: *How did this happen?!* This is where you would typically be embarrassed if people knew you were spending most of your "mental real estate." Sometimes this is a place you can't even imagine a way out of.

Class Three experiences are like:

CLASS ONE **things that feel good and are good for me**	**CLASS THREE** **things that feel good but are not good for me** • avoiding opening the bills • splurging on unnecessary luxury items when I'm carrying debt • moving debt from a high interest card to a lower interest card. This feels like a good decision but you can see on the net worth spreadsheet, the impact is very low • consolidating debt This feels temporarily good, but you are just moving debt around, you didn't get rid of it.
CLASS TWO **things that might not feel good but are good for me**	**CLASS FOUR** **things that do not feel good and are not good for me** • when collection agents call • falling behind on taxes • fighting with my partner about money • opening credit card bills after I've overspent

These are things that usually feel good in the moment, but they have no long-term benefits to your financial health. They are things we'll typically do when we are already emotionally unregulated. They are where we usually go when we find things are hard, frustrating, and/or difficult. This is also the place we tend to live financially if we think, "Well f*ck it, YOLO!"

If you are ever tempted to consolidate or refinance or transfer balances, do this first: Put the debt in the net worth spreadsheet where it is today, and then put it where you want to transfer it and look at the effect on your net worth. *Nothing changes.* You just moved debt around, you didn't get rid of it. As you've seen, you're crossing your fingers hoping you'll make up for it in the budget, which you have not yet mastered.

Most (okay, all) of the people I know who have consolidated ended up *further* in debt in six months than those who didn't. Don't chase a feeling.

Go after results. Pay that debt off, truly. With cash. With real money. The only person who wins when you play these consolidation/refinance/balance transfer games is the new person or institution who is receiving your interest payments.

If you are spending the majority of your time in Class Three experiences, you will end up with a Class Four life. The flow of money energy goes from Three to Four over time, like a gravitational pull you don't even realize is there.

The good news is if you want a Class One life, there is also a money energy flow that will allow you to get there with ease. But before it starts to feel easy, it first requires some work.

To move yourself from Class Three to Class Two, you have to use almost superhuman strength, but only for a short period of time. If you can consistently master Class Two experiences, you will find everything will start to shift for you. The jump from Class Three to Class Two can feel difficult, but that is because you have to master one thing:

Your emotions.

When you let your emotions dictate your behaviors, you'll end up in Class Three every time.

Class Three says: I don't feel like going for a run today.

Class Three says: Oh, I know I've had a quart of ice cream after every meal this week, but one more day won't hurt.

Class Three says: I don't want to have a confrontation with Chad at work, so I'll avoid him.

Class Two says: I don't feel like going for a run today, but I said I would and I'm keeping my promises to myself in spite of how I feel.

Class Two says: I don't need ice cream again. I am going to love my body with some nutrient-dense food to give myself some nourishment.

Class Two says: If I want to make things better at work, I can have a kind but honest conversation with Chad that will get us closer to the workplace culture we desire.

If you start to shift even a little bit, and you do it with consistency, you will see major results in time. I'm not suggesting you have a major life overhaul on day one of getting the hell out of debt. I'm suggesting you start to spend a little more time in Class Two than you did last week and go from there.

Class Two experiences are like:

CLASS ONE

things that feel good and are good for me

CLASS THREE

things that feel good but are not good for me

- avoiding opening the bills
- splurging on unnecessary luxury items when I'm carrying debt
- moving debt from a high interest card to a lower interest card.
- consolidating debt

CLASS TWO

things that might not feel good but are good for me

- preparing a budget so I'm proactive with my money instead of reactive
- reconciling my budget, even a couple minutes a day to make sure I'm on track
- sticking to a list of planned expenses when I shop
- selling stuff on a buy-and-sell
- updating my net worth spreadsheet
- earning extra income
- saying no to family or friends when it comes to spending outside my budget

CLASS FOUR

things that do not feel good and are not good for me

- when collection agents call
- falling behind on taxes
- fighting with my partner about money
- opening credit card bills after I've overspent

Class Two and Class One experiences are all about financial boundaries. When you are absolutely clear on what you want (in this case: being completely consumer debt-free), you need to protect that dream. If you are planting new seeds, it can be wise to put up a little fence to guard against things that will stop their germination. Most people are well-meaning and do not intend to trample all over your new garden, so having a boundary or a fence simply lets them know where they can walk and where they ought not.

But some people who are unsuccessful at planting their *own* crops will drive all over your field and even pee in it while telling you how stupid gardening is. Some, while still having no garden of their own, will give you gardening tips. You must put a fence up around your dreams and a few No Trespassing signs if you expect to yield a crop.

Class One experiences are like:

CLASS ONE things that feel good and are good for me	**CLASS THREE** things that feel good but are not good for me
• looking at my net worth and feeling confident about my finances • knowing when I will retire and understanding how I will make it happen • using money I already have to pay for my lifestyle with my budget • having confident conversations with accountants, realtors, mortgage brokers and financial planners	• avoiding opening the bills • splurging on unnecessary luxury items when I'm carrying debt • moving debt from a high interest card to a lower interest card. • consolidating debt
CLASS TWO things that might not feel good but are good for me	**CLASS FOUR** things that do not feel good and are not good for me
• preparing a budget so I'm proactive with my money instead of reactive • reconciling my budget, even a couple minutes a day to make sure I'm on track • sticking to a list of planned expenses when I shop • selling stuff on a buy-and-sell • updating my net worth spreadsheet • earning extra income • saying no to family or friends when it comes to spending outside my budget	• when collection agents call • falling behind on taxes • fighting with my partner about money • opening credit card bills after I've overspent

When I learned about the Classes of Experiences, my mouth dropped open. I could *clearly* see something I now call "My Line of Integrity."

My Line of Integrity falls right down the middle of this chart.

CLASS ONE things that feel good and are good for me	**CLASS THREE** things that feel good but are not good for me
• looking at my net worth and feeling confident about my finances • knowing when I will retire and understanding how I will make it happen • using money I already have to pay for my lifestyle with my budget • having confident conversations with accountants, realtors, mortgage brokers and financial planners	• avoiding opening the bills • splurging on unnecessary luxury items when I'm carrying debt • moving debt from a high interest card to a lower interest card. • consolidating debt
CLASS TWO things that might not feel good but are good for me	**CLASS FOUR** things that do not feel good and are not good for me
• preparing a budget so I'm proactive with my money instead of reactive • reconciling my budget, even a couple minutes a day to make sure I'm on track • sticking to a list of planned expenses when I shop • selling stuff on a buy-and-sell • updating my net worth spreadsheet • earning extra income • saying no to family or friends when it comes to spending outside my budget	• when collection agents call • falling behind on taxes • fighting with my partner about money • opening credit card bills after I've overspent

See, if I were to take a big marker and draw it smack in the middle of the chart, what I would clearly define is where I fail at my promises to myself.

CLASS ONE things that feel good and are good for me	**CLASS THREE** things that feel good but are not good for me ⇐ *line of integrity*
CLASS TWO things that might not feel good but are good for me	**CLASS FOUR** things that do not feel good and are not good for me

Often, the things on the left (Classes One and Two) are the things I promise myself I will do and be. But where I was living for so long was on the right side (Classes Three and Four). I wanted to *feel* better about things, so I justified so much behavior that allowed me to live a Class Three and Four life. When I started replacing my behaviors with Class Two behaviors the majority of the time, I eventually started living a Class One Life.

We can fool ourselves into thinking Class Three is self-care. But it is actually self-indulgence. True self-support and self-care are found in Classes One and Two.

Often, I get the impression that people think life will just be *so much easier* when they are debt-free, like all their troubles will vanish with that last debt payment. Don't get me wrong: that last debt payment feels euphoric, and I highly recommend marking it with some kind of celebration, even if you are just hoola-hooping in your kitchen singing into a wooden spoon. But money challenges will always be there, just like relationship challenges, health challenges, career challenges, and all the other interesting things life throws our way.

The difference is when we are debt-free, the *kinds* of challenges we have are much less stressful, not because money has solved the problem, but because we have learned to overcome all kinds of obstacles on the path to debt freedom, so our ability to cope is much stronger.

We have to decide whether we want to save more or invest more. We have to learn what kinds of investments suit us best. And with all the decisions we need to make, there will be some decisions we screw up. Sometimes things will just go badly on a vacation, and we'll have to shell out a little cash to reroute home. Or maybe we order something online, and it arrives looking nothing like the photo our order originated from.

The difference is you will have overcome so many obstacles to become debt-free, particularly mastering your own emotions, that these cockups don't destroy you for days or cause you to panic. Mastering your emotions becomes the most difficult work you will do here, but it will serve you for years on end, in so many areas of your life, when you are able to stay calm under financial stress.

Understanding and implementing these Classes of Experiences allows you to become aware of where you are spending your time. If you notice yourself in Class Three experiences or indulging in Class Four thinking, you can simply bring awareness to yourself without judgement and decide, "I'm feeling awfully stressed about money this month; let's go into the budget for a few minutes and have a look, so I know what is true and what is fear." When you can look at the real numbers, you can take real action. You can see that you are $200 behind, and you can make $201 decisions to help yourself. You can feel accomplished once you've taken action and it's this exact competence over time that builds money confidence.

Jenelle says: "I want to thank you so much for your Get the Hell Out of Debt program. After seeing you speak at that event with Anthony Robbins in August you motivated me to make big changes for my family and myself. I worked hard, set up a budget, paid off credit cards, opened a Safe-Zone Account and started paying for things with cash. Wow! It is amazing how well it worked. Today, I am even more thankful for where we are sitting financially with all the changes the world has seen recently."

Chapter Eleven

SINGLE TASK YOUR DEBT PAYOFF

PAYING THE DEBT OFF

> Ashley J. says, "I am amazed at how less stressed I am about dollars! My debt keeps going down. This month I will have paid off my first debt and in two months will have paid off our second debt. We have a full Quick and Dirty Fund. The one thing I struggle with now is the idea of needing access to our Quick and Dirty Fund if we have something unexpected and urgent arise. I don't want to touch that money and that brings up a bit of anxiety."

Oh, Ashley! If only we all had as much anxiety about using a credit card as our Quick and Dirty Fund. This anxiety is completely reasonable because the credit card companies marketed themselves to you as a nice, easy quick-fix for all your troubles. I understand that having cash socked away feels like a safety blanket now, but it's there to protect you against credit card debt. If you save the Quick and Dirty but use your credit card to pay expenses, you will be atrophying those money muscles we are working so hard to build!

Once you've made a list of your debts and know the dollar amounts to the penny, you'll organize them in the way that makes the most sense to you to pay off. This way, you ensure that the minimum payments are in your budget and that your budget can service the minimum payments.

You are going to pay the minimums on all the debts, and then everything extra that you can *squeeze* out of the budget, you are going to put on the *one* debt you are working on.

It's going to likely feel foreign if until now you've been trying to pay down lots of debts at once.

Our brains consume more energy than any other part of our body. When we focus on *one goal at a time*, we wholly direct our attention to the thing we are doing. Therefore, we have more energy to accomplish it, and we accomplish it faster. Multitasking our debts is more exhausting to the brain because we are shifting our focus and often undoing our own work. If you don't believe me, open a daycare *and* try to keep it clean.

Once one debt is paid down, you then squeeze all available funds out of the budget again and knock off the next debt.

As you pay off debts, you transfer the cash from what you would have paid on a debt onto the next one. This is sometimes referred to as the snowball method, the snowflake method, or the avalanche method. I'm Canadian, and I have no idea why all the experts are dragging our climate into this, but essentially you build a bigger snow-thing by adding lots of smaller snow-things to it.

The Squeeze Method

This is essentially what we call gathering extra money to put toward debt. Because I use this term all the time while I teach, I thought I better Google it to ensure it was not trademarked before it ends up in this book. It isn't, thankfully.

But then Google said, "Do you mean the Squeeze Technique?" Hmmmm, did I? And so, I clicked.

Nope. Turns out the Squeeze Technique is used to help with premature ejaculation. I want to assure you if you are familiar with *that* technique, this is not that; however, using this method will prevent you from prematurely blowing your budget.

You must be actively budgeting to take advantage of the Squeeze Method. It doesn't maximize its potential if you wing it because you'll be running up the down escalator, financially speaking, unless you effectively and honestly know your numbers.

You can use this method no matter what phase you are in. If you are in Phase One, you take the money you squeeze and put it directly toward your Quick and Dirty Fund. If you are in Phase Two, you take the money and put it directly on the debt you are currently annihilating. If you are in Phase Three, you take the money and put it directly on the asset you are building.

If you are using the spreadsheet I use (that you have downloaded for free from financialtransformation.ca), then you put it on the "cell" you are working on. The cell refers to the spreadsheet cell. If you are in Phase Two and the debt that you are currently annihilating is your Bank of America Credit Card and the balance is currently $2300, then the cell you are working on is the cell that shows the balance of $2300. If you squeeze fifty dollars, then you have annihilated fifty dollars from that cell and it now is $2250.

Here are some ways you can squeeze:

1. Sell something you no longer use or need, and take that money and put it directly on the cell you are working on.
2. When you purchase an item for less than you had budgeted for (if it's on sale, for example), take the difference between the amount you budgeted and the amount it actually cost and put that money directly on the cell you are working on.
3. When a fixed expense is suddenly less than you were expecting, take the difference and put that money immediately and directly on the cell you are working on.
4. When you have unexpected money appear (yay!), take it and immediately put it on the—you guessed it—cell you are working on.
5. When you get a refund for an item, take that money and put it toward the cell you are working on.

6. When you get a raise at work, take the new money after tax and put it immediately on the cell you are working on.
7. When you win cash, take that money and put it directly on the cell you are working on. If it isn't cash and it's something you'll keep (like a grocery gift card, for example), take the value of it out of the budget in cash, put the cash on the cell you are working on, and use the grocery gift card to get your groceries.
8. When you decide to cut back on something (let's say, eating at restaurants for a month), take that money you would have spent and put it directly on the cell you are working on.
9. When you earn extra money from a side gig, take that money and put it directly on the cell you are working on.
10. When you get a coupon, take...okay, you get the drift.
11. Fill in the blank. Basically anything. Take that extra moola and put it toward the thing you are working on!

If we don't do this, money has a way of disappearing. I've met so many people who received raises that they prayed about, and when their first paycheck came with the raise attached, they didn't even notice because they had not adjusted their squeeze. I have met people who wasted inheritances, lottery winnings, commissions, and bonus checks, simply because they didn't control their spending—their spending controlled them.

Yes, if the amounts you squeeze are small, like $0.23, you can save it up until you have a decent sum. But I encourage you to still update the cell you are working ASAP so the money doesn't go "missing" before it has the chance to live its declared purpose.

Money Bunnies

What you are really doing here is preparing yourself to breed some money bunnies.

Imagine that you had two red bunny rabbits. You would blink, and suddenly there would be thirty red bunnies running around your yard.

This is what happens with debt. Compound interest accumulates, which means eventually you are paying interest on interest, and it starts to feel darn impossible to get ahead. When you are trying to catch all the bunny rabbits, you are running all over your yard and even if you get one or two of them, there are others breeding off in the corners!

What we want to set you up to do is accumulate green bunnies. Green bunny rabbits represent wealth and abundance. If for some reason you acquired a green bunny and you put it in the backyard with the red bunnies, you would not end up with green bunnies. Your debt bunnies would permeate all the wealth bunnies and you might have brown bunnies, but no green bunnies. (Please know that I know almost nothing about breeding so if you are a geneticist, don't @ me. This is simply a silly illustration so you can clearly visualize how consumer debt and wealth do not mix.)

In order to have an abundance of green money bunnies, you are going to have to remove the red bunnies as humanely as possible. In order to grow your wealth as quickly and as healthily as possible, you are going to have to eradicate this debt. Sure. Once in a while you hear of a genetic anomaly where some person leveraged their credit cards on a dream and made a million bucks. But do you know what is *so* common that it never makes the news? How the credit card companies leverage your *hope* and make a trillion bucks on your failed dreams.

Once you have a yard full of green money bunnies, the wealth will start to accumulate in your favor. Now it will be *you* who is earning some compound interest. But in order to truly profit from the bunny-on-bunny action (okay, now this is getting weird), you've got to focus on controlling the debt/red bunny population, one at a time.

Right now, your credit card interest is procreating. Your line of credit is making debt bunnies while you sleep. But if you try paying all your debts at once, *you* will be tired and empty-handed, and your debt bunnies will be hot and heavy. Instead, you need to focus on one thing at a time to create a beautiful, healthy, green money bunny habitat for life.

Sheena says: "We are so grateful to have followed the processes in this program! Our fridge died yesterday BUT we have a Q+D fund ready to pay cash for a new fridge today!

Thank you for this! I have such gratitude instead of stress and fear, which was a normal state for me before Get the Hell Out of Debt. Moving forward after our purchase, we'll go back to topping up our Quick and Dirty fund instead of slamming everything on the debt. A small blip in our plan but still worth it. Thank you Erin Skye Kelly!"

Chapter Twelve

THIS IS WORSE THAN I THOUGHT (INSOLVENCY)

INSOLVENCY

If you have everything organized, and you discover that you can't make the budget balance with the minimum payments, and you've cut all the expenses you can (I mean *alllllll* the expenses you can), you may have a solvency issue. Now, depending on where you live, you might want to do what is called a consumer proposal, an Orderly Payment of Debts (OPD), or (if you are really in the pooper) then bankruptcy. The rules for these vary in each county, province, state, and country, so you will need to do specific research if you go this route, but here is a general overview.

Consumer Proposal

This sounds like a romantic engagement where Lululemon might say, "Erin Skye Kelly, will you take me to be your leggings for the rest of our lives, for as long as we both shall live?" But from the mouth of the government, it is much less romantic.

A consumer proposal is a formal, legally binding process that is administered by a Licensed Insolvency Trustee. In this process, the Trustee (or in some countries, an "Adjudicator") will work with you to develop a "proposal"—an offer to pay creditors a percentage of what is owed to them, extend the time you have to pay off the debts, or both. Payments are made to the Trustee, and the Trustee then sends them off to the creditors as agreed.

When that happens, you stop making payments directly to your unsecured creditors. If your creditors are collecting your salary or garnishing your wages or have filed lawsuits against you, these actions are stopped.

The Trustee then submits the proposal to your creditors. The proposal will include a report on your personal situation and the causes of the financial difficulties.

Creditors then have a time limit to accept or reject the proposal. They can also do this either prior to or at the meeting of the creditors.

As mentioned, consumer proposals are not available everywhere, so you are going to have to research your options if you feel you might be insolvent.

Sometimes people ask, "Well, can't I just do my own proposal and come up with an arrangement with the creditors?" Yes, you can. If you can agree to get everything in writing, then certainly you can make your own arrangements. Some people find the process too stressful and overwhelming, and they prefer to have it handled by someone else. This entire process will definitely negatively impact your credit score, if that matters to you. Most people by this point already have terrible credit, so if you are in this position, you might not be worried about how it will further impact your score. You might just be looking for breathing room.

If your consumer proposal through a Trustee is accepted, then you'll make payments to the Trustee. You'll get to keep some assets as long as you make your payments to your secured creditors, and you'll often have to take a couple financial counseling sessions.

Listen friend, a couple is not enough. In order to avoid going through this process again, you really need to get a handle on that money. So, keep reading. Finish the book. Master Phase Three. No matter what.

Orderly Payment of Debts (OPD)

This is another alternative to bankruptcy, but it's not as flexible as the consumer proposal. Consumer proposals usually give you up to five years to pay off your debts, and, like OPD, is legally binding; however, with an Orderly Payment of Debts you usually have a max of three years to pay off the debts. A consumer proposal eliminates the interest on debts, but with OPD you'll usually pay a small rate. Also, consumer proposals often involve a reduction to the total amount owed, depending on your current circumstances. Consumer proposals can include property tax and income tax debts, which OPDs cannot. That is a very important distinction, depending on what forms of liabilities you actually have.

Since consumer proposals often last longer than Orderly Payments of Debts, the impact on your credit rating can last so much longer. Also, in certain cases, some personal assets may need to be liquidated or cashed in to pay off debt in an OPD, which doesn't typically happen with consumer proposals.

A Licensed Insolvency Trustee can help you determine which restructuring solution might work best for your circumstances.

Bankruptcy

When you absolutely cannot pay your debts, you might choose to file bankruptcy. It's usually imposed by a court order. It will drop your credit score to the bottom of the credit scoreboard, but of course, you are way past caring about that by the time you file bankruptcy. Your Trustee (or Adjudicator, if you live in the UK) will still file the documents on your behalf.

In addition to paying the Trustee's fees, you may be required to make additional payments, depending on how much you earn during the bankruptcy process. You'll submit a copy of your pay stubs or proof of income to the Trustee. They will calculate what earnings you have and assess it against what they believe a family of your size needs to maintain a reasonable standing of living.

The discharge from bankruptcy can happen in less than a year to nearly two years if it is your first bankruptcy, depending on the personal circumstances of your situation. It can be as long as three years if this is your second bankruptcy. Your bankruptcy will remain on your credit bureau in Australia for up to five years, or in Canada for approximately six to seven years (I've seen longer!) for a first bankruptcy, and fourteen years for a second. In the USA, a Chapter 7 bankruptcy stays on your credit report for ten years.

Whether you re-establish credit is up to a lender's willingness to *grant* you credit, as no lender is obligated to do so. If you have spouses or consignors that you share loans with, this process does affect them, so you will need to disclose everything to everyone affected by your financial situation.

There are databases that are publicly searchable that reveal if you have ever become insolvent or been bankrupt. Fortunately, in most parts of the UK, it will only appear for a few months, but in nearly every other part of the world, your bankruptcy is permanently searchable by the public.

But if you are not insolvent, and you know this (because remember, you have done the budget and the net worth, and you are not guessing), then we are just going to hammer away at the debt as best we can.

If you *truly focus*, and you are not insolvent, it can usually be done in under two years. This is a lot faster than consolidation or getting clear of any of the above processes. I know this because of something called Gross Debt and Total Debt Servicing, as you might recall from earlier.

These numbers are the amount of debt a lender will give you based on the amount of income you have. If you really max it out—like, really go for it like Usain Bolt on a hundred-meter dash—then you usually end up with around 50 percent debt-to-income ratio. Meaning if you earn $100,000 combined family or household income, then you usually have around $50,000 in consumer debt.

If you are like I was (not insolvent but not quite solvent either), then here's what you are going to do:

You are going to stop looking for a quick fix and recognize that everything you need is already within you and you are going to do the work to find the energy and resolve to clean up your own mess.

You are going to focus.

You are going to make a solid plan and commit to it and do everything in your power not to break your commitment to yourself.

You are going to recognize that many things do not actually ever go according to plan, so you are willing to be flexible and yet still wholeheartedly committed to getting things done, even when they do not happen the exact way you envisioned they would.

> Ashe says: "In one year we have gone from a negative to a positive net worth. For the first time in my adult life I am confident in my financial health and future!"

Chapter Thirteen

YOUR ORDER OF OPERATIONS

CREATE YOUR PERSONALIZED ORDER OF OPERATIONS

You make a list.

I know. You were thinking I was going to tell you some top-secret formula that involved complicated mathematical equations that you never heard of before. Instead, I'm asking you to make a damn list.

Most of the world's greatest problems have been sorted out with simplicity.

This story has been told so many times that I suspect it is an urban legend. But allegedly, a cosmetics company was manufacturing soap. The company received a customer complaint that they had purchased soap, only to find one box was empty. Immediately, upper management isolated the problem to the assembly line, and for some reason one soapbox went through the assembly line empty and straight on through to the shipping department. The company immediately tasked the engineers with solving the problem to ensure it wouldn't happen again. The engineers ended up creating an X-ray machine with monitors that two factory workers could monitor. They would look for empty soap boxes and catch them before the boxes ended up in the shipping department. The company spent hundreds of thousands of dollars solving this problem.

Another soap company thought they, too, better watch for empty soap boxes to avoid unhappy customers. When they tasked an employee to create the solution, he simply found a strong industrial fan and pointed it at the soap boxes as they came down the line. As the soapboxes passed the fan, the empty ones blew out of the line.

I'm asking you not to overcomplicate this step. Just blow on some boxes.

During the debt payoff process, you can run up against something called decision fatigue, and the mental and emotional fortitude required to get out of debt will feel heavy enough. If you create a complex system for yourself or try to do too many things at once, you will likely overwhelm yourself. The simpler the system, the faster you can focus on execution.

So, make a list. You are going to list out all your debts/obligations.

If you have a small mortgage balance and you want to be mortgage-free as one of your debt goals, you can go ahead and include your mortgage. I do, however, encourage you to take care of the other debts first.

Let's pretend this is a list of your consumer debt.

$13,000 Student Loan	45%	payments of $159.45
$6000 Student Loan	6.25%	payments of $76.10
$31,000 Vehicle Loan	0%	payments of $552.65
$2000 Grandma	0%	payments of whatever whenever
$5000 Mastercard	19%	minimum payment $150

There are four main ways you can structure the list.

1. The Smallest Balance Method. With this strategy, you are listing the debts according to their smallest total balance. If you want to do this strategy, you might list your debts like:

$2000 Grandma	0%	payments whenever
$5000 Mastercard	19%	minimum payment $150

$6000 Student Loan	6.25%	payments of $76.10
$13,000 Student Loan	5.45%	payments of $159.45
$31,000 Vehicle Loan	0%	payments of $552.65

You would pay the minimum payments on all debts (total of $938.20), and then squeeze every penny you can out of your budget by increasing your income, selling items you don't need anymore, and decreasing your expenses. Then you'd put every single one of those dollars toward Grandma's debt. Let's imagine you were able to squeeze an additional $1000 out of your budget toward debt repayment. You could have Grandma paid off two months from now! *Win!*

Then you'd take that $1000, and you'd apply it toward the second debt on the list, Mastercard in this case. So, you'd have approximately $938.20 going toward the existing minimum payments on the debts, and you'd have $1000 toward Mastercard. You'd have Mastercard paid off in less than five months because you'd be paying the minimum $150 plus the $1000 for a total of $1150 to Mastercard per month.

Once that is paid off, you'd take that $1150 and put it on the $6000 student loan. In less than a year, you'd have cleared out three of your five debts, and then you'd have $1126.10 to go toward your next student loan, etc.

The whole time you are doing this process, you are looking for ways to increase your income and decrease your expenses to hammer away at the *one specific* debt you are working on.

2. The Highest Interest Rate Method. I mentioned before that this was popularized in Canada by an outstanding woman named Gail Vaz-Oxlade. She has written a number of books and she encourages you to list your debts in the order of the highest interest rate to the lowest interest rate. Mathematically, this can seem like the most prudent strategy.

If you choose this method, you would order your debts to be destroyed this way:

$5000 Mastercard	19%	minimum payment $150
$6000 Student Loan	6.25%	payments of $76.10
$13,000 Student Loan	5.45%	payments of $159.45
$31,000 Vehicle Loan	0%	payments of $552.65
$2000 Grandma	0%	payments whenever

You would snowball them in the same way, putting all the extra money that you can squeeze out of your budget, starting with the Mastercard this time.

3. The Highest Balance Method. This method has you pay the minimums on everything except the debt with the highest monthly balance. I wouldn't choose it for this particular example because it will take a long time to pay off the $31,000 vehicle, but if you had a high payment on a lower balance loan, it could work to effectively pay off debt quickly. If you did choose it for this particular example, here's how it would look.

$31,000 Vehicle Loan	0%	payments of $552.65
$13,000 Student Loan	5.45%	payments of $159.45
$5000 Mastercard	19%	minimum payment $150
$6000 Student Loan	6.25%	payments of $76.10
$2000 Grandma	0%	payments whenever

4. The Emotional Mastery Method. This is the one most of the people I've worked with have chosen, and we've nicknamed it the Spicy Method as a joke. You put them in order according to what pisses you off the most. Let's say that you hate that you owe Grandma money because she needs to get her piano tuned and her front step fixed, but she doesn't have the money and you are bothered by that. So, you might decide to pay her first.

Then let's say you finished your post-secondary schooling, but you hated the industry, so it bothers you that you carry student loan debt for a career you don't have. You might decide to put those next on the list. Then maybe you are annoyed by the credit card because that interest rate bothers you, but you love your vehicle, so you don't mind making payments (!!!!!). You are the boss of you. So, you might decide to list them this way.

$2000 Grandma	0%	payments whenever
$6000 Student Loan	6.25%	payments of $76.10
$13,000 Student Loan	5.45%	payments of $159.45
$5000 Mastercard	19%	minimum payment $150
$31,000 Vehicle Loan	0%	payments of $552.65

Please know that the order in which you list them matters less than your commitment to annihilating them.

That's the part all the math scholars who try to help people with money get wrong. They forget that behind all that math is a living breathing human who by and large makes decisions almost entirely on emotion.

Humans are born irrational, and yet we all like to continually look for the logical way to do things. This is pure crazymaking if you ask me. In the 1970s, two psychologists called Daniel Kahneman and Amos Tversky proved that humans are not rational creatures. Their discovery of "cognitive biases" showed that humans systematically make choices that have nothing to do with logic, even if logic is laid out in front of them.

When I'm making a decision, I'll go with the one that feels right, and then I look for logical proof to support the emotional decision I've made. Even if there is opposing information that also has merit, I ignore it and look for the logic that supports what I already believe.

Oh, don't you dare judge. You do it too!

		JUNE SQUEEZE!		
June 18	$235.00	sold camera lens	deposited	✓
June 19	$0.59	coins!	deposited	✓
June 19	$20.00	sold puzzles	deposited	✓
June 20	$5.00	sold craft supplies	deposited	✓
June 20	$22.00	sold lululemon bag	deposited	✓
June 21	$10.00	sold file folders	deposited	✓
June 21	$8.00	sold old tupperware	deposited	✓
June 22	$15.00	sold CD's	deposited	✓
June 22	$10.00	sold box of books	deposited	✓
June 23	$15.00	sold craft paper	deposited	✓
June 26	$20.00	sold picture frames	deposited	✓
	$360.59			

Once you've made the minimums on everything, you then choose one credit card to snipe out. We focus on one at a time because we want to highly concentrate our efforts. You can see here *actual* payments I made on credit cards from selling extra stuff on Buy and Sells. Sales were ten, fifteen, or twenty dollars mostly, but at the end of every day, I'd go for a walk (about 1.2 kilometers to the bank one way), get some steps and fresh air in, deposit the cash, and *immediately* put it on the credit card as a payment. I did this *every. Damn. Day.*

Some days I went to deposit at the bank more than once.

If I had cash laying around back then, it would definitely not have gone toward the debt if I didn't have a plan for it. I'd have put it in my wallet, and then used it while at the convenience store, or blown it some way or another.

Once I fixed my eye on the goal, which was annihilating that particular cell in the liabilities section of my net worth spreadsheet, I became unstoppable. I'd walk to the bank to deposit five dollars, and by the time I was home, someone else would want to buy something for twenty dollars. So, I'd walk right back to the bank after they picked it up.

I don't care if you have to load up the kids in the strollers, or if you have to drive them to the ATM in your minivan, or if you have to deposit it on the way to work. *Do it.* Then immediately update your net worth spreadsheet with the updated balance.

I think exercise is absolutely critical to staying sane during this process, so I encourage you to exercise daily anyway. I used to hate outdoor activities. (Did I mention I'm Canadian? We have -40°F/C weather each winter!) But when I correlated it to toughness and being stronger than my debt, it got easier, and eventually more fun to incorporate with the debt payoff. And as a side bonus, I finally released some excess weight I had been carrying.

Because I didn't have a lot of income at the time, I had to sell *a lot* of things, and it was humbling to watch things leave my home that I had paid four times the value I was selling it for. But one of the greatest learnings we can take from this is the market dictates the price.

If there was an upsell market for used yoga hoodies that I paid $85 for, then I'd be selling those for $160 instead of $10. But I sold them for ten dollars because I didn't need the quantity I had in my closet to survive, and I really truly wanted to get the hell out of debt.

I told you it was humbling!

Laura says: "Of all the challenges I have ever done this one has been the most transforming for me. I've made an extra $4500 this month and I've learned a few things:

— 80% of the stuff that is/was in our home was stuff that I bought…not my hubby and that made me feel so yucky.
— I have finally started to see how making small consistent progress works better than 'all or nothing' - man, the pennies make a difference.
— I am so much happier with less. I feel empowered and confident with my relationship with money because I know where my money is going and that makes decision-making crystal clear.
— I really can do anything I set my mind to. We thought it was going to take us over 6 months to pay off our line of credit and we did it in TWO!"

I sometimes have students tell me that it feels pointless to put a $6.00 or a $22.25 payment on their debt when their debt feels astronomical in comparison. But that is *exactly* the mentality that got them into debt. When you think, "Oh, it's just another twenty dollars, that's no big deal. I'll just put it on the Visa," you are slowly digging yourself a financial grave.

A few success tips for the debt annihilation list you write out:

- Write your Debt Annihilation List out at the beginning. I don't care if you choose the smallest balance, or the largest interest rate method, or the Erin Skye Kelly Whatever-Debt-Pisses-You-Off-The-Most Method. I want you to write them out before you start paying off the debts and commit to it. Make certain you are tracking and paying the minimum payments each month through your budget.
- If you have to make decisions on the fly or based on how you feel, you are more likely to screw it up. I say that with love, and also with conviction because I tried myself to do it on account of the fact that I hate rules. This way, when extra money comes into your life, you can put it directly on the debt you are currently annihilating and not have to think about it. Ooooh! Found five dollars on the ground and you are the only one around? *Boom.* Annihilate Debt Number One. Ooooh! Squeezed $17.80 off your grocery list because you shopped with coupons? *Boom.* Annihilate Debt Number One. Ooooh! Sold your Wii on Kijiji for a hundred dollars? *Boom.* Annihilate Debt Number One.
- Once you have annihilated Debt Number One, you do the same for Debt Number Two. You pay the minimum balances on all those debts, and then you knock off Debt Number Two with all your focus and determination.
- Along the way, when you run into *life mishaps* (say you blow a tire on the vehicle) and you do not have room in your budget to cover it, you use the cash designated as your Quick and Dirty Fund.

You do not use an available balance on your credit card! You are *retraining your brain* to manage money differently than you have in the past, and you must not fool yourself into thinking "available balance" is available money! Your available money lives in your Safe Zone Account.

- The next thing you do is halt the debt repayment for a hot minute, and then *quickly* put some new money in the Quick and Dirty Fund until you have the equivalent of one paycheck in that Safe Zone again. *Big deep breath*...and then you resume annihilating the debt on your Debt Annihilation List.
- You do this over and over again until it's boring. And believe me, there are times where it is horribly boring! Sometimes it will feel like you are *waaaaaaiting* for money to hit your account so you can add it to the debt you are paying off. So, make sure you do lots of self-support (Class One and Two Experiences! Like walking! Reading! Drawing! Stretching! Cooking! Whatever!) in order to stay mentally well during this process.

OVERDRAFT

If you have overdraft privileges, and you sometimes use your overdraft, or even if you live in OverdraftVille, I consider that to be a form of consumer debt. This has likely dug a trench in your brain that tricked you into thinking any available room in OverdraftLand equals cash. And it does not. It equals fees for your bank.

If you hang out in overdraft long enough, you start to see that negative number as "your new zero." If you have $700 in available overdraft, and you are at -$550 in overdraft, you might start thinking you have $150 available.

If your brain already does that calculation, I'm very sorry that you were trapped like that! If you are a typical bank client, you are paying on average thirty-four dollars in overdraft fees per OD transaction. Sometimes you'll be charged $2.50 to $5.00 even if you do not use the overdraft! The bank will justify this to you by saying, "Our NSF fees are forty-five dollars, so having overdraft protects you and saves you money."

What in the actual *fluff*?

That's like saying, "You can either have this cookie baked with poison or this one with salmonella. If you are smart, you'll take the salmonella because it does less damage."

We are going to consider the overdraft amount to be a debt, and we'll put the max overdraft balance in the liabilities side on your net worth spreadsheet. Now, if your bank has so kindly given you the luxury of paying them more fees because you have been dipping below zero in your account, we are going to trick your brain. There are two ways to do this.

1. If you have been living with overdraft for a long time, and your overdraft limit is -$1000 or less, we are going to do an "integer flip!" Do you remember integers from school? Me neither. I do remember replying to notes from Ricky S. in math class, though. Let's say your overdraft has been -$500, meaning the bank lets you overdraw your account each month by $500. We are going to "flip the integer" and make your *new zero* be $500. So, in your liabilities side of your spreadsheet, you are going to put $1000. Meaning, you'll pay back the $500 you typically dip below, and then you'll gather up additional cash outside your budget to find another $500.

Once that is deposited, you can cancel your overdraft, and now you are going to *trick your brain*.

You are never, ever, ever going to dip below $500 in your checking account. If you drop down to $498, you are overdrawing against The Bank of Promises You Made to Yourself and you will instantly find two dollars to pay back to yourself. The good news is: you don't charge yourself any bank fees for this. You just make sure that even though you are doing a "Zero Based Budget," you are budgeting to leave that $500 in your account untouched. If the amount of your overdraft limit is -$300, then a positive

$300 becomes your new zero. If the amount of your overdraft limit is -$450, then a positive $450 becomes your new zero.

2. If your overdraft limit is over -$1000, then choose an amount that makes sense for you, perhaps a positive balance of $500 to start. Then as you pay down more debt, you can decide if you need to pad this up or not.

We call this amount "My New Zero." What number is your New Zero? ________

Do not close the overdraft until you've positively padded up the account and you have not been overdrawn for at least thirty days. NSF fees *are* high! We don't want to trade one problem for another.

But do you know what you are saying if you keep that overdraft open? You are saying you do not trust yourself. You are saying, "I'll let the banks take care of me instead of me taking care of me." You are telling yourself that you don't really believe you can do this, and if it's true—that you don't really believe you can do this—then head on back to Phase One and make sure you've nailed that budget.

Sometimes your Plan B is keeping you from having your Plan A.

Keeping a backup plan, like overdraft, may be the reason you keep failing. It shows that you are not fully committed. Imagine if you were exchanging vows with the love of your life and they said, "I promise to love you forever, for richer or poorer, in sickness and in health, 'til death do us part or until someone better looking comes along."

That is not commitment. In order to get where we want to go financially, we absolutely must be committed. Be done with overdraft forever and commit to freedom from debt.

Once you have your "New Zero," you can put that number in your net worth spreadsheet in the asset column under cash, if you want to track your checking account. If you do not keep a minimum balance in the checking account, then do not track it in the spreadsheet. It's questionable whether or not that cash is an asset, but I'll explain that in a little bit!

INVESTING WHILE PAYING OFF DEBT

I can't tell you whether you need to stop investing while you are paying off debt or whether to pause temporarily while you focus on your debt.

The reason is because I have no idea *if you know what you're doing or not* when it comes to investing.

Now please do not take any offense to what I am about to say because we are cool, and remember that I have been in your shoes and I do not judge you for your financial choices or mistakes or anything that has happened to you. That said, I know you are likely reading this book because you and money are not exactly BFFs.

So, it is highly likely that it's in your best interest to stop investing for a year or so while you get out from underneath this debt. You'll then use the same method to build wealth that you used to pay off debt, by squeezing some cash out of your budget and investing it in things you know and understand and can master.

Now, I say all of this with a grain of salt, because if I tell you to stop investing at a time when being "in the market" could have brought you hefty returns, then I will be amiss. I don't know what is happening to your investments at the exact moment your eyeballs are hitting these words. I do not know what is happening to the economy at the exact moment your eyeballs are reading these ones here. So, I cannot possibly predict what you should or should not do when it comes to investing. I just know a lot of people who lost a lot of money because they knew very little about investing.

If I had to make one sweeping, blanket statement, I would say, "Maybe, my friend, it is in your better judgement to put all the cash you can toward becoming debt-free forever. And while you are paying down your accumulated debt dollar by dollar, you could spend this six months, twelve months, eighteen months reading and learning about the kinds of investments you might be interested in. Then, when you are free from debt, put all the cash you're currently putting toward paying your debt off into investments that you know, understand, and will nurture, in order to reach your financial goals."

You'll hear some experts say, "Well, if you are getting eight percent returns in the market, and you are paying nineteen percent on your credit card, then of course it doesn't make sense to invest right now," but that 8 percent and that 19 percent are not true numbers because they haven't factored in compounding and all kinds of things that make them apples versus oranges.

This question, the "should I invest while paying off debt" question, is never about math. It's always about behaviors, cashflow, investor knowledge, and risk versus reward.

If you have no idea what you are invested in or why you are invested in it, then please pause your investing and get the hell out of debt.

> Vanessa says: "Of all the great podcasts out there, Get the Hell Out of Debt is the one I stop, drop, and listen to as soon as I see a new episode pop up!"

Chapter Fourteen

REBUILDING YOUR RELATIONSHIP WITH MONEY

RESPECT AND TRUST AND MONEY

All the money you have represents time you've spent in your life.

If you've received an inheritance, it represents time that someone else spent during their lifetime.

Every time you go to work, you are trading your life for money. Precious hours that are limited and unknown and that you can't get back.

When you consider you also may have a commute to work and you might need to buy dry cleaning or work attire, the at-work meals or take out, you can quickly see that the cost of things is not the true *cost of things*.

Even working from home has added expenses that we trade for our time.

Most of us work so that we can earn money to maybe have a life. But we give up our lives so that we can work. When we add debt and debt repayment to the mix, you can see how quickly time gets frittered away from the things that matter to the excess in our lives.

If your job is sucking up your energy, you are in a double-negative trap. If you find joy in your work and it is aligned with your life's purpose, and you are energized by your job, you are extremely blessed.

Many people ask if they should work at a job they hate in order to pay off their debt. The answer depends on whether it will shorten the amount of time they have to trade for their life overall. If you enjoy your job, but *not* taking another one means that you will be in debt for longer, you are still trading your precious, beautiful time on earth for debt. You'll have to decide what's more important to you: getting the hell out of debt or being in debt for a much longer time while enjoying your work.

It's possible to do both, by the way! It's possible to do your life's work and enjoy it and get the hell out of debt. And it's also possible to grind it out for a bit and get the hell out of debt. Then when you are debt-free and less stressed, you can choose a job that is enjoyable where you don't accept the job offer because of the pay. This is a very personal choice.

Here's a question to consider:

Do you trust yourself with money?

Seriously. Spend some time journaling on that one. What comes up for you? Many people who are in a long-term relationship with debt lack money confidence, and this can often be traced back to something along their financial journey that caused them to not trust themselves with money.

If you do not trust yourself with money, it's okay. We are going to use abundant thinking to repair and build our relationship with money. First, you're just going to have to decide that you can be trusted with money. Done. Simple. Just decide. Then, you'll *consistently* take the following action to reinforce that belief. That's the start of the Abundant Cycle, which is a new belief and money-handling system you'll introduce into your life.

Some ways to start respecting money:

1. Do a budget to give your money a purpose. *Check!*

   You've already done this. Doesn't it feel good to check things off a list? My friend Jenn loves checking things off checklists, so sometimes when she makes herself a to-do list, she puts things on the list she's already done so she can feel good about checking them off. This one's for you, Jenn.

2. Track your net worth to allow your money to achieve its purpose. *Check!*

   The more you do your budget and your net worth, the more you show your money that you care. If you were married to Ryan Reynolds but you never actually said, "Hey, how are you doing? How was your day?" two things would happen. The first is that he would troll you on social media on your birthday, and the second is that your relationship would break down. That could very well be what has happened over the years. Your relationship with money has deteriorated because you weren't paying attention to it.

   Maybe you were never taught how to have a relationship with money or do a net worth spreadsheet before now, and that's sucky and unfair and it makes me want to pout on your behalf. But many people also weren't taught how to have healthy relationships.

   There was a time in the '80s and '90s where Canadians were taught this nutritional formula called "The Canada Food Guide" that dictated our health. There were four groups: Dairy Group, Meat Group, Fruits/Vegetable Group, and the Bread Group. Essentially you were to choose a certain number of products from each group for optimal health. Butter was part of the Dairy Group. There was a time when they called for a daily serving of potatoes. Doesn't that just seem *ridiculous* now?

   This says to me that your past does not dictate your future, and we all have the ability to evolve and grow. We can do this without blaming our past. Let's build a healthy relationship with money by caring for it properly and still be open to being wrong or learning new things.

3. You're going on a treasure hunt. Gather up all your loose change. Check those old jacket pockets. The console in your vehicle. The couch cushions. When you have money laying around, you are signaling that you do not have due care and attention.

You're going to put this money in a designated jar. Now, I do *not* want you running out to Target or Temple & Webster to buy a cute jar for your money. That is actually *disrespectful* to your money when you have debt. When you hit Phase Three of this program, if you want to buy a cute jar to put money in (you won't), and you budget for it, knock yourself out. For now, you're going to just use whatever empty spaghetti sauce jar you have or whatever you have that you can repurpose and put all the coins in there. And then, you're going to give that jar a purpose.

If you decide that all the coins you've now collected are going toward paying off a specific debt, write that directly on the jar. Yes, you can use a label. Or fancy chalk paint. But for the love of god, please don't spend money on this. We are cleaning things up, not delaying the process or making a new mess of things. (Honestly, if you step foot into a craft store, you know you are not getting out of there with only the item you went for.)

So, if you write "ABC Credit Card" on the jar, then every spare dime you find from now until that card is paid off is first going in the jar, then getting deposited, and then paying down the dang card. Sometimes you have to convert the money; sometimes you have to find a really kind bank teller to help you. But you are going to do it because you *respect* money, remember? When you've designated this $0.05 to go toward ABC Credit Card and you go digging in the change jar to buy some wine, you are disrespecting money. Once we've given that money its purpose, we don't stray from that purpose. If you have a jar that you've designated as your "wine fund," then you don't take money out of there to get a haircut. Master your budget. Pay attention to the pennies and the pence and the shrapnel of coins. Refocus and give them a purpose. Pay due care and attention so you don't continue this pattern of broke.

4. You're also going to get a money clip for your cash.

Now if you don't have a money clip lying around because maybe you weren't born in 1930, then you don't need to buy a fancy money clip. You're going to use a paperclip. Remember, let's not disrespect our money by prolonging the debt. We are going to respect our money and honor where we're at. I don't care if you have to use an old shoe to collect your money for now. You're going to focus on giving your money a home and a safe place to be where it can also mate. You know what I mean? Like if you put a few dollar bills together in a little private paperclip, there might be some more dollars there later. I'm just saying. It's one of the most mysterious parts about money that I have never been able to figure out because it's not a scientific formula. I can just tell you that it happens to almost every participant in the program when you can trust yourself with money. When you can be trusted with money (and I'm talking even the dimes and the nickels in your ugly spaghetti sauce jar), more money seems to come into your life.

5. *Do not allow any loose change to lie about in your car.* If you need spare change in the car, then you're going to have a special place for it. It's going to be all lumped together. You can call it drive-thru money (or car wash money, or money to donate to someone who needs it more) and put it in a baggie. But you have to give it a name. And if you do not want to keep change in your car, then it goes in the money jar in your home that you have designated a purpose for already. If I could turn the world upside down and shake change and coins out of every vehicle, we'd have enough money to heal a lot of the hurt in the world. Don't waste even a cent of it.

6. When you find money on the ground, you're going to thank God for it. Or thank the universe for it. Thank baby Elmo for it. I don't care. Just express gratitude out loud for it. I mean, first you're going to look around to be sure it doesn't belong to somebody else. Once you have done that, I just need you to be loudly grateful. Then you're going to give it a purpose. So, if you find a quarter on the

ground, of course you're going to pick it up, hold it in the air like the opening sequence from *Lion King*, say thank you, then put it in your pocket immediately. *And then you're going to decide where it goes.* Does it go home in your change jar? Maybe it goes to a charitable cause you love as part of your monthly donation you are already making. You're going to decide its purpose the minute it enters your life, before you spend it. And then you're going to spend it according to what you decided. Look at you. Keepin' promises.

7. Pay your bills with gratitude. When you pay the electricity bill, you'll say out loud to no one and everyone, "I'm so grateful for the privilege of paying this electricity bill. I enjoy that I can flick on a light switch and experience seeing the faces of the people I love. I am grateful that I can read at night. I love that I can use appliances to cook and savor tasty meals."

   Maybe you're paying a mobile phone bill. You might choose to declare, "I'm so grateful to pay this bill. It has kept me in contact with people I love during hard times. I love that I can see people's faces from around the world with the tap of a digital button. I love that I can play games, take photos, and learn about whatever topic I'm curious about any time of day. It's a privilege to be a mobile phone owner."

   I'm not trying to put words in your mouth, but you get the idea! Find a way to be grateful for these expenses that often feel like a burden when that paycheck rolls around. It's easy to be grateful for the paycheck. But it takes practice to be grateful for the expenses. Those are all expenses you chose at one time to meet a need, and if you can't find a way to tie back gratitude to the expense, it might be time to reevaluate that expense and cut more from the budget.

8. You'll always do what you say you will. You'll honor your word and show money that you can be trusted with it. This is about strengthening your personal integrity. Integrity is not a moral word, so this is not about you being a good or bad person. This is about your

ability to keep your word to yourself. Your words are your contracts with the world and with your soul. When you are budgeting, you are looking ahead at the month and predetermining, to the best of your ability, what you want to happen with your money. You aren't aiming for perfection, but you are aiming for accuracy. We know it isn't always going to work out as expected, but you are committed to doing your best. You are also committed to not derailing yourself based on a feeling.

Remember *waaaay* back at the beginning of this book where I said one of the Success Principles was "Feel Your Feelings," but the very next Success Principle was "Do Not Let Your Emotions Dictate Your Behaviors?" This is what I'm referring to here. It's one thing to have a surprise bill, but it's another thing entirely to have a surprise bill after you just splurged un-budgeted money after some late-night shopping following a fight with your sister. Your word is gold. It's worth more than all this money you are budgeting anyway. When you get to that place where you can trust yourself to keep your word to yourself, you will absolutely be free. Financially free. Emotionally free. Mentally free. Spiritually free.

Let's imagine you are budgeting next month and you decide you want to give thirty dollars to charity. But then you overspend in another category and you now only have twenty-five dollars to give to charity. You must decide that you will find that other five dollars somehow. You can pay close attention to your variable expenses and find ways to save. You must find a way, and you have to find a way without backing down on your word in another area. So, if, for example, you have a fifty-dollar debt payment to your sister, you can't only give her forty-five because you said you'd give thirty dollars to the charity. You have to keep your word wherever possible. When you do this, when you start to consistently keep your positive word over and over to yourself, you will start to develop drag-queen-level confidence.

Respecting money will be a work in progress. You might find yourself falling into old habits, like "throwing a penny over your shoulder for good luck" or whatever wasteful money habits you might have had. (Side note: throwing a penny over your shoulder *is* good luck, but only for the people walking behind you!)

This is not about "loving money." There is an ancient phrase that says, "For the love of money is the root of all evil." It doesn't say, "Money is the root of all evil." Money can't be evil. Money is just a tool. Your running shoes are a tool. A screwdriver is a tool. A thermometer is a tool. No one says, "Running shoes are the root of all evil." But when you become obsessed with something, it causes problems in our brains and our lives and our relationships. I don't want you to *love* money. I just need you to respect it to get the results you want. Save your love for the people in your life who deserve to have you show up and care for them unconditionally.

Kim says: "I have been waiting for today so that I could share my news…this morning I paid the last of my final debt, in full! It has taken lots of slow learning, failing, judging myself and getting up again, quieting the voice that said I could not do it, and strengthening the voice that knew I could. I'm so grateful for the folks I have met who have supported me along the way and cheered me on. Thank you Erin Skye Kelly for creating a space to learn, fail and grow. First time in my adult life that I can say I am debt free!"

Chapter Fifteen

LIVING IN ALIGNMENT

Here's your next assignment.

CREATE YOUR LOVE LIST.

I want you to make a big ol' list of things you love to do with your time and people you love to spend time with. Go on. I'll wait.

Don't worry about what you think the right answer is. I just need you to create an honest to goodness list of things you love and people you love without apology.

Here are some of mine:

I love surfing in warm waters.
I love listening to my kids laugh out loud.
I love drinking tea with honey and wearing those giant fluffy reading socks.
I love playing basketball with my kids.
I love taking pictures of my kids.
I love forty-five-minute walks in nature.
I love watching movies with my kids and learning what makes them laugh.

> I love my Get the Hell Out of Debt community and celebrating when they've paid down debt or made other progress!

I don't care if you have material items on your list. I almost wrote down "I love my Apple watch," but I hate when it buzzes and tells me to stand up. *Mind your own business, Apple watch. I am writing a book.* You put whatever you want on that list, no judgies.

Now that you have your Love List, I want you to have a peek at your last thirty days of expenses.

Each of those payments represents time in your life that you gave away to work in order to have money. Each of those payments *cost* you something in terms of time. So, if you earn twenty dollars per hour, and something in your monthly expenses costs you twenty-five dollars, it might actually equate to that item costing you two hours of your time.

By the time you commuted to and from work, had some money deducted for taxes, factored in the expense for lunch you needed to perform that work, maybe the item actually cost you forty dollars, or two hours of work to generate twenty-five dollars net pay to purchase the item.

Let's pretend the twenty-five-dollar item is some new luxury shampoo.

As you look through the payments, ask yourself:

1. Am I fulfilled and grateful for this expense, or would I rather have that time back to do one of the things I love? Or spend that time (i.e., two hours) with someone I love?
2. Is this expense in line with my values, or could I have achieved the feeling I wanted by being resourceful and not spending the money (i.e., not spending the twenty-five dollars)?
3. How can I choose to be grateful for this?

Maybe you answer the questions like:

1. In retrospect, I don't think working two hours for fancy hair products makes sense for me. If I didn't have the shampoo and instead

I had two hours off, I would spend it at the dog park and baking homemade cookies to deliver to my grandmother.

2. It turns out financial freedom is my goal, and I have this debt. I want to be financially free more than I want to have this hair product, which is only marginally impactful to my life compared to being debt-free. My sister always has leftover toiletries from the hotels she stays at, and because she travels well, those sample products are decent (and free!). I'll contact her and see if she'll save some for me.
3. I can be grateful for this bottle of fancy shampoo, and I'll use it sparingly to last as long as possible. I'll treat myself to my next bottle of it when I become debt-free!

Or maybe you answer the questions like:

1. I have unruly hair, and I feel better about myself when I use this expensive shampoo.
2. This is not really in line with my values, but I'm tired of trying other products and not finding something that works for me.
3. I am grateful for this shampoo because I worked hard for it, and I will treat it like a luxury-spend while I cut back in other areas to get the hell out of debt.

It doesn't matter what your answers are. There are no right ones! This exercise is designed to get you thinking more about the time-value of money. The true cost of your non-renewable resource: your life. This process can help you with purchase decisions in the future, and it can bring awareness to how you show up with the people you love. If we are aware of how our time is allocated in life, we can be more fully present when we are with the people we love. When we are at work, we can be fully present and alert and engaged and productive. When we are at home, we can show up lovingly and fully present and alert. When we live from a place of multitasking our time and our brains, we are never really anywhere because we are thinking about the places we are not.

Wendy paid off $59,000 doing the Get the Hell Out of Debt program. When she was finished, I cried giant tears for her. (It's a thing. Some people cry when *Old Yeller* dies, and I cry when people pay off all their debt.)

I said, "Do you trust yourself with money?"

And she said, "Getting better. It's been tough. Like a really a tough mindset to change. I remember you once said that when you give money a purpose and you respect money, more money will keep coming into your life. And when you prove that you're good with money, the universe will keep giving you money to work with. And it's really so true. Like unbelievably true. I remember before Get the Hell Out of Debt I'd be thinking: "Hmm, where did my check go? Maybe I didn't get it this month." But I'd log into the bank and not only did I not notice it was deposited, I'd spent it. So since Get the Hell Out of Debt, I've learned to pay attention to my money, and designate where I want it to go. Otherwise, it just disappears."

Chapter Sixteen

FINANCIAL BOUNDARIES

While you are putting your custom system in place and working diligently dollar by dollar to annihilate your first debt, I want to talk to you about some things you may have struggled with in the past:

- How you spend your money
- When you spend your money
- Where you spend your money
- Why you spend your money
- What you spend your money on
- So basically ev.er.ry.thing.

1. We need clarity around what our financial goals are. If we do not have clear financial promises to ourselves, we are more likely to honor someone else's financial agenda.
2. We need to practice language and behaviors that support our financial promises.
3. We need to articulate our financial boundaries to those we are in relationships with.

4. We need to honor our feelings when an attempt to cross a boundary happens—*and it will happen.*

Let's start with number one.

We need clarity around what our financial goals are. I'm guessing if you are here, your number one financial goal is to get the hell out of debt and stay debt-free. You're going to need to make that crystal clear to yourself. What does that mean exactly to you? Does debt-free mean that you don't have credit cards? Or does that mean you don't have any credit cards, loans, lines of credit, student loans, car loans, second mortgages, or other obligations? If you are unsure, I recommend you start by working to pay everything off except the mortgage. If you want to be mortgage-free (I mean, it's next-level awesome), then we'll tackle that in Phase Three. But clearly articulate in your journal what debt freedom means to you.

For number two, we need to practice language and behaviors that support our financial promises. This is basically looking at your goals every dang day and taking action toward them every dang day. People who do not have debt issues don't need to look at their money every day. People who do not have health issues do not need to think about their breathing, or their gait, or their blood sugar levels, or whatever they are tracking every day. So do not compare yourself to someone else who has an entirely different financial journey.

I've heard money experts who are wealthy and who have never struggled with debt say, "Don't waste your time budgeting." *Ummmmm. Thanks for your insight, Rumpelstiltskin.* You have to track what you want to change and the thing you can control. When you look for "financial behaviors" on this debt journey, those could be any of the following activities:

* Selling something you no longer need
* Doing contract/side work that you are skilled at
* Overtime
* Cooking for others
* Anything you can think of that is legal and can squeeze that debt down

As a side note, I currently have an amazing student, Jacqueline, in the Get the Hell Out of Debt program who became unemployed due to Covid. She recently posted that in spite of that, she increased her net worth by $6807.70 by staying true to her goal of being debt-free.

She is Italian and fabulous in the kitchen, and she has been selling lasagnas as one of her directional activities. She takes pre-orders, which allows her to budget and plan ahead, and ensures she isn't stuck with excess pasta. When there are no lasagna orders, she can do supporting activities like taking photos of her lasagnas to upload to social media, watching financial education videos in her extra time, reconciling her budget, and more. She has no desire to be a chef and she isn't going to do this forever. She's simply committed to a goal.

Number three: using effective language to talk to friends or family about our financial goals is important. Knowing what to say and how to say it is important when it comes to honoring your goals and not getting derailed by other people's opinions. If you are seeking validation from your friends, you might get derailed. If you are looking to teach them something or be "right," you might get derailed. Remember that you must stay in your own lane, but there are times when it can be important to your financial wellbeing to have conversations that:

a) Do not invite other people to weigh in on your financial journey.
b) Set standards for how you will manage social situations financially.

For example, you might say:

"I've set a financial goal, and it is in my best interest not to spend so much money out at restaurants. I'm either going to come less often, or order smaller portions for a time, but I still want to be included in the invitations, even if I have to decline."

"I have realized the extent of my overspending and I'm working to correct some financial habits that have landed me in debt, so I won't be able to pick up the tab for a while. I'm open to doing a potluck meal if that works for your family too."

"I've humbly accepted that if I continue on the financial path I've been on, I might never be able to retire, and so I'm going to start making decisions with my future in mind. I'm not asking you to change any of your spending, but I hope you are open to the change in pattern if I have to decline the girls' weekend trips for a while. I want to join you and I love spending time with you, but I want to come when I've paid for it up front and don't come home with a credit card hangover!"

Number four: note that in all of these, you are *not* asking other people to change. *You are not asking other people to live by your money story.* You are simply sharing what you can or cannot do, and you are asking them to respect your choice.

You must never do this with an expectation. If you have a desired outcome in mind, you are manipulating the situation and that means you are not staying in your own lane. This is not about you getting help from others or convincing them to change their lives for you. If they decide to make changes of their own accord, great. But you must not be upset if your friends go out to dinner without you, and you must not derail when you see photos of the girls out and about while hashtagging #bestweekendever. You must continue to celebrate your own goals and work toward your own successes so that you can be truly happy for others and not let that get in the way of your debt-free life.

IN ORDER TO BECOME FINANCIALLY FREE, I MUST HONOR THESE ELEVEN PROMISES TO MYSELF.

When I started working my way out of debt, I was overwhelmed. I owed so many people so much money and they all were calling at once, and rightfully so! I had made them a promise I didn't and couldn't keep. My money story was now affecting them. In order to get out of the mess, though, I had to put up some boundaries. There was no way I could continue the journey without some sort of emotional backbone, a structure to help me fortress myself in this storm. This is the list of eleven promises I still live by today. These are written out and attached to my money clip in my wallet.

1. *If I want to be financially free, I have to set financial boundaries.*

I could not continue to try and live this unnavigated, boundary-free life. I had forever been trying to make everything work for everyone else. At some point I realized if I was going to do this, and I was going to pay back every penny to people I *legit* owed, I had to have some solid rules and boundaries.

For instance, one time this well-known person in my community ripped me off, then negatively impacted my business with a bunch of gossip and B.S. But to my face, they were charming and playing innocent. I remained kind and polite. But later it hit me: it was my lack of boundaries that guilted me into paying them for value I never received, for an agreement they never made good on. This person took food out of my kids' mouths, and continually tried to use me for personal gain, while simultaneously trying to destroy me financially. I have no ill will toward them*, and I wish them love, joy, and inner peace. But my lack of boundaries was an opportunity for them to use me, and it wasn't until I decided enough is enough that I was able to make headway with the rest of my financial plan.

*Okay, sometimes when I see their face on a billboard my first reaction is to give it the middle finger when I drive by, but then I choose to send them love.

2. *I absolutely must put my personal financial wellbeing before that of others.*

This is not about using others for *your* financial gain. This is about prioritizing you and your family before helping someone else. If you do not have enough money in your budget to meet your obligations this month, you must not make a donation to someone's GoFundMe. You must not put your wellbeing at risk to help someone else with their emergency. When you are in a position of strength, *yes*, I want you to be a source of generosity for others. But if you are not properly executing your own promises to yourself, you are creating a problem that someone someday might have to bail you out of.

This goes for time as well. If you are constantly running around helping other people and you have a giant emotional mess at home, you are not truly helping anyway. You are looking for validation, or some other form of approval, or meeting a need to be liked. Instead, let's clean up our own side of the street.

Take a break from rescuing or helping others for a while, and instead focus on mastering your money so that instead of giving people scraps, you can actually contribute to their lives in a meaningful and abundant way. I promise you, if people found out you were putting your family in financial struggle to help them out, they would not feel good about that. And if they do feel good about that? You could re-evaluate your relationships and why you have them.

3. *I have to refuse to rescue others from their financial problems.*

It is not my responsibility to fix people or teach them. I'm looking at you specifically if you have a broke partner or you are dating broke people consistently. You are a partner first, not a coach. Don't "should" on your sister with "you should pay off that credit card," or "should" on your partner with "you should tell your boss you need a raise." You are either doing this work in partnership or you are zipping your lip and leading by example. Additionally, you must *never* cosign and you must *never* pay off someone's debt to "help."

If someone needs you to cosign, it is because the bank does not believe they will pay the money back. But the bank thinks *you* can. It can be so painful to tell someone no. But unless you are Daddy Warbucks and you are happy to pay the whole debt on their behalf anyway, do not cosign.

If you do ever pay off someone's debt, you must have *zero* expectations that they will stay debt-free. Because if they aren't doing the work to learn proper money management, they will be right back in debt in about a year. And if you have any attachment to the outcome, you will feel disappointed and you will have wasted your money. Save yourself the hundreds of dollars and send them a copy of this book instead. It's likely going to sit in a pile unread, but at least you have a *hope* of helping.

4. *I must be honest with myself about my financial circumstances.*

The future often looks so bright that we forget how we typically behave. This is why credit card companies exist. They know you will *forget* that when you buy something today and think you can handle it "later" that later will come with its own set of problems. When we look at a calendar, all the days ahead are blank and beautiful and stress-free. We can't possibly anticipate that in three months and four days we are going to blow a tire. And that in four months, we'll end up with the flu and miss some work. And that in seven months, the sewer will back up. Or, you know, a pandemic will alter the course of history.

Additionally, if we are trying to look a certain way to impress people or to feel a certain way, we are setting ourselves up for financial disaster. This is a really yucky story, but for many years I worked in the mortgage industry. Someone in a position of authority in my industry used to convince new mortgage brokers to finance or lease a car they couldn't afford and buy a bunch of fancy clothes on credit cards in order to give the appearance that they were more successful. He would tell them it would help them attract better clients. He would convince them it was a wise investment for their business, but what he truly believed behind the scenes was financially macabre.

His theory was that they would work harder and stay longer because they had debt.

Dunnnnn dunnn *dunnnnnnnnn!*

Inevitably, what ended up happening was people who were supposed to be giving sound financial advice were leveraged to the max and gave bad financial advice in order to make more sales to pay off their own bad financial decisions.

I'm not sure it ever really worked out for anyone. Many people had to quit the industry because they were on commission pay (which fluctuated), and the stress of not being able to pay their bills or providing for their families meant they had to take salaried jobs that often paid less but allowed them to meet their obligations on time.

I vowed then and there that I would never wear anything or drive anything in order to pretend to be something. I would just *be*, and I would impress clients by what I knew, how I could help them, or who I was deep down. If they were unimpressed and needed me to drive a $250,000 car to be impressed, they were not the kind of people I wanted to spend my precious life with anyway.

5. *I absolutely have to do what is in my own best financial interest.*

Okay, confession time. I used to buy things from salespeople:

- If I felt sorry for them.
- If they were new on the job.
- If they were a friend of mine.
- If they were struggling financially.
- If they walked me through a sales pitch and I felt like I had already invested time.
- If there was a really "good deal" on something I was already going to buy.

Basically, I would put their financial needs ahead of mine. I didn't know how to say no. I thought I always needed a good reason to say no, but when I'd explain why I couldn't, the salesperson had a trained response to my objection. I'd usually end up giving them the sale just to make the transaction end. And even when I gave them my money, a transaction I willingly participated in, I felt gross. It wasn't an "enthusiastic consent," you know? It didn't feel honoring to my spirit.

Later, when I was working in real estate and mortgages, we'd learn "Objection Handling," which was how to turn a "no" into a sale. And even when this would work, and I could turn a rejection into dollar signs, it always felt disgusting. I abandoned manipulating the sale and instead worked to attract clients who were open to financial literacy. I *finally* saw in others what I couldn't see in me. When you put other people's best interests ahead of your own, no one wins. When you compromise your truth for someone else's benefit or you take advantage of someone who doesn't have financial boundaries for your own gain, it feels damn disgusting, and it lacks integrity. But, when you legitimately operate at a financial standard that matches someone else's, the transaction is joyful for both parties.

If it feels like a no, you can say *no, thank you.* And you can walk away. Your sashay out the door might save you thousands of dollars in the long run.

6. *I need to plan my own retirement and be responsible for me in old age.*

If today I am not looking out for myself in my old age, I can't trust that I will get the level of care that I desire. By living my life with poor financial boundaries, I am likely to need to rely on people who do not have my best interest at heart in my elder years. Assuming I am fortunate enough not to be taken advantage of monetarily as a financially illiterate senior, I might also be leaving the burden of my problems to the children. If they witness a lifetime of me behaving with little or poor boundaries, they may also then feel the need to take on my problems (demonstrating that they too have poor financial boundaries) and instead of planning and saving for their own lives and retirements, they are dealing with my lack of self-accountability, which negatively impacts my children and grandchildren.

7. *I have to protect my privacy, and I must not share my financial circumstances with those who ask about it casually.*

In some social circles, people love to talk about money. And in other social circles, they never talk about money. As you are learning your own personal comfort level discussing financial matters, it is important not to be baited into a conversation that someone does not have the right to. I've witnessed people at parties "casually" discussing money and income and careers, only to find out someone in the group was some pyramid schemer trying to figure out if anyone had money or assets. By the time people saw the dollar signs in his eyes, it was too late. They had already "overshared."

If you do not feel comfortable sharing your financial situation with someone, you do not have to say a peep. No one is entitled to that information unless you are in some sort of formal or professional agreement with them and you trust them.

8. *It is necessary, even though it might feel mean, that I avoid people who undermine my financial wellbeing.*

If you have people in your life who mock you for your finances (whether you have a better financial picture than them or worse), it's okay to limit your time with them and exposure to them. If you have people in your life who make you feel stupid for the things you don't know, it's imperative to limit your time with them and your exposure to them. If you have people in your life who stiff you with the bill, who don't pay their fair share, or who simply set you up to fail, you must limit your time with them and your exposure to them.

9. *I must avoid situations that will incur more debt.*

I think I've been to every spice party, plastic dinnerware party, makeup party, candle party, and nail sticker party known to mankind. Some of these are legitimate products I use and some of them were, at first, an excuse to fill my socialization cup, but they ended up draining my wallet.

If you are going to be tempted, you have two choices. You can say to the host up front, "I'm on a debt-free path right now, so I will not bring my wallet and I will not buy anything, but I am happy to promote your link on my social media or leave some catalogs at work." Or you can always decline and make a mental note to use your friend's website to buy gifts and products in the future when you've budgeted for them.

But there are just some situations in life where you *know* you are going to go deeper in the hole, and until your boundaries are ironclad, it can be wise to avoid those situations. You would never say to an addict in the first part of recovery, "Let's meet at the bar to talk...you can order water." It would just be an obscene suggestion. I'm not saying you are a debt addict, but I *am* saying you are in recovery. So why put yourself in a situation where you are bombarding your senses?

10. I must be a healthy financial role model for my family.

It's important to me to give my kids the tools I didn't have. It will be up to them to use them, but I don't want them unexposed to how money works and spending their teens and twenties making giant messes that their forty-year-old selves have to fix. (It's also why I created the "How to Teach Your Kids About Money" program that you can find on my website. It's necessary that they see me succeed *and* fail. And when I make money mistakes, I speak openly of them. I don't speak specifically to the numbers, as I try not to say anything that I would not want repeated on the playground, but I talk in terms of concepts they understand.

The kids also handle their own money. They have ever since they were three and four years old. They make their own decisions about spending, but they each save money for investments. They give some away to the charity or cause of their choosing, and they sit down once a month and update their net worth spreadsheets. The spreadsheet is color coded the same way it is for you: red is liabilities and green is assets. The only difference is the red section says, "*Stay away from here, buddy,*" which I wish someone had said to me when I was young!

If I don't teach my kids about money, the banks will teach my kids about money, and the bank has a very different agenda than I do. The bank is going to teach my kids habits that will allow the bank to profit off them, so it is up to me to set an example for my kids. That way, the kids can also make decisions that are in their own individual best interest.

11. I must also honor other humans' financial boundaries. I will stay in my own lane.

When someone else shares their financial boundaries with me, it is up to me to respect those. I do not get to try and get that person to "overcome an objection." I also must not ask anyone else to play by my money story. If I am struggling financially, I cannot ask a small business owner to discount a product so that I can afford it. That's unfair to that business owner, and it's me asking them to play small. Instead, I have to rise up and find a way to afford it if I see the value in it. I can choose to save up and buy things when they go on discount, and it's always important to save money where I can. But my financial limitations must not be imposed on others. Additionally, if someone cannot afford my products or services, I honor where they are by letting them experience their own growth. I do not need to convince them to prioritize my products over something else in their budget. I have to allow everyone their own experience when it comes to life and money, and this is by far the thing that brings me the most peace.

> J.F. says: "Mastering my financial boundaries has increased my net worth by 300% and ended the cycle of generations of low income. This means it has changed the life of both of my daughters, who will be the first generation to experience wealth on my side of the family. With every financial boundary I have set, I've learned to believe in myself a little more…and I get to show that to my kids! Financial boundaries have changed everything."

Chapter Seventeen

MORTGAGES

THE DEATH PLEDGE

Mortgages.

One of the most expensive forms of debt is a mortgage, which literally is the Latin word for "death pledge." You are likely to have this debt for most of your adult living years. The average Canadian is fifty-eight years old before they are mortgage-free.

The Australian Housing and Urban Research Institute (AHURI) found that nearly half of people between the age of fifty to sixty-four still carry mortgage debt.

Fifty-nine percent of Americans aged fifty-five to sixty-nine still carry mortgage debt, according to Zillow research.

Sixty-one percent of Brits between the age of forty-five to fifty-four still carry mortgage debt, according to the Office of National Statistics. (UK)

When you consider that most of us mortgage our homes and settle into the idea of fifteen, twenty-five, thirty, or forty years of debt, it's no wonder that debt feels common. Most of the time, we are so excited to be "approved" for a mortgage that we don't read the fine print. And because we are so busy thinking about where our furniture will go and what window coverings we want, we miss the opportunity to ask great questions that will impact us long after the dog has chewed the corners of the couch and the window coverings have been replaced.

People get so focused on the interest rate, but it's *how the interest is compounded* that matters more.

Let me show you what I mean.

If Jessica and Nick both start out with a penny, and we tell them we are going to double it, that's the interest rate. They have the same interest rate, which is 100 percent. But we are going to compound Jessica's daily and Nick's once a month/every thirty days.

Here's what Jessica's finances look like:

Day One: $.01

Day Two: $.02

Day Three: $.04

Day Four: $.08

Day Five: $.16

Day Six: $.32

Day Seven: $.64

Day Eight: $1.28

Day Nine: $2.56

Day Ten: $5.12

Day Eleven: $10.24

Day Twelve: $20.48

Day Thirteen: $40.96

Day Fourteen: $81.92

Day Fifteen: $163.84

Day Sixteen: $327.68

Day Seventeen: $655.36

Day Eighteen: $1,310.72

Day Nineteen: $2,621.44

Day Twenty: $5,242.88

Day Twenty-One: $10,485.76

Day Twenty-Two: $20,971.52

Day Twenty-Three: $41,943.04

Day Twenty-Four: $83,886.08

Day Twenty-Five: $167,772.16

Day Twenty-Six: $335,544.32

Day Twenty-Seven: $671,088.64

Day Twenty-Eight: $1,342,177.28

Day Twenty-Nine: $2,684,354.56

Day Thirty: $5,368,709.12

And here's what Nick's looks like:

Day One: $0.01

Day Two: $0.01

Day Three: $0.01

Day Four: $0.01

Day Five: $0.01

Day Six: $0.01

Day Seven: $0.01

Day Eight: $0.01

Day Nine: $0.01

Day Ten $0.01

Day Eleven: $0.01

Day Twelve: $0.01

Day Thirteen: $0.01

Day Fourteen: $0.01

Day Fifteen: $0.01

Day Sixteen: $0.01

Day Seventeen: $0.01

Day Eighteen: $0.01

Day Nineteen: $0.01

Day Twenty: $0.01

Day Twenty-One: $0.01

Day Twenty-Two: $0.01

Day Twenty-Three: $0.01

Day Twenty-Four: $0.01

Day Twenty-Five: $0.01

Day Twenty-Six: $0.01

Day Twenty-Seven: $0.01

Day Twenty-Eight: $0.01

Day Twenty-Nine: $0.01

Day Thirty: 0.01

Day Thirty-One: $0.02

They both have the same interest rate, but because of how the interest is compounded, Jessica ends up a millionaire and Nick barely has two pennies to rub together.

So that is more dramatic than most episodes of *Real Housewives*, but can you see how interest rate is just *part* of the equation that determines the cost of your mortgage?

The number you are looking for in all your mortgage documents is something called "the Total Cost of Borrowing." It's usually buried in the fine print. What you want to know is: over the life of the loan, how many dollars are coming out of your pocket in total?

In many cases, your banker or mortgage broker won't know this. We were trained to get you fixated on mortgage rate and "sell" you the best rate. But when you are truly comparing two or more mortgages, you want to know the total cash coming out of your jeans at the end of the loan, so you can properly compare apples to apples. When your mortgage broker *does* know Total Cost of Borrowing on your first ask, please give them a high-five and say, "That's from Erin Skye Kelly."

In addition to figuring out what the Total Cost of Borrowing is, you'll want to be well-versed in the prepayment privileges for your mortgage. Depending on what country you live in, you might have restrictions on paying off your mortgage early. In Canada, many lenders allow you to prepay part of the mortgage off each year, but the rules vary greatly from bank to bank and even mortgage to mortgage. One popular bank in Canada allows you to make a 10 percent lump sum prepayment toward your outstanding mortgage balance each year without penalty. Another bank allows you to prepay up to 25 percent of the total balance, plus they allow you to increase your mortgage payment by 25 percent each month in addition.

Before you make any prepayments, you'll want to always be sure that the extra money you are putting on the mortgage *is* going on the principal. Usually that will be the case, but I'd hate to give that blanket advice and find out that you are one of the odd scenarios where the lender will only apply the payment to your next payment or something that doesn't benefit the big picture.

They also might make you do these prepayments at specific times. Some lenders allow you to do it once per calendar year. Others allow you to do it once a year based on the mortgage anniversary. (Meaning if you got your mortgage in August, you can make a one-time payment from August to July before the date resets.) Some allow you to make payments as often as possible up until you hit the max prepayment privilege, and others allow you to make payments but not less than one hundred dollars at a time. Be sure to know all the expectations your lender has and what you've agreed to before you go bending over backwards to reach your wallet.

If you currently have consumer debt, such as lines of credit, loans, credit card balances etc., *and* you have a mortgage, you aren't going to worry too much about the mortgage now. But when it comes time to renew your mortgage and you have achieved consumer debt freedom, you will absolutely want to look into the mortgage option that has the most flexible prepayments or paydown options, if you desire to be mortgage-free.

If you live in the USA, you may be able to write off your mortgage interest against your income to reduce the income tax you pay. This is not a thing in Canada, Australia, or the UK, unless your home generates income or you have home office-type deductions. Regardless, my American friends, you must not use this as an excuse to overborrow!

If you currently have a mortgage, your action item is to go through the mortgage documents and learn what the following terms of your mortgage are:

- The payment, if you don't know it off the top of your head
- The frequency (how often you make payments)
- The interest rate on the loan
- How often the interest is compounded
- The total amortization of the loan
- The term of the loan (in some countries, this is different than the amortization)
- How flexible it is or what the paydown options are
- What the Total Cost of Borrowing is for this mortgage
- What the penalty is if you, for some reason, needed to break the mortgage contract

We're going to do more with this in Phase Three, but for now, you need to know these numbers and sit with these numbers. You definitely do not need to consolidate your consumer debt into these numbers. Whenever you are considering a purchase, it's important to consider your long-term financial goals. If you only plan on being in an area or a home for two years or less, it might make more sense to rent. You'll run the numbers in the net worth spreadsheet and the budget to be sure, but once you've factored in real estate commissions when you sell, closing costs, and other expenses related to moving, you may discover that any equity you might have had has been chewed up by these expenses.

If you plan on being in the area long term, and you are unsure whether you want to buy or rent, know that the math is near impossible to predict because we don't know what expenses you will incur over the next couple of decades. If you have a home that you've purchased but it requires a lot of repair and maintenance, that can be costly. If you rent and the landlord has a lot of repair and maintenance and you are paying market rent or lower, you might end up saving money. (And if you do, make sure you squeeze that budget to invest for the long term.)

If your landlord decides that they want to sell, that might mean your moving situation is out of your control. If the vacancy rate in your city increases, you might end up with lower rent, or if it decreases, you might end up with higher rent, which is a cost you don't have control over. No matter what you decide in terms or renting or buying, you want to be sure your monthly housing costs are well below your income.

Janna and Jeff say: "You opened our eyes. We went from our lives-running-us, to us-running-our-lives.

"In 3 years we became 100% debt-free and 100% mortgage-free. And it's fabulous! We recognized we weren't spending our money in alignment with our values. We didn't want to spend $3000/month on a home, which was a good percentage of our take-home pay. We realized we didn't need to impress anyone. We sold our big furnished house, and we right-sized our life. And it's so fabulous. Oh my gosh. But more than that, like it's so freeing! This smaller space is easier and more aligned with us and it has just brought us so much more joy than we could ever imagine! It's really made us intentional with our money and we will be retired in a just few years now that cash flow has improved and we are actively mastering our money together."

Chapter Eighteen

PLOT TWIST

ASSETS AND LIABILITIES

By now you've mastered your net worth, and you are chugging along making debt payments. Now brace yourself for a giant plot twist. This is the point in the reality TV show where you find out the girl who is getting one of the final roses is actually a lesbian and she was only on the show to try and break into a music career, but her girlfriend from her hometown found out and told the producers and they are going to confront her at the most dramatic rose ceremony ever.

How your bank views assets and liabilities is very different from how a wealthy person views assets and liabilities.

In our section earlier about assets and liabilities, we determined the bank says these kinds of things are assets:

- Tax-free savings accounts/ISAs/Roth IRAs
- Traditional 401(k)s/RRSPs/Pensions/Superannuations
- Savings accounts
- Checking accounts
- Cash

- Mutual Funds
- Stocks
- Real Estate
- Jewelry
- Art
- Furniture
- Business
- Rental Properties

And these were examples of what your bank considers to be liabilities:

- Credit cards
- Lines of credit
- Student loans
- Mortgages
- Second mortgages
- Secured lines of credit
- Loans from family/friends
- Vehicle loans
- Leased vehicles
- Medical debt
- Department store cards

Seems straightforward. But here's the twist: the bank wants to know your net worth *so they know how much they can lend you.* A wealthy person wants to know their net worth so they have a clear picture *about their financial freedom.* That means that the metrics they use are very different.

Instead of valuing our assets and liabilities the way the bank does, let's look at a new way to view them.

Your New Wealthy View of Assets and Liabilities:

Assets are things that consistently put money *in* our pockets. Liabilities are things that take money *out* of our pockets.

And by "pockets," I don't necessarily mean your actual pockets, but I do mean that they are making a return, which means if you invest ten dollars, you have more than ten dollars within a month or two.

If we start to view everything through that lens, it definitely changes whether some of those things above are assets and liabilities.

TAX-FREE SAVINGS ACCOUNTS/ISAS/ROTH IRAS

This one gets tricky now because while you are in your wealth-building years, these are taking money out of your pocket to prepare for retirement. They are not technically assets today, but they will *become* assets. So, we'll leave it on the asset side for now.

TRADITIONAL401(K)S/RRSPS/PENSIONS/SUPERANNUATIONS

Again, this is usually something you are preparing to turn into an asset later, meaning that it will put money in your pocket when you are retired, so we will leave it here for now.

SAVINGS ACCOUNTS

If you have money in a savings account and it earns a little bit of interest, we would say sure, this is an asset. But it barely squeaks by the criteria.

If it is your Quick and Dirty Fund, however, we do *not* count it as an asset. This is because it is essentially marked as money that later will be used for expenses. It's for when your hot water tank blows. It's for when you get that flat tire. This money is not making money for your financial freedom; it's mostly preventing you from a financial disaster. It's still important, and if you insist, you can leave it in the green column, but only because a net worth statement doesn't have a neutral column. I don't include my Quick and Dirty in the asset column because to me it's not an asset. It's simply money I haven't spent yet.

And *no*, you *do not invest this money* to turn it into an asset. You will buy *assets*, and *those* will be your assets. You still need this whoopsie-daisy-I-had-an-emergency account, so don't mess with the safe zone and make it unsafe.

CHECKING ACCOUNTS

This is where you are going to start to get really mad at me. Your checking account typically does not earn interest and it doesn't not put money in your pocket, so you won't consider this an asset. Don't worry about trying to make it earn interest so that it becomes an asset. Simply accept that this account is where you keep the money in your budget you haven't spent yet.

CASH

You get where this is going. If it's just sitting there, it's not an asset. It's sure better than a credit card in your pocket, but cash in and of itself is not putting more moola in your pocket, so it's not an asset. (Think of it this way: you'd never take five twenty-dollar bills and "invest" in a one-hundred-dollar bill.)

MUTUAL FUNDS

Hopefully these are growing for you (after you take into account any fees). If you are taking money out of your pocket today to fund a mutual fund account as a future asset, then right now it is a liability or obligation (*gasp!*). It doesn't mean you don't contribute today, as ideally it will become an asset later. But we want to be clear that if it isn't putting money in our pocket today, we don't see it as an asset yet. If, however, your mutual funds are paying you dividends, those dividends are an asset because they are putting money in your pocket today.

STOCKS

Obviously if these pay dividends, then yes, they are an asset. But as long as they are just going up and down, we don't consider them a true asset because the gain hasn't been realized. What that means is you haven't actually taken the money, so tomorrow it could bottom out and you can lose money. When you are updating the green column of your net worth spreadsheet, you won't update it with the daily stock balance. You will just update your total portfolio value of your stocks once a week or so.

REAL ESTATE

This is the one that p*sses everyone off. Many years ago, I told my assistant that her house was not an asset, and she was so angry with me that she did not speak to me for two whole weeks. The fire was fueled, however, and she paid that sucker off in just a few years. I'm happy to p*ss you off, too, if it makes your financial circumstances better. "Your house is the biggest investment you'll ever make" is what we, in the mortgage and real estate world, were trained to tell you. But if you consider how much money it takes out of your pocket or whether you rent or own, your house is a liability. If your home is paid off and you have some sort of rental suite that generates more money than your taxes and utilities and all the things required to keep that roof over your head, then yes. You now have an asset. But if you are paying mortgage payments, property taxes, electricity, heat, and water out of your pocket, you have a big fat liability.

JEWELRY

That rock looks nice on your finger, but putting your hand in your pocket doesn't make this an asset. Selling it doesn't make it an asset. (That's a way to generate quick cash on a one-time deal.) You can take that cash and buy an asset that consistently puts money in your pocket if you'd like. But don't go hocking any sentimental jewelry. Enjoy it. Feel good wearing it. Just don't list it on your net worth spreadsheet as an asset.

ART

Same rule here. If you own an art gallery that people consistently pay admission to see and you have constant cash flow, then yup, you have an asset. If you bought a fancy painting at an art show, you have a fancy painting.

Hear me out, though: I do want you to own items of quality. I do want you to own original art that is meaningful for you when you can afford it. I just don't want you to delude yourself into thinking it's an asset. Sure, in history, there have been a few art pieces that have gone up in value *even though it wasn't an asset*; however, it's more true that most pieces of art have gone down in value as seen at nearly every garage or rubbish sale. Support the artists you love, please. (One of my favorites is Kal Barteski.) Cherish their work. Choose it over department store prints or knick-knacks. Teach your kids the value of it, so you are buying generational pieces. But you likely will not need to put it in the asset column of your net worth spreadsheet unless you have an original Picasso and even then you'll have to convince me.

FURNITURE

Just no.

BUSINESS

The question becomes: does it meet all its obligations and taxations and pay everyone (including you) fairly and still provide positive cash flow? If yes, then it's an asset. If no, then it's a liability.

RENTAL PROPERTIES

If the income exceeds the expenses, then yes, it's an asset. If the rent does not cover the payments or you are breaking even, it's a liability.

Here's a trick question: if you purchased the property for $100,000 and today's value is $120,000, and the rent is $1000 per month but the expenses are $1120, is it an asset or liability?

High five if you said liability. Even though it has *appreciated in value,* it's not an asset because we define an asset as something that consistently puts money *in* your pocket. The appreciated value isn't the true price because the market dictates the price when it comes time to sell.

If you purchased the property for $100,000 and today's value is $80,000 and the rent is $1000 per month but the expenses are $800 per month, is it an asset or liability?

High five if you said asset. Even though it has depreciated in value, it's an asset because it is putting money in your pocket every month.

Your primary job if you own a rental property is to ensure it cash flows every month. Ideally, it also appreciates in value. That's a double-decker-awesome sandwich. But when you are being drained every month financially to keep things afloat and pay for liabilities, you are running on a life deficit.

This doesn't mean that you don't ever buy a house. Or a rental property. Or that you don't buy mutual funds or investments unless they immediately put cash in your pocket. We just need to be making sure they are offering us a return as much as possible.

But do you see how consumer debt makes it *extra* difficult to become wealthy? Most or all of the debt you have is likely because you borrowed money to purchase a liability. You created an *expense* in your budget to pay off something that decreases in value over time.

Doesn't that seem *ludicrous*? Are you as mad as me, or am I the only one that gets spicy here?

This is not about never buying TFSAs and ISAs and stocks and homes. This is about committing to never ever, ever, *ever* borrowing for a liability *ever* again. Never *ever*. Find a ring from the bottom of your jewelry box and put it on your left hand after having a personal commitment ceremony with yourself and decide to *not* be with your credit card for as long as you both shall live. I already know what your first dance song could be.

When you are going to borrow money, the question becomes: "Is this something that puts money in my pocket?" If the answer is yes, you can *think about* borrowing. I'm saying *think about*. There are lots of things to consider, including, "Can I acquire the asset without borrowing?" But if the answer is no, this is not something that puts money in your pocket, then you can walk away with your head held high because you made a commitment to yourself and you and debt are never ever getting back together, remember?

* * *

Now I know what I am about to preach is not why you are here. You did not come here looking for parenting advice. But honest to *gawd*, every time I teach a workshop or a seminar and I ask, "What are some liabilities?" Some sarcastic asswipe jokes, "My *kids!*"

Kids are not liabilities. Don't be a jerk. Don't even let your brain joke about that. Here's why: if you are like most parents, you wanted these babies, and you loved them before they were born. You couldn't wait to hold them, to throw a ball with them, to dress them up in Halloween costumes, and to celebrate them every year with a party where they smash icing into their cake hole.

And now, because you got yourself into a financial clusterfeckhold, you are blaming these tiny humans for draining you. Even though you are joking and you think you're funny, they are picking up on that.

Parenting is hard, there's no question. But as I have mentioned, I have learned that when I am well-rested, drinking enough water, exercising wherever I can squeeze it in, budgeting, and staying on top of my self-care, I am amused by my children's antics. When I am exhausted, emotionally drained, pulled in too many directions, unwell, and filling my face with garbage, I am *not amused* by my children's antics. It is never about the kids, and it is always about me.

Kids can feel your stress. They sense when they are a burden to you. All those little bits of frustration you have with them and all the times you ignore them when they are seeking connection form little imprints in their head about who they are and what they deserve.

I am not a perfect parent by any means, but I would bet my bottom dollar that part of the reason you are in this financial pickle is because somewhere along the way, when you were a kid, you picked up an imprint about your value and you've lived it out ever since. And if you want to improve your life, my friend, you start with your own four walls.

When your kids are fighting for your attention and you are in the middle of cooking dinner, for example, try turning the burners off and getting down on their level so you can see them eye to eye and really listen to them. Be interested in them. Pay attention, even if it means cold noodles or burnt pot roast. They won't remember the meal, but they will remember how they felt. You could also engage them in conversation while you cook. Have them pull up a seat on the other side of the counter and talk them through what you are doing as you are doing it, so their beautiful, curious little brains can be engaged while you connect.

I know you are tired, and this might seem overwhelming day-to-day. But we want to engage our children in *what is possible* with money. We want to say things like, "It's not in the budget this week, but if we can figure out *how* to gather the money/resources for that, we absolutely will!" instead of, "No, we can't afford that. Don't ask."

By teaching them not to ask, you are teaching them not to advocate for their needs.

The other reason you do not even let your mind joke about your kids being liabilities is because you are teaching them that money matters more than they do. When you joke about how expensive kids are and how much all their activities cost, you are effectively saying, "I wish I didn't have to pay for this."

Mama, I know you are doing the best you can. And I'm not here to criticize you. But sweet heavens, I cannot stand when parents say their kids are liabilities. Thank you for coming to my Ted Talk.

> Twila says: "Not sure if anxiety is an emotion but I felt very anxious and stressed and overwhelmed around money. Now that it is all written out and I have a plan, I feel much more in control and hopeful. I just said to my husband last night – 'wow did I ever spend way too much time stressing about money when this feeling of being in control feels sooooo much better!'"

Chapter Nineteen

VEHICLES

We're going to talk about vehicles now that we've established that no matter what, vehicles are not an asset.

This hurts some people right in their feelings because their cars are an extension of their identity.

I do not want you to think about cars in terms of what is a good investment or what has the best horsepower or interior features or least depreciation. I want you to think of, "What will get me where I need to go? What is the purpose of my vehicle?"

Maybe it's to get you to and from the place where you earn income. Maybe it's to safely drive little people to extracurriculars to give them some cool life experiences. Maybe it's to impress people because you had a boss that told you it will make more people do business with you (*eyeroll*). I'm not here to judge you for that. I just need you to be honest with yourself about what you need the vehicle for so that you can align your vehicle needs with your values.

What I know is that if you are like most consumers, you are letting the car industry tell you the purpose of your vehicle. The car industry is telling you that 0 percent financing is a no brainer. The car industry is telling you that your souped-up truck makes you a rugged man or that your minivan makes you a responsible and caring mom, or that your sports car makes you great in the sack. But I have learned to tune all of that out because I know very wealthy people who drive unassuming vehicles, and I know very broke people who drive luxury cars with luxury $650/month payments.

Now, when I hear 0 percent financing, I don't hear "free money" like the mass majority of people hear through marketing tactics. When I hear 0 percent financing, I still hear "a loss of millions in retirement" and I'll show you why.

Let's imagine that Carla turns sixteen and finances her first vehicle. She chooses something moderately priced, but from the age of sixteen until the age of sixty-five, she has on average a monthly vehicle payment of $350.

Then Mercedes turns sixteen and finances *her* first vehicle. She chooses something a little fancier and ends up with a $500 per month car payment every year until the age of sixty-five.

Portia turns sixteen and works two jobs to have her vehicle "freedom," and she ends up with a $650 monthly car payment from the age of sixteen until she retires at sixty-five.

Now let's imagine you turned sixteen and decided you would never have a car payment. You drove older vehicles that simply got you where you needed to go. You didn't always have the important stuff like the cassette players or the three-CD changers, but you simply made do in order to avoid having a car payment. Instead, you started squeezing your budget to invest the money you would have otherwise been putting toward a payment.

Assuming you invested that money for a lifetime and had a conservative-to-moderate 8 percent rate of return by the time you turned sixty-five:

— If you had been putting $350/month away, you would have $2,387,648 by the time you retired.

— If you had been putting $500/month away, you would have $3,705,426 by the time you retired.

— If you had been putting $650/month away, you would have $4,817,054 by the time you retired.

You might have your arms crossed and your lip pouted, and you might be saying, "Yeah, well, it would have been nice to have that kind of money when I was sixteen, Erin." But the point is this: your fancy car payment is likely one of the contributing factors to your financial struggle. It doesn't matter if it is 0 percent or not. That giant chunk of cash every month is not giving you freedom. And this is the bullsh*t we are sold on: a newer vehicle is reliable.

Do you hear how illogical that sounds?!

Imagine having maxed out credit cards, lines of credit, no cash in the bank, and now a $30,000 brand-new vehicle with $500/month payments. None of that sounds reliable to me.

We are far better to have a $5000 used vehicle and $25,000 cash in the bank to get ourselves out of any trouble that we are hoping the "new car" will rescue us from. When you have cash in the bank, you can pay a tow truck. When you have cash in the bank, you can call an Uber. When you have cash in the bank, you are relying on your own resourcefulness. So, don't believe for a minute that having a new car means having a reliable car. Don't rely on a vehicle for anything. Rely on *you*.

Now I'm definitely not a car person. I don't care what you drive; it doesn't impress me. And what I drive won't impress you. But here are a few things to keep in mind as you plan for your next vehicle if you are going to ignore me and go to a dealer.

1. The price is never the price. There are usually underlying costs that are not advertised. Additionally, there are often advertised incentives or discounts, but when you show up on the lot to check out the car, you can discover that you are not actually eligible for the incentives. Get all the information up front and all of the fine print in writing, and give yourself forty-eight hours to review it at home or away from the dealership where the new car smell can't sway your decision. Also make sure the incentives are applied *after* you've figured out a fair price.

2. If you are seeing advertisements for low monthly payments, it could be a lease with low mileage, or it might require a very large down payment or a magical credit score only available to people who have not been bitten by life. If a deal seems too good to be true...well. You know that it probably is.
3. Before you ever step foot on a lot, do your research. Check out consumer reports or Kelley Blue Book for information on cars in your price range. If you want to buy used or sell your vehicle privately or trade it in to the dealer, Kelley Blue Book is where you'll want to do your research because it has different expected prices for each of those categories.
4. If the car salesperson winks at you and does finger guns, *leave.*
5. Your goal is to find the "invoice" price of the car, not the MSRP (manufacturer's suggested retail price). The "invoice" price is what the dealer paid the manufacturer for the car. This will help you figure out an appropriate price.
6. It's always better to have a completely paid off car before you buy another one, especially if you are financing. Otherwise, you'll roll your debt into more debt, and your debt will snowball *you.* We are almost always financially upside-down in vehicle purchases when we finance them at the best of times, so don't take your past mistakes and push them further into the future.
7. Understand the full purchase price of the vehicle and not the monthly payments. Look for hidden fees and taxes, car preparation and delivery fees, licensing fees, administration fees, freight, and inspection expenses. Even with 0 percent financing, there are hidden costs. The dealer is not in business to give you things for free. To stay in the business, the dealer has to make money.
8. Don't talk about your trade-in right away with the dealer. Handle the new car and the trade-in separately to maximize your cash. Often, you'll come out further ahead if you sell your vehicle privately, and then use that cash toward your next vehicle purchase.

Kelley Blue Book can help you determine this. I am embarrassed to tell you this, but I was in my thirties before I ever bought a car on my own. I used to outsource this job to the men in my life because I had an unconscious belief that this was a "blue job." I'm here to tell you if you also have that unconscious belief, it is so empowering and freeing to do this work on your own, and it is not nearly as complicated as you think. And this is coming from someone who called the carburetor a garburator for many years.

9. Remember that add-ons *add up*. Carefully consider what features you need *before* you get into the dealership and start adding on rust protection and the VIN etching and all the other doohickies. Know those options ahead of time and research them. Some features will make sense to have the dealer provide, but many things can be done afterwards for a savings. Some don't need to be done at all.
10. *Do the math* before you buy the extended warranty. Often the total cost of the warranty, especially if you are financing your vehicle, is far more money than it's worth. If you can, instead deposit that amount of money in a savings account that you are specifically reserving for vehicle maintenance and repairs. If the vehicle purchase is going to eat up all your cash, you cannot afford that vehicle.
11. Figure out your total ownership costs. How many miles do you typically put on a vehicle in a year? What are your insurance costs? When you've narrowed your vehicle search, phone your insurance company to get a quote before you sign anything. Research what it costs to have the vehicle with all expenses, not just the payment amount.
12. If you are financing the vehicle (barf! *Don't!*) make sure you've looked into your own financing and that you aren't just assuming the dealer's financing is the best. They often are paid a flat fee or a referral fee or commission on the financing, so it's not likely they are looking out for your best interest.

In all seriousness, here's the bottom line: do whatever you can to reduce your monthly vehicle expenses. Take the difference between what you were paying and what you are paying now and put that money directly on your debt. When your debt is paid off, start paying yourself that car payment, and buy your future vehicles in cash. Remember, we do not ever borrow for a liability!

When you hit Phase Three, you'll be investing for retirement anyway, but anything you can squeeze out of that former car payment will help you build wealth and stay out of debt.

> Allison says: "Vehicles have been paid off for several years now. Will pay cash for any future purchases, but that is when this one is 'miled out' and the wheels are falling off! For me vehicles are the worst investment we make."

Chapter Twenty

A COMPLETION CEREMONY

At some point, you are going to pay off your first debt.

(*Butt wiggle happy dance!*)

Now we have to mark this occasion with a ceremony. You'll do this every time you pay off a debt, and you'll do it up big style when you pay off *all* your debt.

Many major life moments are marked with ceremony. If you have been carrying this debt around for longer than some of your friendships or relationships, it is important to truly let it go forever. We've learned through history and culture that rituals actually help people perform better. So, if we are singing happy birthday to a one-year-old and taking photos of them covered in icing from a cake they'll never remember tasting, why wouldn't we mark your progress toward a lifetime of financial freedom?

Here's how to do a basic debt completion ritual.

You first find something physical that marks the debt. Maybe it's an old credit card statement or something you purchased with the card that you now do not even need or appreciate. You'll hold it in your hands and talk to it.

Yeah, you can go ahead and call me unbalanced. But you know what is actually unbalanced? Paying 19 percent interest on a credit card. Carry on.

You'll thank the debt for what it brought you in your life (the trip you went on, the memories you made) and you'll say goodbye to the pain it brought (the payments, the extra time spent working). If you feel angry, I truly want you to express that anger. Maybe you have to stomp your feet or have a little hissy fit. Give it the finger. It doesn't matter what you do, I just want you to have a fully expressional experience. And once you've let it all out, you can destroy the physical representation. If it's a statement, you can burn it. If it's a recyclable biodegradable balloon, you can pop it. If it's ice cubes and tequila, you can put it in the blender and drink it. Just kidding.

It might sound like this:

Dear credit card number three,

Thank you for allowing me to have that experience on spring break with my friends in Mexico and for buying me replacement clothing when I returned home without my suitcase. Thank you for covering my butt with those parking tickets when I was being a bit reckless and impatient, and thank you for charging a ridiculous amount of interest so that I was forced to take note and pay attention to my finances.

I'm ready to let go of your high interest rates, your late fees, your overpayment fees, and all the other nickels and dimes you slipped past me over the years. I'm done with the convenience of you when what I truly desire is freedom. I'm ready to say goodbye to picking up late night shifts and work and missing out on more time with the people I love because I'm trying to pay you off all the time. I'm ready to be completely free of you and have actual cash set aside for emergencies so that I'm not relying on you and then feeling punished by you. I'm absolutely done with all the interest payments and all the debt payments that have prevented me from taking control of my financial future.

I'm saying yes to me, which means I am saying goodbye to you forever.

lights it on fire
walks away in slow motion while it explodes in the background
flicks hair
doesn't look back

The point is to mark the moment with a goodbye ritual and then commit to not going back into this situation again.

If this is not a debt you intend to use again, you can choose to close it. (It's not always as easy as calling the creditor and closing the account. Sometimes you have to fight through a really strong sales retention department because they want to keep you using that credit.)

If you want to eventually go back into debt again (see what I did there), you'll keep two trade lines open (trade lines are accounts that are listed on your credit report) with at least a $1500 limit on each. But you will *not* touch those trade lines until Phase Three when you create your new identity as a debt-free person and determine whether you will live debt-free forever or not. That's so you can keep the credit score people happy, even though it seems like the credit score people are only happy when you are not happy. In the meantime, bye Filipe!

> Julie says: "Since starting Get the Hell Out of Debt, I've improved my net worth by over $300,000. As a single woman totally on my own! Without selling a kidney online! Sure I still have a bit of debt and a mortgage. But I have a secure plan to eliminate that last little bit of debt thanks to this community."

Chapter Twenty-One

DEBT BURNOUT

You're going to want to dogear this page or bookmark this chapter or highlight some of these words, my friend. This *is* going to happen to you and coming back here when things get tough might be the lifeline you need in those moments.

Paying off debt can feel exhilarating initially. You are all excited, you have new information, you are feeling financially literate and in control of your money for the first time in a long time. The momentum can be strong in the beginning. But as time continues and you start living a debt-filled Groundhog's Day of repeated tasks—budget squeeze, payoff, budget squeeze, payoff, budget squeeze, payoff—you might look up from your budget and notice other people going on trips. Or Google ads have got you surfing the clearance department of your favorite online shop because you accidentally thought about shopping and the internet cookies picked up your brainwaves. Suddenly, you are in what is known as the Messy Middle.

Over time, this process can feel emotionally taxing. It's tough to keep on track for long periods of time without feeling burdened and restricted. If you let your emotions dictate your behaviors, you are likely to say f*ck it and rack some debt back up again. The efforts you've put in over weeks come undone in a matter of hours.

Directional Activities vs Supporting Activities

Knowing the difference between directional activities and supporting activities will be key. My friend Rael Kalley coined the term "directional activities," and I've never heard a better phrase to describe this.

Directional activities are where we need to focus—actions that take us directly toward our goals. When we have a new fitness goal, we might think, "I need new gym shoes, a gym bag, a lock for the locker, a cute new Lorna Jane top, and I have to clean out my pantry." But none of those things actually get us closer to the goal. Those are not directional activities.

Actually exercising is the thing that gets us closer to the goal, no matter what shoes we have. *Actually exercising* is a directional activity. All the extra stuff just drains our energy and creates work. Certainly some of those things are supporting activities, which means they help you prepare to get closer to the result, but they don't actually get you closer to the result. If all you did was supporting activities, you'd never have results—and that's exactly what happens. If you busy yourself with too much busy work, you'll run out of energy to take action, which is the *actual work.*

When you are starting out, the budget and the net worth are directional activities, but over time as you move through the process, they become supporting activities. The actual directional activity is making a payment to pay down your credit card. If you never do that, you never achieve the result you want.

Here are some examples of both supporting and directional activities once you are in Phase Two of the program.

DIRECTIONAL ACTIVITIES	SUPPORTING ACTIVITIES
• selling things I no longer need and putting that money on the debt I am annihilating • squeezing money out of the budget and putting that money on the debt I am annihilating • working overtime and putting that money directly on the debt I am annihilating • offering some kind of side-creation or part-time work and putting the extra money I earn directly on the debt I am annihilating	• reconciling the budget • reading financial articles • watching the videos and doing the homework in the online version of the Get the Hell Out of Debt course • having interesting conversations with my partner or my kids about finances • following social media accounts of people who are committed to debt-freedom • researching the kinds of assets I might like to invest in when I get the hell out of debt

Create *your* list of directional activities to focus on and your list of supporting activities. Know that when you are struggling and feeling like things aren't moving fast enough for you, and when you've done all the directional activities you can, you can choose self-support items from the list of Class Two Experiences you created, or you can choose from your list of supporting activities to help you stay focused.

DIRECTIONAL ACTIVITIES	SUPPORTING ACTIVITIES

Nicole says: "Directional activities gave me the ability to see how the actions I take support the outcome I desire. While supporting activities allowed me to grow at a rate I was both comfortable and uncomfortable with. Both provided me with the tools to master my time, commitments, and ultimately find my purpose."

PHASE THREE

Chapter Twenty-Two

YOU'RE DEBT-FREE!

You did it! *You did it!* You paid off all your consumer debt!

One of my favorite business owners, a woman named Laura who owns an infusible jewelry company, asked:

> *"I'm scared that when we get out of debt that the "maintenance & building" part will be harder. I clearly need to work on the mindset around this… It's like my yo-yo-ing with weight loss. Losing it isn't my issue, it's making changes that are real and permanent- that's what holds me back. What are ways to stay consistent after we've gotten rid of all the debt (or lost all the weight)? I have a feeling these are super linked for me."*

First, we have to create a new identity for you. Using the Abundant Cycle, we want to truly see ourselves as financially free people who *do not borrow* money.

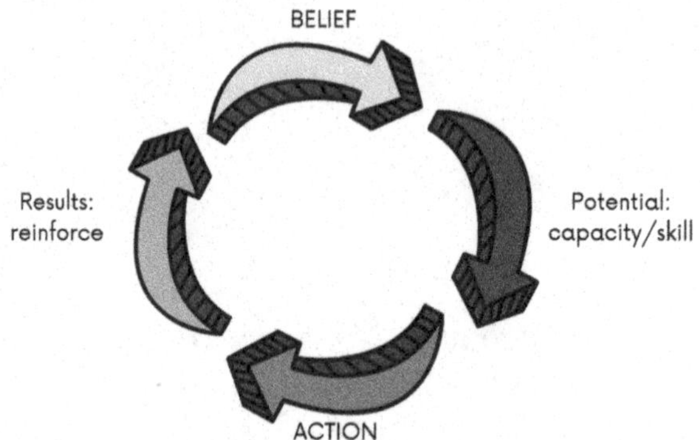

An abundant thinking cycle works like this:

1. First you choose a thought or a belief, such as "I am excellent at managing my money." You might not have been a great money manager in the past, but that is because you had "lack" thinking, and that is what we are working to change, so simply focus on what it is you want.
2. Then, let's look at your potential. Could the statement "I am an excellent money manager" potentially be true? Of course! Certainly, there are people less intelligent than you who have become debt-free and started to build wealth. Do you have the capacity or skill for this? Of course you do! And if you don't know something, there are so many places you could learn or so many books to read. So even if you don't have the skill now, you can certainly acquire it!
3. Now we must line up our actions. We must *act* like an excellent money manager. We have to *do* the things that excellent money managers would do. Would an excellent money manager borrow for a liability? Nope! So, we mustn't do that either. Would an excellent money manager budget ahead of time? *Yes!* Let's do that. Figure out what actions line up with this new belief you are creating and do those things.

4. Next, every single time we get a result that *even implies* you are an excellent money manager, we are going to celebrate the heck out of that! We are going to say to ourselves, "*See!* I *knew* I could do it!" Every time you make progress, it reinforces that the belief is true, so we are going to *look for evidence* every day that this belief is true. You are going to Sherlock this belief into existence by taking action and getting results that *prove* this belief is true.

And you are going to do this over and over and over again until it undeniably *is* true.

Let me clearly show you why you absolutely must start your abundant life with a belief or a thought:

When it comes to weight loss, many people are focused on the *result.* That stupid number on the scale (seriously, do you still have a scale? Throw that f*cker out!) must never be the *goal.* It can be the *result* of the goal, but the goal must be something you can control. So rather than focus on that stupid scale (you better have thrown it out by now), you focus on drinking lots of water, moving your body every day, and nourishing it. Your body is going to do what your body is going to do.

I don't know about you, but I decided to start dieting in Grade Nine when I was ninety-five pounds and I decided I should be ninety pounds. *I mean, how stupid is that?* But I dieted myself all the way up to nearly 200 pounds in my life.

And I did that because I was focused on the f*cking scale.

I would start a diet, usually on a Monday (bonus if the Monday fell on the first of the month). After completely binging the night before because "Tomorrow is day one of my diet!" I would follow the diet strictly, and about four days in, I'd check the scale. *Yessss!* I would have lost a few token pounds.

I would be so excited that it reinvigorated me, so I'd stick with the diet. And then a few days later I'd step on the scale again, expecting to see *victory* because I'd done everything I'd been doing before, and *whatintheactualf*ck?!* I'd *gained* weight.

Maybe it was Shark Week. Maybe I had to have a big poop. Who knows. But by focusing on the number as the goal, I would be derailed in an instant. Because I didn't have the results I wanted, I would give up. Eat some more pizza. Self-loathe for a while. All because I didn't know how to properly set goals and track the parts I *can* control: what I put in my chaihole and how often and how vigorously I move my body.

If instead I had made myself a little chart and checked off how many days I worked out in a month, or how many times I ate green things, or how many pounds I could lift, or how many directional activities I did, I would have had entirely different results.

But even when I'd lose weight, I used to still see myself as "overweight." No matter how much or how little I weighed, I hadn't yet learned to create a new identity in my mind that I was a fit, healthy person. Whenever you undertake a personal transformation, you have got to live into a new identity that you create.

This is not about being something you are not. This is about growing into the person you are already capable of being.

I did finally wise up to this diet nonsense and worked on the inside stuff (believing I was fit and healthy and sexy), and the outside stuff melted off. Those daily trips to the ATM to deposit money from the items I sold online didn't hurt, either!

If you want to live a financially free life, you can't see yourself as broke, and you must not do "broke people things." Broke people things are: borrowing for liabilities, using one credit card to pay off another, consolidating debt.

You absolutely must do wealthy people things. Wealthy people things are regularly investing in retirement before spending money on other things and keeping liquid savings on hand for emergencies. You have to see yourself as financially free and live in accordance with that. You take action toward those things, and you reinforce the belief that you are someone who is financially free.

We also need to talk openly and honestly about something important here. Being broke is very different than being poor. Being broke is a privilege. Being broke is "I made bad choices" but the privilege is that those were choices to begin with.

People who live in poverty are there not because of financial mistakes but because of systemic issues that run so much deeper than "I bought some dumb stuff on my credit card when I was in university."

Poverty is often rooted in discrimination. It's usually not random. And it is usually damn near impossible to escape.

It is my biggest challenge because those of us that advocate for financial literacy have to teach you this idea of personal responsibility. But by teaching it, the implication is that if you are poor you are just not trying hard enough, and that is catastrophically untrue. Until we can all work together and figure out how to change the system, taking personal responsibility is our only option. But we must recognize that personal responsibility varies and is inherently discriminatory.

When I'm talking about "broke people things," I am not talking about systemically poor issues. Those are much deeper issues not covered by this book; however, when you start doing "wealthy people things" and you've created and lived into a new identity as a wealthy person, I hope that you use your finances and your resources to support organizations and individuals that are actively fighting food insecurity, lack of education access, lack of healthcare and medical access, social injustice, and any other issue that you feel called to.

I'm certainly not someone who will tell you what you need to do with your wealth, but I have a hard time seeing how, after you work so hard for so long to pay off all your debt, you would feel entirely fulfilled by shopping, trips, and indulgences. I know deep inside you there is a cause that resonates with you, and while I want you to take some of your money and treat yourself and your loved ones, I also want you to connect intimately with the part of you that is called to serve in a big way.

I've heard people say that they donate their time to charity and that's enough. It's not. Charities are typically amazing at stretching a dollar, and your donation can often mobilize so many more manpower hours than you alone can give. It's important to remain in a posture of financial generosity, so you can remember that you don't own any of the money you have. Your role is simply to manage it and manage it well.

Who *are* you? Let's spend a moment thinking about this identity. Use your journal to write out the first thing that comes to mind.

Who are you when it comes to money? When it comes to family? When it comes to your community and your world?

How do you show up for others? How do you show up for yourself?

How do your new financial debt-free habits line up with these things? What is your belief system around allocating your resources to serve your family and your community and people who are not as blessed as you?

> Tammy L. says: "I paid off $72G in consumer debt and I will never use a credit card again. I think about money differently now. It excites me to build wealth and give instead of satiating my feelings with impulsive spending. Erin Skye Kelly's approach is about so much more than becoming debt free. She's the kick in the ass I never knew I needed."

Chapter Twenty-Three

YOUR NEW CREDIT CARD IS CASH

EMERGENCY FUND

You have proven to yourself that you are exceptional at paying off debt, and the transition from debt to wealth-building should be seamless, but it's not. This is much like how many people who have been studying for years in school find the transition to the working world challenging. Many people who have been on a certain healthy food plan for months find navigating a restaurant menu difficult. You've got to ease into trusting yourself while proving you can do it along the way.

If you are worried about "falling back into debt," then play along with this strategy. Pretend you are still in it! We need to move you to the wealth-building part of the process, but first we have to save up some money for emergencies.

1. You're now going to work to ensure that no emergencies will derail your finances ever again, and you are going to start taking the money you were using every month to put toward debt and *create a proper cash emergency fund.*

Here's a little guideline if you are unsure how much you will need.

If you work in an in-demand industry and you are solid in your skills and career (you don't get fired very often, and you keep on top of technology and innovation in your industry), then you need three months of expenses banked away.

You'll know your monthly expenses because you've been budgeting, so you'll add up all the expenses and multiply the expenses by three.

If you are self-employed and your services are in demand and your industry is in demand, *or* you are employed in a field where your job is more at risk (meaning it would take you three to four months to find a new job if you lost this one), you will need six months of expenses.

If you are a business owner or self-employed, or you work in a volatile industry, or have a lucrative position, you will need nine months of expenses.

That is a lot of money. But for now, you'll accumulate it. Once you've been building wealth consistently for two years, I'll let you take half of this emergency fund and invest it in something fairly liquid but non-registered. Non-registered money is money that is not tax-sheltered, and registered money is usually best left for retirement purposes. It's *very important* that emergency fund money isn't registered because in an emergency, you don't want to be cashing out your future retirement to pay for today. Plus, there are often taxes withheld at time of withdrawal, depending on how you've invested it. Right now, your job is only to put it in a high-interest savings or checking account on top of that Quick and Dirty in your *Safe Zone* where there are no fees.

2. You're going to put this money away for *two years* before you reevaluate how much you need for emergencies. That gives you a good head start to fully understand what kind of emergencies you might experience, and once you've hit the two-year mark and you've built up some investments that are registered, you can reduce the amount of cash in your emergency fund *if you've not ever needed it. This is only for those of you who believe money "should" not be sitting in a savings account because it's not doing anything.* But in those two years,

you are going to be investing and growing your assets, so hopefully you'll have a change of heart about cash for emergencies.

Then in a couple years, if you have a smaller emergency fund but lots of investments, if you lose your job or a worldwide pandemic hits, you will use the cash on hand for the first few weeks. But as time carries forward during those weeks and you have a handle on the time horizon, you can cash out some of those non-registered investments (the liquid ones) to use for emergencies. Cashing out an investment usually takes three to five business days so that still gives you lots of time. Again, this is only if you believe you are "wasting" money by having it sit in the bank account. Remember that when it is invested and non-registered, the growth on it will be taxable.

But here's how you trick the brain.

3. You're going to put that amount—the amount you've determined is your proper emergency fund amount—and temporarily add it to your liabilities. You *owe* yourself now!

Let's say you've determined that your emergency fund amount needs to be $5000. And let's say you've got $1200/month that you had previously been putting toward debt that is now ready to be handled. If you do nothing, this money will disappear. So you are going to keep paying off "debt," but this time it's imaginary debt, and it's to you.

But this debt-that-isn't-really-debt will get you practiced at not using "open available balances" on your credit cards. Remember: an available balance *is not money*.

You'll continue to budget as before. You've got the equivalent of one paycheck in there already. You'll put $1200/month toward your emergency fund, *plus whatever else* you can squeeze out of the budget. In less than four months, you'll have your emergency fund set and ready to go, and you can delete it off the liabilities side of the spreadsheet. If you've got it in a high-interest savings account, you can move it over to the asset side of your spreadsheet if you are insistent, but remember this is not technically a true asset. This is simply a representation of monthly expenses you haven't paid out yet because you don't know what your emergency is going to be.

As you are doing this, you will start researching the types of investments that interest you, so you don't waste a minute of investment time because you are overwhelmed or indecisive about where to put your new wealth-building money.

Once your emergency fund is funded, I want you to do something fun with your money. Not from your emergency fund and certainly not from your credit card (if you even still have that thing).

Please plan ahead. Budget and pick something meaningful to you. Otherwise, if you let your emotions decide, you'll be sitting in consumer shrapnel, wondering what happened to all the lovely habits you spent months developing.

Take some time, figure out what your freedom present is going to be, and pay cash for it.

Make sure you tag me on social media—I love celebrating your successes!

AN ACCOUNT TO PAY YOUR INCOME TAXES

This is simply a brief note to say: I want you to start paying attention to your income taxes and the amount you owe the government every year. Most people pay their taxes as a reaction. I want you to proactively prepare and know what your tax situation will look like. Especially if you are a business owner, or if you are self-employed, I want you to carefully assess whether you've been financially prepared for your tax bills every year. If not, I want you to start putting money aside each month into a no-fee account to pay those dang income taxes. It's time to shift. This money *can* be held in the same emergency fund account if you want to keep it simple, but it is over-and-above your emergency fund money. Otherwise, simply open a separate account called personal income taxes. (You'll hopefully already be doing this inside your business for your business taxes. Right? *Right?!*)

You can also potentially use this money to *reduce* the amount of taxes payable by investing in one of the tax-deferral options available to you, but whatever money you've put aside for paying your income tax at the end of the year that you *don't* use can go toward wealth-building and investing!

So now:

- You are a budget guru.
- Your net worth is consistently increasing.
- You've paid off all your consumer debt.
- You have a proper cash emergency fund.
- You are proactive about your income taxes.

It's time to become an investor!

The biggest investment mistake is not usually where people put their money. The biggest investment mistake people make is not starting.

If you get overwhelmed by details, you are less likely to begin. Often when people are looking for investment advice, they are:

1. Looking for someone to just tell them where to put their money and what to invest it in.
2. Asking questions too advanced for someone who has no actual assets.

No one is going to be able to make investment decisions for you. It's as personal as, "How do you like to wear your hair?" If this was the 1990s and you said, "I want the Rachel cut," you know it isn't going to look nearly as cute on you as it did on her because you are not Rachel Green. There is no one-size-fits all investment plan, so you truly have to devote a bit of time each day to research.

Another challenge to keep in mind: you might read or hear things about investments, and you'll look for professional investment advice in places you won't find it. I'm going to tell you the truth, even though it pains me to say this. Most skilled financial planners don't want your $1200/month. Many of them get paid on commission of their total book value (the asset total that their clients have), and because there are only so many hours in a day, they usually only take clients that have a minimum of $250,000 in liquid investable assets.

If you're just starting out, you likely don't quite have that much yet. So sometimes the answer is just to start, and amass some money while you learn. That way, when you are refining your investment skills, you'll know things like "how your portfolio is weighted," and you'll know what financial products you are comfortable investing in, and you'll know your risk tolerance.

When you are starting out, it can feel a little bit like throwing spaghetti at a wall to see what sticks. It sucks that really experienced financial planners aren't terribly interested in helping you (unless you have an "in" somewhere), but we do need to respect that they got where they are because they learned how to master their time.

> Rachel (not the one with the famous haircut) says: "I am coming up on a full year of budgeting every paycheck. Getting closer and closer to being debt-free and now I feel more gratified about tracking my money than spending it (most of the time.) Considering I used to get surprised by every credit card bill, and cry in frustration when I opened them, this is a milestone for me. Forever thankful to 'Get the Hell Out of Debt' and ESK for helping build actual money muscles!"

Chapter Twenty-Four

BECOMING AN INVESTOR AND LAYING OUT YOUR OPTIONS

You're going to start by creating an at-a-glance-chart for yourself so you can see what your potential options are when it comes to starting out as an investor.

TAX-FREE GROWTH	TAX-DEFERRED GROWTH	MORTGAGE PRE-PAYMENTS	OTHER

COLUMN NUMBER ONE IS TAX-FREE GROWTH

These are accounts that protect your investment from being taxable. You put in your after-tax dollars (money you've already paid tax on, like money from your paycheck) through one of these accounts and then any of the interest you earn on these accounts cannot be taxed.

Otherwise, any time you earn money from an investment, you *have* to pay tax on it (unless you buy the investment *through* a tax-free growth account).

These are accounts like the TFSA (tax-free savings account) in Canada. If you're in the US, it's Roth IRAs, or if you're abroad, it's ISA, or investment savings accounts. These are accounts where you can deposit money and the growth is not taxable. So, if you set aside $10,000 from your budget and you decide to invest it in a mutual fund *through* your tax-free growth account and over time it grows to $20,000, you will have experienced a $10,000 gain.

Because you invested this through your tax-free growth account, you do not have to pay income tax on that $10,000 gain; all of the growth is yours to keep. And you already paid the income tax on the $10,000 initial deposit, so basically, no more tax on that money.

In your country, you will have a limit as to how much money you can invest in your tax-free growth account, and this number is available to you as a taxpayer. You will need to look it up on your last tax return or contact your country's tax revenue service to get your exact number.

If you've never invested in this before, and you have it available to you, you probably have a lot of contribution room. If you've been making investments or contributions to this type of account, you probably have less contribution room. So that's your homework. Figure out how much contribution room you have in that account.

You'll write that number in the first column under Tax-Free Growth.

COLUMN NUMBER TWO IS TAX-DEFERRED GROWTH

These are accounts that your government says you can invest your money in now, but then pay tax on when you are old and wrinkly.

You put in "pre-tax dollars" (money you will not be taxed on today) through one of these accounts and then any of the interest you earn on these accounts will be taxed when you withdraw it, presumably when you are much older.

Remember, any time you earn money from an investment you *have* to pay tax on it. And when you buy the investment *through* a tax-deferred account, you are delaying or deferring the payment of the tax until you are a senior citizen.

This is a registered retirement savings plan (RRSP) in Canada. In the US it would be like a traditional 401k, or if you're abroad, it would be a pension in the UK or a superannuation in Australia.

In your country, you will have a limit as to how much money you can invest in your tax-deferred growth account, and this number is available to you as a taxpayer. You will need to look it up on your last tax return or contact your country's tax revenue service to get your exact number. Your number is unique to you as it depends on how much you've already invested, your annual income, and the number of years you've been a taxpayer.

Once you know your maximum limit, write that number in the second column under Tax-Deferred Growth.

Both Column One and Column Two are "registered" accounts. Think about it as, "These accounts are registered with the government," meaning the government will track these accounts for taxation purposes.

COLUMN NUMBER THREE IS MORTGAGE PREPAYMENTS

If you are a renter, you can skip this column. If you currently have an existing mortgage, you'll need to look up what your prepayment privileges are. If you are hoping to get a mortgage one day, you don't need to do anything with this column; we are currently just laying out what options you have for all the money you were previously putting toward debt.

As a homeowner, if you can increase your mortgage payment amounts, record that number here. If you can make a lump sum annual payment, record that here along with any pertinent dates and terms that affect your mortgage contract.

COLUMN NUMBER FOUR IS "OTHER"

This would be any taxable investments, any rental properties, registered disability savings plans, or any sort of other type of investments that you either have or that you'd consider getting. You'll do the same as you did with the other columns: record any relevant numbers and dates that can help you see everything at a glance.

This is going to be the basis by which you make some decisions. You basically spread it all out and look at it and see what makes the most sense for you.

Let's imagine you have $52,300 in unused contribution room available to you in tax-free growth. You have $18,300 in unused contribution room available in tax-deferred growth.

In your mortgage prepayment options, let's imagine you have a $120,000 total balance on your mortgage. This year you can put up to $12,000 max until August 1st, and then after August 1st until next year, you can put another $12,000 down, but you can also increase your monthly payment by $300.

TAX-FREE GROWTH	TAX-DEFERRED GROWTH	MORTGAGE PRE-PAYMENTS	OTHER
Contribution Room $52,300	Contribution Room $18,300	Contribution Room $12,000 maximum pre-payments until August 1 can also increase monthly payment by $300	

So now let's imagine you've paid off all of your debt, and you have at least $1500 a month available for investments. Just like you did with your debt, you will decide what your wealth priorities will be. You're going to look at all of the options and then make a decision. There's not a right or wrong answer when you're starting.

Eventually, as you become savvier, you're going to find that some options will make more sense than others. But like I said before, waiting to make the "right decision" often prevents people from making any decision, so getting started, paying attention, and tracking your progress is the best gift you can give yourself now.

If you can't decide between two options, the best way to manage is to put both scenarios in your net worth spreadsheet and see what happens. "If I do this on my mortgage, what does it look like in ten years? If I do this in this investment, what does it look like in ten years? What does it look like in five years? What does it look like next year?" Play with the numbers and see because the numbers won't lie—but our emotions often try to trick us!

And remember that math matters less than behavior. There's always going to be someone—your brother-in-law, your Great Aunt Mildred, your coworker who knows everything—who tells you there's a better mathematical way to do things, but do them your way anyway *because the habit-building is the most important part in the beginning.* Don't invest in anything you do not understand, of course. But decide today what you want to start with, and start. Once you know what you're investing in, you can change your strategy if it makes sense to do so especially once you've hired trusted professional advice. But make a commitment now for your dollars so you make a commitment to your learning and growth.

Choose how much of your $1500/month is going to go toward investing. Choose how much is going to go toward mortgage pay-down if that's important to you. Choose how much is going to go toward education, or upgrading to three-ply toilet paper. Decide ahead of time, commit, then act.

CHOOSE YOUR WEALTH-BUILDING ORDER OF OPERATIONS

For instance, maybe you determine that you will max out your tax-free growth options first, then pay off your mortgage. This is because you can withdraw from the tax-free growth investments without penalty if something happens, or if you decide to make a lump sum contribution to your tax-deferred growth once a year (because you can't withdraw from your tax-deferred growth without a tax hit).

Much like you did with your debt, you'll make a list and attack your goals that way! You can start squirreling away your $1500/month into an account you designate as your "Squeeze Account" and have your investments automatically withdrawn from that one squeeze bank account so you don't have to think about it once it is set up. Having a separate, no-fee Squeeze Account from your regular checking account can set you up for success. You'll take the money you squeeze from your budget and transfer it from your checking/daily banking into this Squeeze Account so you don't accidentally spend it. Then you can have your investments come out of the new Squeeze Account when *you* decide.

Because you are in Phase Three, I'm happy to have you automate some of the wealth-building. I wanted you to be very conscious and intentional about money in Phases One and Two, so I am not a fan of automatic withdrawals in those phases. But once you've proven you've mastered your numbers and are now in Phase Three, feel free to automate if you can consistently make wealth-building an automatic part of the budget. Anything extra you squeeze out of the budget becomes a wealth-building bonus.

Play with the numbers, but most importantly, *make a decision and then immediately act on it.*

Christy says: "I felt a physical weight releasing from my shoulders the minute I paid off my last debt. Learning how to be in control of my money and financial choices was absolutely liberating and I haven't looked back. Thank you Get the Hell Out of Debt for teaching me the tools to change my life."

Chapter Twenty-Five

CHOOSE YOUR WEALTH-BUILDING ORDER OF OPERATIONS

Pinky swear you're only going to invest in things you understand! Don't ever put money in an investment that you feel confused by or that came as a hot tip from someone else.

On that note, people often ask, *what should I invest in?* And I can't answer that for you because I don't know what you're going to understand. It's truly important that you pick something that you understand. So, I'm going to run through just the basics of a few different investments. Now, your tax-free growth account or tax-deferred account are not actual investments. If you are like, "Hey, you've said that before," then that tells me you are getting it! Those are cases or jackets or buckets that your investments are held in, in order to determine the taxation on them. But within those different accounts/buckets, you can hold stocks or mutual funds or ETFs or all kinds of things that *are* the *actual* investment.

So, once you've opened your tax-free savings account, or your ISA, or your Roth IRA, you still have to then invest the money you've deposited *in* something. You are only investing *through* those accounts to determine taxation as those accounts are registered with the government, but your *investment* is not with the government.

Let's say you have one hundred dollars in cash.

You can put it in your mattress and it will never drop in face value. But it *will* drop in purchasing power. What this means is if you buy a cart of groceries at the beginning of the year and that cart costs one hundred dollars on January 1st, the cost is likely to go up in time.

Based on what's happened in the last decade or so, if you pulled that one hundred dollars out of your mattress twelve months later to buy the same cart of groceries, you wouldn't have enough. The price of those groceries would have increased and now cost $102. The proper word for this is inflation.

In 1913, a loaf of bread would have cost you about $0.06. A hundred years later, the cost of bread increased by 2439 percent to $1.42. If your great nana had put $0.06 in an envelope and wrote "do not open until the next century" on the front and you finally just opened it now and saw her note that said "Treat thyself to a loaf of bread, my future loin fruit," you would laugh hysterically.

Forget about the Kardashians…you need to at least be "keeping up with inflation" and that's why putting money in your mattress isn't the best way to save for retirement.

This is also why savings accounts are not a great retirement option. If inflation is increasing by 2 percent a year, and your savings account is paying 1.5 percent, you still are falling behind in your retirement. If your retirement isn't growing at least at the rate of inflation, you are lowering your standard of living in your old age.

And let's get real. It's not good enough to simply "keep up" with inflation. That means you are only investing your one hundred dollars today to take out the equivalent of one hundred future dollars.

You want your money to mate. You want to put in one hundred money bunnies today so that you have 1000 money bunnies in the future. Since you are putting your money away anyway, why not let it bang? Yes, there is some more risk involved (this is true with all kinds of banging), but you are an adult, and you have managed all kinds of other risks before.

Knowledge is the thing that reduces risk. We know this is true because we watched a marmy teacher put a condom on a banana when we were still in school. Sex ed, as uncomfortable as it might be, has a positive effect on society because it increases knowledge and improves attitudes related to sexual and reproductive health.

When it comes to investing, learning what you can might be uncomfortable and awkward at first, but it will improve your knowledge and your attitude when it comes to money, which has a direct effect on your financial health.

You have to pick what you want to invest your cash in, so that it can actually grow. So here is a brief synopsis of just *some* of the more popular investments.

STOCKS

They're probably the most well-known when it comes to investing. You likely know someone who bragged about their stock purchase at some time. (Secret insider tip: we all brag about our wins in the stock market, but we are usually pretty quiet on our big dumb mistakes.) This can lead you to believe that the stock market is the magic lottery ticket to wealth.

This is not true; it can definitely be a gamble, especially if you don't know what you are doing.

When you buy stocks, you're taking a share or a part of a company. Because most of us can't afford to invest in a whole company today, that company can divide itself up into parts, and you can buy a portion of it, or "shares" in the company. This allows the company to raise money, and in return for your money, you are entitled to some of the company's profits, in relation to how many shares you own. These shares have a value and they can be bought and sold on the stock market.

There are many stock markets around the world, and you can access these opportunities through brokers or brokerages, depending if you want a human to help you, or if you want to do it yourself.

What it means to you: You can start investing in companies that are of interest to you and potentially increase your net worth.

What it allows you to do: When there is high demand for the stock, the price of your shares will increase. When the company isn't doing too well, or there is a decrease in demand for the stock, the price of your share will decrease. Obviously, you want to "buy low and sell high" so learning about different strategies will be important as some people prefer to buy stocks for the long term, and others prefer to trade frequently. There are also many advanced strategies to reduce risk. You'll need to first figure out what strategy works for you.

BONDS

Essentially you are lending money to an entity. Companies can issue corporate bonds, governments issue bonds, the US treasury issues treasury bonds. After the bond matures (which means after you've had it for a certain amount of time), you earn back the money that you spent plus interest.

The interest is usually predetermined or fixed, and the rate of return for bonds is much lower than it can be for other types of investing. But bonds are also considered lower risk. That's often the way investments work: the higher the risk, the higher the return, but also the greater the potential loss. The lower the risk, the lower the return, but you might not lose as much money. When you become a sophisticated investor, you can often see opportunities for higher returns with not much risk, but that comes from education and experience over time.

What it means to you: You can have a bit of certainty with your investments, compared to the uncertainty and fluctuations that happen in the stock market.

What it will allow you to do: You can put money into a bond and know you'll get it back. Twenty-one years ago, I lent money I barely had to this friend named Shawna for textbooks, and then she disappeared. She apparently quit her college program and changed her name to Ocean. Even though I have not seen or talked to her in over twenty years, I am bonded with her for life over this. Ocean, if you are reading this, that money is now a gift because that was a very expensive lesson in boundaries I apparently needed to learn. The only money I'll "lend" now is in a proper bond investment.

MUTUAL FUND

A mutual fund is a pool of many investors' money and a pool of companies or stocks. Actively managed funds have a fund manager, who is usually some fancy person who went to some fancy school and wears a fancy suit to work. They choose everything that's going to go in the fund. You're paying them a percent, usually a large percent, like 1 to 2 percent. (Doesn't sound like a lot, but it's a lot when you consider they get that money no matter how well they do their job, and they take it the entire time your money is invested with them. It adds up!) But they do the stock picking for you, and you are supposed to get a return on that money.

Some mutual funds only invest in stocks. Some invest in bonds and stocks. So, it's important to read about the fund you are choosing and have a general idea of the types of companies the fund has. All that information is available to you publicly, and usually through the bank or brokerage you are doing your investing through. Don't read it before bed though, because they make those bits of information (called a prospectus) boring AF, and you'll fall asleep on page two.

What it means to you: This is a very easy way to get "into the market" and usually for very little money each month.

What it will allow you to do: Buying mutual funds is one way to start increasing your net worth while you learn about other investments too. Because you don't have to watch these investments as closely as you might watch individual stocks, you can spend more time increasing your knowledge while leaving your money to (hopefully!) make money bunnies.

EXCHANGE TRADED FUNDS.

ETFs. They're *kind of* like mutual funds. When you buy a mutual fund, the price you pay on a mutual fund is the price at the end of the trading day. (Once the stock market is closed, they take the data from the various company trades and come up with the mutual fund price for that day.) The price of an ETF fluctuates throughout the day. An ETF provider gathers up assets, including stocks, bonds, commodities or currencies, and creates a bucket of them, and gives it a specific name or "ticker." Investors can buy a part of that bucket, just like buying shares of a company. These were invented when mutual fund investors were irritated that their mutual fund returns weren't as good as the general market returns.

What it means to you: ETFs give you a way to get involved with buying and selling a bucket of assets without having to buy all the components individually. ETFs can often have wildly fluctuating returns, so if you are starting out, you'll want to be clear on the type of risk you can tolerate. If you are putting money away for a long time, don't let these fluctuations bother you.

What it will allow you to do: ETFs are often recommended to new investors because they're more diversified than stocks and they're cheaper than mutual funds in terms of the fee. (Usually, but not always! Be sure to read the fine print before you make an investment.) Sometimes they are actively managed, but sometimes a robot does it, which means lower fees. (I know, I used to think that Optimus Prime was handling my money, but it just means that brokerage is an online platform or "robo-advisor" and not some dude with file folders.)

CDS/GICS/TERM DEPOSITS

The next type of investment that's quite common is a CD (certificate of deposit) in the USA, a GIC (guaranteed investment certificate) in Canada, or term deposit elsewhere in the world. It's a low-risk investment. You give the bank a certain amount of money for a set amount of time. When that's over, you get your money back plus a little bit of interest.

What this means to you: You are usually just handing your money over to someone else to stuff in their mattress or their bra. My friend Brandie has this magical ability to hold things in her lady-gonch. Once, I gave her something to hold for me, and when she returned it, she also pulled out a wallet, a phone, a set of keys, and an apple out of her top. Your money will be safe in Brandie's bra, but you can't retire with it. (I mean, *she* certainly can if she decides to monetize these tricks.)

What it will allow you to do: It will allow you to feel safe if you worry about fluctuations in the market. Because this money won't dip in value, you'll get all of it back, plus a couple apples.

ANNUITIES

When you think "annuities," I want you to think "old age." You wouldn't invest in an annuity while you're starting out. It's a contract with an insurance company that gives periodic payments. Usually when people are well into retirement (think around seventy-five years old), they'll convert their investments to an annuity to have a guaranteed income stream.

What this means to you: They're low risk, but they are not high growth. You wouldn't be looking to *build wealth* within an annuity. You're looking to *take your wealth out* when you have an annuity.

What it will allow you to do: When you are eating supper at 4:00 p.m. and watching daytime TV game shows on full volume, this will allow you to budget for the rest of your living years by knowing how much money you can withdraw comfortably without going broke.

CRYPTOCURRENCY

These are fairly new investment options, but in the last ten years they've really gained popularity. Bitcoin is the most famous type of cryptocurrency, but there are lots of cryptocurrencies out there. They're digital files, and because of something called blockchain technology, it's really tough for crypto to be counterfeit. They are typically "decentralized" meaning they are not part of any government system, which makes them less prone to interference or inflation. You can buy and sell them on crypto exchanges. They even have ATMs for crypto. They can have wild fluctuations so they can be quite risky, and it's not a typical place to start for first time investors, but like anything, the more knowledge you have, the more informed you become in your decisions. Heads up that in some countries now, you can buy cryptocurrencies through a regulated platform. Make sure you know if your platform is regulated, if that matters to you.

What this means to you: You can transfer money between two parties without the interference of a bank or third party.

What it will allow you to do: Crypto allows you to hold money outside of the systems that are usually affected by typical market conditions.

REAL ESTATE

If you're buying real estate, what you're doing is providing a home or business space (if you're buying commercial real estate) and renting that out in order to get some sort of return on your money. You can buy real estate as an individual, or you can buy it as part of a real estate income trust. There are all kinds of ways you can purchase real estate, but the idea is if you are buying it, the goal is to always have more money coming in than going out. That's what makes it cash flow. Although it's not very liquid (meaning the day you list it for sale is rarely the day you complete the transaction), it can often be a stable source of cash-flow income—if you take the time to learn how to do it effectively.

This is how I started investing as a teenager. I think my first down payment was about $5000, and because I was young and dumb, I didn't have much to lose. True story: the reason I chose my first rental property was because I loved the mint green carpet. This is definitely not how I make investment decisions today.

What this means to you: Real estate is an investment that is usually easy to understand because you can physically see it, whereas most other investments are theoretical concepts.

What it will allow you to do: Have someone else pay down the mortgage for you while putting a little cash in your pocket, *if you invest properly for cash flow.* It could also mean a giant pit you shovel money into every month.

Those are just some of the investments that you could look at if any of those interest you, but it's by no means a comprehensive list. It's not even enough to say, "I am now financially literate!" True financial literacy comes from understanding the value of your potential and existing investments. To be fully fluent, you'll need to be actively investing.

I wanted to provide a basic distinction of some of the options out there because as I mentioned to you earlier, I often hear people say, "I have a retirement account!" and I'm all, "What is it invested in?" And they have no flippin' clue. This is your opportunity to research more if there is something that interests you.

I want you to have a clue. I want you to have complete comprehension of what you are invested in, why you are invested in it, and how the investment grows. I want you to understand how it will impact your cashflow at retirement so that you can live the life you dream about.

Amélie says: "Since transferring my tax-free growth money into a self directed account and starting to buy/sell stocks I have increased that account by 28 percent! That account had only been fluctuating up and down with the market by a couple hundred dollars for at least five years. Thank you to Get the Hell Out of Debt for giving me the tools and confidence to try investing!"

Chapter Twenty-Six

WE START BY STARTING

One of my participants, Wendy, said the most brilliant thing. She had been trying to find the right time. It's a classic procrastinator move, and if you are an overthinker, I know you've done it too. It's when you are waiting for the right time to begin something. Sometimes you plan and schedule and get exhausted from the planning, and then you never begin. Sometimes you can research your plan to death and get overwhelmed and never start. Wendy finally became sick of not making progress because of being overwhelmed and announced, "I have started by starting."

Months later, she was well on her way to her goal.

IF YOU HAVE NO IDEA WHERE YOU WANT TO START, START HERE

Open up a TFSA/ISA/Roth IRA

These are accounts that are set up for growth but that you can access before retirement if you'd like. Some banks and institutions will tell you these accounts are where you save for major purchases. But I'd like you to take advantage of the tax-free growth in these accounts for your wealth-building, not for your consumer shopping. Don't withdraw this money to buy a car. Or go on vacay. Use this money for true and proper financial freedom.

If you do the work, you can use this money's baby bunnies to buy the car, or go on vacay, without ever draining the account of the initial mating money. Basically, you keep the principal invested and potentially spend the interest or profit only.

Contributions to these accounts are *not* tax-deductible, meaning that you will have already paid income tax on this money before you invest it, but any money that investment earns is not taxable.

What's important right now is you can look and see how far you've truly come…and trust that with the experience you've had so far, you can do this too.

In time, as you grow as an investor, you'll have more conversations with people about investing. You'll be drawn to articles and books about investing. You'll catch the news when it comes to investing.

This is all already wired inside your brain. It's a system called the Reticular Activating System, or RAS. The more clarity you have around the results you want, the more your brain goes on a covert operation to make it happen. When I bought my first grey Jeep, all I saw on the road for years were Jeeps. I didn't tell my brain to do that; it was just braining around, doing brain things.

When you start investigating and getting clear about investing, your brain will start its mission of seeking out investments. The job of the RAS is to filter things. If you noticed *everything all the time*, you would go quite crazy. Your brain has to bring some things front and center and push other things back, and that's the entire job of the RAS. Once you decide what's most important to you, your brain is relentless in bringing you information, and you can choose if you want to act on it or not.

Your RAS will catch the things you need it to know. We just have to activate that RAS and let it work for us.

Truly, the important part is to simply start. If you buy the Jeep and it turns out it doesn't have enough horsepower (or in my case, enough cup holders), then you just make a new decision on your next vehicle. But this time you have the experience of buying the first vehicle to help you make a better decision on the next.

GET STARTED BY STARTING

1. You'll first make sure you are eligible for your IRA/TFSA/ISA by hitting ye ol' Google machine.
2. Then you're going to decide which institution you are going to open your account at. You'll ask a few of your friends, the ones who are actively preparing for retirement, to see what their experience with that institution has been. Then, you'll research to find out if there is a fee to open or maintain it. Also, check to see if the company provides customer support online or only in-person at a branch (you want to be able to access it when you want it, so choose a service level that makes sense for your life).
3. Do they offer the types of investments you want? Exchange Traded Funds (ETFs), target-date funds, mutual funds, stocks, bonds? If you have no idea what you want, you may want to ensure they have a variety of options as you learn. You can always start with good ol' mutual funds, which require no active management from you but do come with typically heavy fees, around 2 percent (which again, doesn't sound like much but can actually eat away at your profits). If you have an 8 percent gain on your investment, but there is a 2 percent fee, that's 25 percent of your gain. As you learn more about the other investments, you can diversify, but the institution you invest with will ask you a few risk-tolerance questions to help you decide on the best fund for you while you learn. This is how I started, and I'm so glad I did, fee-heavy as it was.
4. If you plan to trade frequently (stocks, for example), find out how much each trade costs. There is often a fee, and those fees add up quickly if you are not paying close attention to them. Some brokerages have monthly fees, and some have per-trade fees. You'll choose the best fit for you.

5. The good news is there are bloggers and nerds who pay attention to this all the time, so you can check in with nerds in your area to see what they have analyzed to be this year's best institutions and accounts. But before you just take anyone's advice on the internet, check to see if they are getting a kickback or affiliate payment for their recommendation, just so you are a critical thinker when it comes to a person's motivation when giving you advice.
6. Next, you're going to open the account. You'll need your ID, and you might be asked to designate a beneficiary, which is the person who gets this moola when you croak. You'll want to keep this up-to-date, especially after major life events like marriage, birth, divorce, or death of a beneficiary. The reason you want to designate someone (or sometimes even a charity) is because if you do not select someone, the funds go into a legal process after you die, so your loved ones might not even end up with it. Much of your money will get chewed up by some of the legal fees that will be incurred as this is processed. Yuck. Take the time to choose a beneficiary, but make sure your estate has enough to pay all your taxes after you die. You don't want the tax man coming after your beneficiaries for money later (this can happen, depending on where you live). Once you add the tax man to the list, it is way too many people for you to remember to haunt when you're dead. Best to make sure you are thinking of these things while you are alive and well.
7. Now, you are going to choose what you are going to actually invest in.

    There are usually three ways you can do this.

Number One: The first is simply by hiring a financial advisor, which is usually someone who is selling that company's products and is paid a commission to do so. They usually have some sort of formal training, will give you advice, and will often place your trade for you. You can also choose an independent advisor, and sometimes they charge a fee for their service instead of earning commissions. You'll want to choose a fiduciary when possible, which is a person or entity legally and ethically who must act in your best interest above their own. In many countries, the financial industry operates on a "duty-of-care" model, which simply means a financial advisor must operate "fairly, honestly, and in good faith," which is a little more whimsical than a fiduciary.

Number Two: You could buy a target-date fund or a mutual fund that is designed by the company you opened your account with. This would match you to a fund that is supposed to perform a certain way and aligns with your risk tolerance and your time horizon.

Number Three: You could also design your own portfolio by picking your own choices from the various institutions you are familiar with.

In the beginning, most people start with number two, but I would love to see you get to the place where you are capable of number three, even if you choose not to also have a number one. You ultimately are responsible for your own results in life. That investment advisor doesn't care about your retirement as much as you do. Your financial planner doesn't care as much as you do. They are all doing their best, but at the end of the day, you still have to know what is going on with your dollars to feel comfortable with your choices. You are the most invested in your retirement out of anyone, so you might as well pay attention to it now and become proficient in it.

People often want to know what the rate of return on their investment is going to be. With debt, you know straight up you are paying 17.5 percent interest on that credit card, for example. But with investing, the rate of return fluctuates. You can look at historical rates of return to get an idea of how something performed in the past, but depending on what you invest in, you won't know the exact rate of future return. Just like your past performance is not an indicator of your future success, the past performance of an investment isn't a guarantee of its future success. Once you've had your money invested for a while, you can learn what is called your "return on investment," or ROI. This is calculated by taking the net return of an investment and dividing it by the cost of the investment. So, if you invested $1000 and your investment was now worth $1200, you would take

$200/1000, and that would give you 0.2 expressed as a percent (0.2 x 100) = 20 percent return or 20 percent ROI. This number becomes very important to you as you learn.

Once your account is open, you are going to continue squeezing as much out of your budget as you can toward your investment(s).

You don't necessarily need multiple accounts at multiple institutions. The reason you'd open up another account would be because the institution you are currently with doesn't have the product you want to invest in. If you do open multiple investment accounts, you'll need to track them somehow, so it can be meaningful to create a worksheet in your net worth spreadsheet. (If you are in the Get the Hell Out of Debt online program, you can use the one I use by going to the video in Phase Three that is called "Contribution Tracker.")

We do not open multiple accounts at multiple institutions because we are trying to achieve "diversification," which is a term you've maybe heard, that implies spreading out your risk. We don't achieve diversification via institutions, we achieve them through the investments themselves. Often when people are spread out over institutions, it turns out they're invested in most of the same things (i.e., a "Balanced" fund with one bank/institution is often composed of many of the same holdings as a Balanced fund at another institution). But you are going to *know* what is in your portfolios, so you can make informed decisions, versus letting a banker or advisor convince you their portfolio is better or different than the one at the institution across the street.

TAX-DEFERRED ACCOUNTS

These are accounts that you set up with retirement in mind. The contributions to these accounts *are* deductible from your income, which can reduce the amount of income tax you pay in the year that you claim contributions. No income that you earn in the account gets taxed *until* you withdraw it in your retirement years.

These investments help reduce the amount of tax you pay today. They exist to encourage citizens to help save for their own retirement needs, and they presume this is a benefit to you because the assumption is that when you retire, you will earn less income. So, the money you withdraw will be taxed lower than it would be taxed if you were paying it today.

There are typically penalties for withdrawing from these accounts early, so you'll need to be sure you intend to keep the money in there long term, and you'll also need to understand what penalties could apply to you.

If you look up your contribution maximums, you can contribute automatically to these (or check with your employer to see if they can deduct from your paycheck). Or, if you aren't sure of the contribution amount that will maximize your tax savings, you can always invest under a *tax-growth strategy* (the retirement account that grows tax-free and there are no penalties to withdraw) and once a year, pull out the number you need to put in a *tax-deferred account* to reduce the amount of tax paid.

EMPLOYER-MATCHED CONTRIBUTIONS

Yes! Do this. Whatever the employer matched amount is, do that. I don't have more to add except it is a heck of a blessing to have an employer match option because if they are matching your contribution, it is like your money is doubling. Free green bunny! Make sure you pay attention to the total number being contributed on your behalf because it will affect your contribution room. You have to be mindful of *both* the amount your employer contributes and the amount *you* contribute to be sure you aren't going over your limit.

When you are looking to invest, if you are starting out and have a fair amount of time until retirement (fifteen years or more), you typically will want to invest in growth strategies.

As you near retirement, you'll typically want to choose more conservative investments (meaning there is less risk, but the return might also be lower). This is because you don't want to face a drop in the market and lose your investment value before you retire.

I say all this with a giant caveat: you never know what the market is going to do. Anything can happen between now and the time you retire. But not taking action is almost always the strategy that leaves you broke, so at some point, you are going to have to put some money where your goals are, and now that we've freed up all that cash that was previously going toward debt, you can start there.

And once you've started, you're going to look for books and courses on investing and continue your learning. You got through this money book, didn't you? You can keep going and learn even more now. Your financial literacy now is way stronger than it was back at Chapter One. You'll know so many more things if you choose to read five investing books this year as you get the hell out of debt. I've listed some options in the recommended reading section.

> Michelle says: "The concept of the amount of money being equal to my time struck me pretty hard. I can't turn back the clock, but since Getting the Hell Out of Debt, I have spent my time so much more wisely. I am very motivated to have more of my money going to my future rather than continuing to pay for my past."

Chapter Twenty-Seven

A LIVING PAYCHECK

THE MOST MORBID CHAPTER

Now we're going to talk about you as a dead person. I know this sounds super morbid, but we really do have to get to the point where we accept the fact that we are going to die. Death is part of life, unfortunately, and while nobody wants to think about it, one of the *least* loving things we can do for the people we leave behind is to leave them in a giant financial mess while they are already mourning and grieving.

It's like going to the grave with two middle fingers in the air and screaming, "I'm out, bitches!"

Now I am not going to tell you whether or not you need to get a specific insurance product. I'm not licensed for that. Know that I'm not here to sell you anything, but I do want you to fully understand how insurance works when it comes to protecting your income.

Insurance can both:

a) Be the thing that prevents a financial disaster.

b) Be very expensive and harm our budget.

Knowing the right amount of insurance for you is going to be important because you've got to make sure you have the right risk coverage while also protecting the wealth you build.

Life insurance protects the money you would have earned had you lived long enough to earn it.

The exception might be if you already have significant assets to cover the cost of dying. I hate to say that, but death does cost money. The cost of dying includes things like debts or lost income, your funeral expenses, paying your taxes, or hiring a caterer to feed your family those sandwiches with the crusts cut off that you never eat any other time except at funerals.

The best way to take care of your loved ones (if you don't have significant assets to cover those costs) can be life insurance. Now you might say, "I don't want a funeral. I don't want any of that stuff. Don't worry about that. Just put me in a cardboard box!"

I hear you. It's going to still cost someone money.

Or maybe when you talk to your partner like I did, they tell you that they want to have a funeral pyre and when you ask, "What is a funeral pyre?" They say, "Erin! It's like what Darth Vader had. You float on a lake and then archers torch your body with flaming arrows," and you cannot even believe you sleep next to someone who is going to make you ask for "flaming archer recommendations" on Facebook while you are in the depths of despair, but you agree because love makes you do funny things.

So, we're going to need to be prepared with some insurance. But the question is always how much insurance you need.

In order to figure out what your life insurance needs are, we have to figure out two things. The first is:

1. Who do you owe?

Who do you have to pay in terms of mortgages or debts or funeral costs or taxes? What kinds of expenses might your death put upon somebody who is still living?

2. And who do you love?

Who would you be providing for after you pass, and for how long would you need to do that? Let's say, for example, you were the main income earner in a family, and you're married to somebody who is a stay-at-home parent and you have children under the age of four. You might want to be sure that the stay-at-home parent is able to continue raising the kids the way you would have planned, had you been alive. You might even want to continue that legacy for another sixteen years. Or you might want to continue only until they're school-age; you're going to have to decide how long is appropriate. And knowing these answers helps determine how much life insurance you need.

Let's look at a few types of life insurance.

Group Life Insurance

This is your workplace benefits package, and it's usually one to two times your annual salary. So, if your annual salary is $50,000 a year, you might be covered in a lump sum payout when you pass away for $50,000 to $100,000 and that would go to your named beneficiary. If you choose your partner as the main beneficiary, for example, they would receive $50,000 to $100,000 (depending on what your group package says you're entitled to) when you push up the daisies.

You need to familiarize yourself with what your coverage is like! The advantage to group coverage is: it's non-evidence coverage, which basically means you don't have to have a ton of medical tests or anything upfront in order to qualify for the insurance. And usually, it's dirt cheap compared to other types of insurance.

The disadvantage is it's generally not nearly enough for most deaths and anything above and beyond the amount they grant you is something you usually have to qualify for, and if that's the case, it's usually no longer cost effective. Either way, the cost typically goes up every year. Another disadvantage is it's not portable. And it's the biggest disadvantage, to be honest, because if you ever quit a job or get fired suddenly, this coverage is no longer applicable.

Then if you've aged like the rest of us, when you get to your new job you might not qualify for new insurance because of your age, health, or other risk factors. Often there are waiting periods for new benefits. And to make matters more stressful, you might have an uninsurable period between jobs.

Creditor or Lender Insurance

This is attached to a debt. It's the institution that lent you money that gets paid if you die. As an example, we'll use mortgage insurance.

It's one of the fifteen million pages that the banker or broker tries to get you to sign when you get your death pledge. Let's imagine you have a mortgage balance of $200,000. When you pop your clogs and you have this type of coverage in place, it will cover you for $200,000, but it pays off that mortgage directly. The advantage is that it's better than nothing. Without it, your loved ones may be forced to sell the home sooner than they're ready. And there's really not a whole lot to the application. There are usually a couple of boxes that you check and that determines the coverage, so that part can be quite simple.

But the disadvantages are mighty. The first disadvantage is that it protects the lender, not you. Your loved ones don't see any money directly, and they have no choice in how that money is directed. Imagine that I lent you money (hahahaha, not happening, don't ask) and then I took out an insurance policy on you, but then I made you pay for the insurance policy. That's what's happening with mortgage insurance.

The biggest disadvantage is that mortgage insurance is based on something called a decreasing benefit, but not a decreasing premium.

Let's say you start off with a mortgage of $200,000 and you (through the lifetime of your mortgage) pay it down to $50,000, and suppose you die when the mortgage is $50,000. You're paying the premium based on the mortgage amount of $200,000, but they're only covering you for $50,000 when you pass away. The *nerve.*

The other issue is that it's underwritten *after* you die, which means that it's not guaranteed. The insurance company has to decide whether or not you deserve the insurance. They're still happy to take your money the whole time you're paying those premiums. But upon your passing, they might say, "It looks to me like there was a preexisting condition here," and they can choose not to pay your mortgage off.

To contrast: with independent personal life insurance, you can get coverage for the $200,000 and even if you pay your mortgage down to $50,000 when you are living, your beneficiary gets the check for $200,000. They can choose to pay off the $50,000 and bank the other $150,000, or they can choose to take $200,000 and get head-to-toe tattoos. It's up to them.

Now, please go through all of your documents and if you find that you do have mortgage insurance, I don't want you to cancel it until you have other insurance in place and you have compared policies. It *is* better than nothing.

Personal Life Insurance

You own this insurance; you benefit from the insurance. Well, *you* don't benefit…the people you leave behind after you die benefit, 'cause you're dead. But you know what I mean? I'm trying to keep it light here. It's yours and it follows you everywhere regardless of your job or your location or your life changes, and your loved ones benefit, not the bank. It's often less expensive than the other types of insurance.

Once it's approved, it's guaranteed as long as you were telling the truth at time of application. It can be tempting to fib about some of your habits or proclivities, but it is best to be forthright. It often involves a medical personal history questionnaire and sometimes can require a paramedical exam, which means somebody is going to take your blood. Maybe make you pee in a cup. They check your blood pressure, that kind of a thing.

The disadvantages are that based on those results, you can be denied coverage. But! That can be temporary or permanent. If you are declined because maybe you are in a weight category that the insurance company doesn't like, and it's something you can control and choose to manage differently, you may have the option to reapply when the risk of health issues decreases. (I'm going to level with you here: you can be carrying more weight than someone else and be healthier than them, but still be uninsurable. The insurance system can be a little archaic, so you might have to practice patience and mindfulness when you apply for insurance.) The other disadvantage is if you become uninsurable, your existing insurance can get very expensive when it renews.

Under personal coverage, there are really three main types: life insurance, critical illness insurance, and disability insurance.

The first is term life insurance, and you want to get this type of insurance when your insurance need is significant. Let's say you're buying a home or you're in a two-income relationship or you've got kids. You can get a term based on a certain number of years: a ten-year policy, a twenty-year policy, a thirty-year policy, whatever the length of time that you decide. You can usually cancel it at any time. It just means that you have insurance, as long as you keep paying the premiums for that term, and the term determines the price of the premium.

At the end of the term, you can still get insurance...you just probably have to pay a higher premium because your risk has gone up. (You can also reapply at any point during the term in an attempt to secure a comparatively low rate for longer, and provided you've remained healthy, you won't see the same drastic increase in premium had you waited for it to renew.)

Another form of life insurance is permanent life insurance. It's sometimes called whole life insurance or universal...there are all sorts of different names for it. Basically, it's not on a set amount of time like a term. Meaning you have the insurance for the rest of your life, whether you die at age thirty-five or 105, and the policy increases in value over time. Think of this as "owning" the insurance for life, versus "renting" term insurance when you temporarily need a significant amount.

Cash builds up inside these permanent policies by dividends from the insurance company, and the death benefit increases with the dividends.

The disadvantage to this is: it's very expensive insurance. Oftentimes, if you compare the cost of term insurance with the cost of permanent insurance, you'll end up with more money if you buy term insurance and then invest the extra money yourself. *But!* What we know to be true is most people don't bother. Most people get term insurance, and then they just spend the rest of the money. (*Ahem.* *cough* *That used to be me.* *cough*)

You will often hear an insurance person call permanent life insurance a "forced savings program." Permanent life insurance is guaranteed to pay out, but because of that, it is not cheap.

So, here's your homework. Your first assignment is to figure out what type of life insurance you have, if any.

Go through your documents and see if you've got any group or any creditor or any personal insurance.

1. You need to know what amount of coverage you have and what premiums you pay every month.
2. Then you need to know why you have this insurance. What is the risk you are covering yourself for? Family history of breast cancer? Diabetes? Early death? Think about what illnesses are likely to affect you.
3. Who benefits from it? Who is the beneficiary of each policy? Is it the lender? Is it an ex-spouse and maybe you've forgotten to update your beneficiaries? Would your current spouse love that idea?
4. And then consider which stage of life you are in because you'll need to review if your risks when you got the insurance are still the same as the risks you have today.
5. Then you'll want to know *how* it's structured and *when* it's structured, meaning you want to know what the terms and the premiums and the riders (insurance speak for "options" or "extra features") are. Familiarize yourself with when it renews and when it pays out or *when it doesn't*...so watch for any exclusions or modifications.

I want you to go through this research process so you can be clear on your insurance and your coverage, just to see if there are any gaps or anything you need to be aware of in case something happens to you. I mean *when* something happens to you. (We know one day you'll turn to dirt. We just hope it's not for a really long time.) I want you to become long in the tooth, but let's just make sure the people we love are cared for in case we kick the bucket before we accomplish everything on our bucket list.

Your primary focus remains paying off debt if you are still in Phase Two. So know that unless you discover you are grossly underinsured, it's important to still focus on the task at hand. Pay off those dang liabilities.

When you are over insured, it impacts your ability to pay off debt. I'm giving you this information so you can start to think about these things and make informed decisions when it is budget-appropriate for you.

And when it is time, please find an insurance broker or financial planner to help you.

In insurance circles, they often say: "If you found a goose that lays golden eggs, what would you insure: the goose or the eggs?" Most people will choose the goose. But when it comes to real life, what we actually do is we insure our stuff, our vehicles, our home, its contents, but we are very slow to insure our income.

It *boggles* my mind that you can spend hundreds of dollars on a new smartphone, and the company then convinces you to buy a phone care plan to insure the phone in case the phone breaks, which it will. *I beg your pardon, Phone Company: you know you are selling me a product that will break or become obsolete and you feel no remorse about that, and furthermore, you want me to insure* your *inadequacies?* It's *madness*, but we as consumers buy these extended warranties all the time, and yet we don't insure our *own* lives.

The second type of personal insurance is critical illness insurance. This is a lump sum that pays if you're diagnosed with one of about twenty-five really critical conditions. This protects the income lost from limitation or lack of benefits or medical expenses.

And the third type of personal insurance is disability insurance. This is ongoing monthly payments resulting from either the illness or injury, and as long as you structure the policy properly, it protects your after-tax income for as long as you would have continued to work.

And the facts are not awesome: the likelihood of a forty-year-old becoming disabled before the age of sixty-five is about 33 percent. The likelihood of you suffering a critical illness before the age of sixty-five is up to about 22 percent. And the likelihood of you dying before the age of sixty-five is only 4 to 6 percent, but of course that would be devastating to the people you leave behind. But here's the part that's scary: *your combined likelihood of becoming either disabled, critically ill, or dying before the age of sixty-five is 49 percent.*

And I know you're thinking, "But Erin! I'm indestructible! This isn't going to happen to me!"

I believe you're indestructible. Look at all the hard things you've done so far in your life, and you are still here. You cannot be stopped by a global pandemic. You are currently annihilating your debt and winning a war against a system that is designed to keep you broke, to keep you controlled. This chapter is not meant to scare you. But the probability of your insurance premiums increasing every year that you don't have coverage is 100 percent. The longer you wait to get insured, the more expensive insurance becomes. Don't use that sentence to panic-buy insurance. Use that sentence to hurry the hell up and get out of debt so you can live free from financial worry.

The probability of becoming *uninsurable* at some point is also 100 percent. You will reach a point in your life where suddenly you no longer qualify. You're too old. Your bones are creaking too much. You've had some sort of disease or there's been enough medical issues for you that an insurance company just doesn't want to touch it.

And then you have a 99 percent probability of dying eventually. (Okay. I know, you know, it's 100 percent, but I just wanted to give you some sort of win.)

With a critical illness payout, you can do whatever you want with the money. You can pay for uninsured or private medical expenses. You can replace lost income, especially if you have a person who needs to support you while you're going through something and they take unpaid time off from their work. You can go to Bora Bora for one last hurrah in your floppy hat because you just got diagnosed with something awful. The insurance company doesn't care what you do with the money.

It's designed to allow you to focus on your wellbeing.

The big question is, can you cover your bills for three years without borrowing from your investments, going into debt, or burdening any loved ones? And I say three years because that's the typical duration of this type of claim.

Of course, there are some that are shorter and some that are longer, but the point is, most of us could not pay our expenses for three years with no income.

And having a savings account with three years of expenses in it doesn't make a lot of financial sense, so it is wise to let a little bit of insurance cover those what-ifs.

Just like life insurance, you can get critical illness and disability insurance in terms. Some policies even offer return-of-premium options, which means if you never make a claim, you get 100 percent of your money back. That's the "forced savings" plan we were talking about earlier that insurance brokers love to sell. Now, obviously, if you have a bunch of money invested and that money can earn money, then you're going to be a savvy investor and take care of yourself financially. But if you're just starting to get the hell out of debt and you don't have a lot of assets yet, sometimes these other types of insurance can be beneficial for protection. You really do have to weigh the cost with the benefit and analyze what works with your budget.

The reason the insurance company sells you on these forced savings programs is because you're giving them money, but they're turning around and investing it. They keep the growth on the money. They use your money to breed money bunnies. That's how they make their money. So for critical illness insurance, the questions you're going to ask yourself are:

Where do I have gaps in my wealth-building strategies?

Where am I vulnerable?

And how much of my cash flow is dependent on me being able to work?

You're going to have to calculate your monthly expenses, which you've been doing with your expense column in your budget. Then you're going to have to figure out where you're vulnerable. If it turns out you can no longer earn an income and your partner can't work either, then you're going to have to figure out how to bridge any gaps.

Disability coverage is a "living benefit" in that it provides a monthly, ongoing, usually-tax-free payment if you're unable to work as a result of illness or injury. Essentially, it replaces your monthly paycheck. What you need to do is calculate your monthly after-tax income. (That's what you get in your pockets after you've paid taxes, otherwise known as your take home pay.) Then you multiply that number by twelve. And then by the number of years until you turn sixty-five or until you plan to retire. Calculate the difference between that number and what you've already put away now (that's not earmarked for retirement or other financial goals) and *that difference* will tell you how much disability coverage you might need.

Now, you're going to want to know this information when you get a quote, but you might get a quote and decide, "You know what? That premium is way too high for me." You might choose to take less coverage right now while you're building up some retirement savings, but it *at least gives you an idea* of where the gaps are. Disability protection is the most expensive of the three, the three being life insurance, critical illness, and disability. That's because of the odds of disability, and the amount of cash flow required to replace the income when you are on disability, is high. The maximum percentage you will qualify for is typically two thirds of your income. That tends to be equivalent to your take home pay, but the insurance companies also want to make sure that the number isn't so high that Bob and Doug don't drink a case of warm Canadian beer and get any ideas about shooting each other in the foot with a shotgun to collect a payment.

Having proper personal insurance can mean if you have a workplace injury, you're covered. If you have cancer, you're covered. If you are skydiving drunk and naked—well, if you live—you might be covered.

For how long becomes the question, and this is where it gets tricky. This is why you're going to need to have a professional really look at it. Most people just assume "I'm good. I have benefits." But here's the term you want to look out for in the fine print: *the definition of a disability*. There are two phrases that can getcha: *Regular Occupation and Any Occupation.* If your documents say that you have a regular occupation period for two years only, that means that whether you're a neurosurgeon or a professional LEGO builder (which sounds awesome, by the way), you will only receive benefits for being unable to do that job for the first two years of your disability.

If after two years of your disability, you have the ability to say, "Would you like fries with that?" you're going to be deemed capable of working and no longer eligible for benefits, regardless of any loss or decrease in earning potential. So, it's really important to know what type of occupation your disability insurance covers you for, and for how long. That's a sneaky one… you don't want to find out too late that your degree in astrophysics is irrelevant to your insurer who wants you off the insurance payment and onto the food court pavement.

Now, you have a couple of options. You can contact an insurance broker, or you could contact a financial planner. A financial planner is somebody who knows your overall situation, goals, and plan. They're not just selling you insurance. They have a full scope of how you're going to build wealth in the long run. You need to arrange to have a full insurance needs analysis and quote done. It costs you nothing to apply except your time. And it can provide you with valuable information that will help you budget and plan.

And as a side note: please give a little extra love to the people in your life and community who *do* say "Would you like fries with that?" Those jobs get a snub sometimes, and they are really important jobs, especially to those of us who love fries. If you are currently working a job in fast food and getting the hell out of debt, I am giving you a standing ovation right now. Please put this book down for a moment and take a bow.

OH YEAH. SINCE WE ARE ON THE TOPIC OF DEATH AND ALL…

Next, I want you to update your power of attorney or personal directives.

Most people don't like to think about doing their will, but you're going to have to do that if you really care about the people you say you care about.

You want to make your transition as burden free as possible on the people you love.

You're also going to create a document that lists everything your executor or spouse would need to know when you bite the dust.

This makes it as easy as possible for your power of attorney, or next of kin, or executor. You're going to keep it in a very safe place. You can store it digitally as well. You don't have to send it to anybody today, but just make sure somebody that you trust and love knows where to find it if something were to happen to you. Make sure to protect your privacy and safeguard all of your account numbers, but make it accessible so that if something does happen, somebody doesn't have to solve a mystery to figure out where everything is. You can even type all of this information digitally into your net worth spreadsheet so it's all in one place. Just make sure you keep it password protected.

Legacy Letters

Lastly, I want you to think about all of the things you want the people in your life to know when you pass. If you have children: what do you want them to know about who they are and how much you loved them? Maybe the day of your passing, you aren't able to speak, or maybe you have a fight with somebody you love and then something tragic happens. Leaving a legacy letter allows them to truly hold onto your love. I know this is sad and you're not going to *want* to do this, but it is really an important lesson as part of the overall Get the Hell Out of Debt program because it forces you to really remember what it is you're living for.

Try and keep the list as short as possible for now, so you don't overwhelm yourself into doing nothing. Five to six core people is plenty. (Unless you have seven kids, then do seven of course!) If you are having trouble cutting the list down, keep it to your spouse, if applicable, and your children.

If there are older people in your life, you can write those people letters and give them to them now. You know. Because, odds.

And also, because too many of us have things left unsaid: I still think legacy letters are a crucial part of your estate planning, but I also don't want you to have to leave this planet before people learn what they mean to you.

The purpose of a legacy letter is to give them *your words* to hold on to in their time of grief. They are meant to be encouraging, uplifting, and full of *unconditional love*. (Not "Mommy is watching you from heaven, so you better clean your room!")

You'll put each letter in its own envelope, addressed to the recipient on the front. Make each letter individual and unique and meaningful. The words you know *they* need to hear after you depart. You can include photos and sentimental items if you choose, but if there is anything of material value stated in the letter, be sure it is also documented in the will so your peeps don't run into a legal issue.

Here are some sample phrases to help you. You can keep the letters short and sweet if you prefer. The most important thing is you get them done. Please use your own words. But if you are stuck, steal a sentence starter or two from this list:

> I am so proud of you for…
> Thank you for…
> I am so grateful for the time we…
> One of my favorite memories of us is…
> A few of the things I love about you include…
> You blessed my life by…
> I could not have asked for a better…
> You were the greatest joy in my life because…
> I love you unconditionally and…
> I'm deeply appreciative of…
> Here are five things I've always loved about you…
> Here are five things I've always admired
> and respected about you…
> Here are three memories of us that make me laugh…
> Here are three memories of you that warm my heart…

In case you ever doubt yourself, here's a list of all the amazing characteristics you have…

Here's a sample legacy letter:

I love you wholly and completely for who you are. I am so grateful that I got to spend my time on earth with you. There is nothing about you or my experience of you that I would have changed. If I could do one thing over, I would go back to some of my favorite moments in time, and pay closer attention, stay more present, so I could soak up your awesomeness a little longer. But I have carried them in my heart every day just the same. My wish for you would be that you would use your unique talents and gifts without reservation. Some of the talents and gifts I've noticed you have are: (you'd fill this in here, obvs.)

But at the end of the day, this life is yours to live, and you know you best. I trust that you will always trust that.

I love you.

I'm grateful for you.

I am with you.

I am telling you: this work is *just as important as the will*, in my mind. You aren't going to hear that from a lawyer of course because they are focused on the legal stuff and making sure your loved ones are resentful as hell for cleaning up your money stuff so they can bill more by the hour.

Kidding.

(Kind of.)

And I want you to get the will done. *Get the will done.* But make sure these letters are included with it.

Now, if you cannot afford a will today and you are in the online Get the Hell Out of Debt program, I have a draft template you can access. It's better than nothing. It may or may not hold up in court, so you've really got to look into what is appropriate in your area, but it at least gets your brain organizing your life. Set yourself a goal to get all of this done in the next four or five days. And then you can breathe deeply and focus on paying off debt and building financial freedom so that you can truly live the life you want to live while you're blessed to be here.

Homework:

Because I am not done with the most morbid chapter of all time…you need to make a paper tombstone.

This is a giant envelope or small box that has everything in it someone needs when you perish. You'll need to keep it locked up safe somewhere like in a fireproof safe or a safety deposit box or in the box of dehydrated kale in the pantry because no one will ever look there.

Inside it you will have the following:

- Insurance documents
- Personal directives documents
- Your will (or your draft documents at least!)
- Your legacy letters
- Anything else you feel will make your survivors feel loved and cared for while taking work off their shoulders while they grieve
- The name of anyone you know who can launch flaming arrows at my husband's funeral pyre. Kthanx.

> Trisha M says: "Geez Erin, I was crying by the end of this one. Legacy love letters, what a beautiful idea but just the thought of it has me bawling. I am going to have a box of tissue by my side when I do those."

Chapter Twenty-Eight

FINANCIAL FREEDOM

Have you thought about what financial freedom means to you? When I ask people what financial freedom means, they often give me very abstract but beautiful answers.

"It means I can take my kids on a trip around the world."

"It means I can buy my dream home with cash."

"It means I can spend as much time as I want marching for the causes I believe in."

"It means I can retire my parents."

These are all such beautiful daydreams. And I want you to continue to dream. But I want you to have a clear understanding of how it is you are going to get there.

Deep breath. Are you ready?

You will be financially free when your passive income exceeds your expenses.

Did you catch that?

You will be financially free when your passive income exceeds your expenses.

Active Income is the income you earn from a job. It requires you to trade time for money. You give your time and you earn a paycheck or salary.

Commissions are also active income. Although you are not always being paid for the time you put in when it comes to commissions, sometimes you are paid for the results you get…you still have to actively earn that income.

Passive Income is ongoing certain money you earn without having to actively trade time for it. It's money you earn while you are sitting in a hammock drinking lemonade. It's money you earn when you sleep. It most often comes from investments you have—truly cash-flowing assets like we talked about earlier. Things that put money in your pocket.

Residual income, ongoing money you earn for work you previously did is a form of passive income. Rental income can be a form of passive income. Dividends can be a form of passive income.

You will be financially free when your passive income exceeds your expenses.

Here's what you do to know your financial freedom number:

You look at your budget and check out your monthly expenses column. What is the total of your monthly expenses?

Remember our pretend pal, Peggy? Her monthly expenses were $2096.30. Once she has her debt paid off, her monthly expenses drop by $350 to $1746.30

That means that Peggy needs to earn $1747.30 in passive income in order to quit her job and spend her days reading library books and sipping chai lattes. If Peggy decides to take up trumpet lessons for $100/month then she needs $1847.30 in passive income in order to be financially free.

If she knows she has $800/month coming in pension dollars when she retires, that means she now only has to create $1047.30 in passive income to be financially free.

Here's the point in telling you all this: it is often less than you think it is. Provided you can budget like a pro, you can often see and understand your retirement better than just winging it. I recognize the budget examples I gave you in this book in no way reflect real life; these are kept simple to help this book maintain its readability. The point is that you are more in control of your finances and retirement than you know.

I was on the phone with my friend Jackie this week. She's intelligent, social, and a true leader to so many women. She's one of those people you instantly love. Jackie is part of a home-based business that sells shampoo and hair care products. She said, "I don't really earn that much from it, about $1250 a month." I nearly spit out my tea. I asked her what she was doing with that money, and she said, "Nothing much, it just sits in the account in case there is a good sale on product and then I use it."

I quickly punched $1250/month into my compound interest calculator and spoke to her in my all-caps voice. "Jackie. Do you realize if you start investing that money *consistently,* and you learn proper investment strategies, and you and your hubs do not spend a cent of your shampoo money that in twenty-five years with a moderate eight percent rate of return, you will have over one-point-two million dollars in the bank?"

Her hair would have stood straight up if she wasn't using product. And the $1.2 million is assuming she doesn't grow her team, but simply maintains the current size of it. She's young. She has time. She loves her company and the people in it. She has the ability to be creating residual income, but she had no idea the power she had in her hands. (Hair?) $1250 isn't enough for Jackie to retire on right now. But handled appropriately and with intention, it has the power to change her family's lives.

A few years ago, Pamie took the Get the Hell Out of Debt course. I adore Pamie. She is funny, smart, extremely fun to be around, and she is the kindest human. She made hard decisions while doing her debt paydown and drove a rust bucket of a vehicle for a while. She saved for major purchases (like her gorgeous mountain wedding!) and paid cash. And then when she got the hell out of debt, she kept going. I showed her how to create passive income streams in the home-sharing/hospitality industry and she accumulated about ten apartments. She started cleaning the first couple herself to save money. Then she realized what it was costing her in time, and she paid a cleaner. Then when she realized what it was costing her to have them cleaned, she started a cleaning company to clean her short-term rentals and contract out to others. In just over a year, she was managing all the properties from an app on her phone from her house, and she created almost $50,000 in gross passive income.

Once she paid her expenses, she was very much cash positive and earns more in a year from her home-sharing business than most people do in a part-time job. Except Pamie is not trading 1,040 hours per year for that part-time income. She's systemizing her income to be passive: creating a check-in-check-out system for guests that doesn't require her to be there. She's focused on creating a phenomenal guest experience with a system that she manages a few minutes a day on her phone. I would have called this chapter "passive income whilst you're in the loo," but Pamie is too graceful and proper and professional for that.

If Pamie keeps going, by my math and estimations, she will be financially free in her early forties. And her retirement and passive income will allow for luxury travel and dinners out and fun adventures with friends and her hubby. And most importantly, supporting Kamva and Lili, two friends in South Africa. Every year Pamie raises money for their schooling so they can continue to receive the best education available to them. And I know this matters to you, dear reader, because your purchase of this book helped provide financial education to people in need. At the end of the day, becoming financially free isn't only about money freedom. It's also about creating the time freedom you need to contribute to the causes and people that matter most to *your* heart.

When you are in Phase Three, if you stay focused on growing your assets and staying away from liabilities, you can make your dream life happen so much faster than if you leverage yourself back into debt to try and get there.

> Kendall says: "Thank you for teaching me to be an adultier adult with this knowledge!"

Chapter Twenty-Nine

YOUR LEGACY OF LOVE

I just want you to take a moment and honor the person you were when you first picked up this book. That's a pretty brave thing to do. It required both courage and vulnerability and openness to the possibility that you might still have something to learn. You arrived at this point in your life with accomplishments, failures, love, and pain, and your debt-free wealthy life is also going to contain accomplishments and failures, love and pain. It's not going to be perfect. But you are no longer the person you were. You've grown your capacity to feel, to show up, to love, to play fully. And when you live your life, you will always have two choices: love or fear.

Every decision you make going forward comes down to these two things. Every action you take comes down to these two things. I already know what you're going to choose. You're going to choose love.

I know this because if you have read every word in this book, it means that you chose you. You made a commitment to you, and you followed through. And love is more powerful than fear.

When you engage with your family or friends, old patterns and old fears might creep in. You might be tempted to "should" on the people you care about. You might feel momentarily tempted to help coach them unsolicited or fly across a table and slap their credit cards out of their hands at dinner.

But you won't. You won't jump in with a bunch of suggestions or blurt out what they need to fix. You see them as perfectly beautiful, imperfect, messy, wonderful humans, just like you. And you love them wholly and completely for who they are.

You would rather stay present and listen to them share their views on the world, hold space for them, and love them than tell them how to improve or why they are wrong, or judge them for collecting credit card points. In fact, you've released the need altogether to try and control or change any circumstances because you are at peace. You live a calm, peaceful life, and sure things can get stressful and busy and schedules can get out of control sometimes. But deep down you have inner peace.

And the people who matter most to you are the ones that you save your energy for. You are able to stay in your own lane and allow those you love to have their experiences too. You no longer find it frustrating when those you love have a different opinion than you. You now recognize that their opinions are shaped by their experiences, their fears, their insecurities. And so, you meet them always with love.

Love is the only transformative power there is. You now know that discipline and control and quick math and consolidation will not get you the results you want, but doing consistent daily action with love will.

You find the humor in situations and circumstances. You know that every moment is a blessing. You know that while you're creating a compelling future, the only moment you truly have is now. Throughout this book, you let go of negative thoughts and negative patterns, and you are prepared to be tested. You know that sometimes these things will crop up again, but now you're going to see them just as that: a test or an obstacle to overcome.

You'll simply acknowledge a challenge when it shows up, thank it for the information it brings you, and let it go.

You know that all you need to do to change your pattern is make a different decision, and then reinforce that decision. There are going to be some challenges as you set some new boundaries. In order to feel truly competent and truly happy and keep your word to yourself, you're going to have to choose yourself before others.

This doesn't mean you will ignore people or behave selfishly. It simply means that now you fully understand that someone else's happiness is not more important than your own. You now understand that by avoiding hurting other people, sometimes it means you were hurting yourself and you've forgiven yourself for this. You have forgiven others for this, but now it's time to be who you are created to be. Show up for you so that you can more powerfully and beautifully and peacefully show up for others without the burden of financial difficulty, without the burden of debt, without the heavy weight of fees and monthly payments and being uncertain about retirement.

You understand that power has nothing to do with control over others and everything to do with mastery over yourself. You are a master at keeping promises to yourself. You are ready: ready to live financially free, ready to love and be loved. Take a moment now and decide in advance how you feel about your finances this coming week. Decide in advance how you will show up to your money this week. Decide in advance and clearly see in your mind that your net worth is increasing right now. You are proactively engaged in life. You lean in; you do not react to life. You are life. You recognize that life is not happening *to* you. It is happening *for* you.

Take a moment again and decide in advance how you will greet your friends, your family, your coworkers, and your community this week. You are ready to take care of yourself and go after your dreams. You deserve the life you dream of. You are capable of it because you first created it in your mind. Take a moment and think about the moments you're most grateful for regarding your money. This month, maybe you learned something in a new way. Maybe you have a partner who is lovingly supporting your goals. Maybe someone you know introduced you to this book because they, too, believe in you. Take a moment, breathe deep. And imagine that you're sending that person some love.

And when you're ready to close this book, carry that peace, love, presence, and gratitude with you as you go.

Glossary

Annuities: a guaranteed paycheck every month that you purchase with your own retirement savings. This allows you to have cashflow every month, but you still need to be a master budgeter in your old age to make this work.

ATO: Australia's revenue service (the people who collect your income taxes) are called the ATO, which stands for Australian Taxation Office.

Bujo: this is nerd-speak for bullet journal. You will find all kinds of journaling inspiration if you search the hashtag #bujo on social media.

CD or Certificate of Deposit (USA): you give the bank some money, and they guarantee to give it back plus a wee bit of interest. You do this if you are an uncertain investor or you cannot afford to lose any money. You do not do this if you are hoping to get rich.

Classes of Experiences: this is how we look at our behaviors and habits to see what is out of alignment, or what is in alignment, with our beliefs. This concept originated with Tony Robbins.

Consumer Proposal: a method of managing insolvency in some parts of the world when there is no way your current income will meet your obligations.

CVV: the code on the back of your credit card that is there for security purposes. Mine was once 666. Eeeesh.

ETFs or Exchange Traded Funds: this is an investment fund, but it's traded on the stock market like individual stocks or shares of a company. ETFs are not typically managed by living breathing humans the same way that mutual funds are (computers often do the work) so they usually come with lower fees to the investor.

Executor: the worst job on the planet. Ugh. (For most of us!) This refers to the person who is designated to carry out a dead person's wishes after they die. It usually involves a lot of paperwork and a lot of hassle. That's why I want you to make your executor's job easy. No one likes a dead arsehole.

401(k): in the USA, this is an employer-sponsored retirement account. You put a percentage of your salary (before tax) into a retirement account and because it's designated as a 401(k) you don't pay income tax on the investments (stocks, bonds, mutual funds, etc.) until you withdraw them when you are old and wrinkly.

403(b): in the USA, this is a retirement plan for certain employees of public schools, some hospitals, or non-profit organizations. The major difference between a 403(b) and a 401(k) is that the 403(b) plans are for not-for-profit organizations while the 401(k) plans are for people who work in the for-profit sector. We don't go into detail in the book about these, but you would put them in your green column under registered investments if you had a 403(b).

GIC or Guaranteed Investment Certificate: this is a Canadian version of a term deposit. It's a glorified savings account where you can earn interest for lending the bank your money. They turn around and use your money to make lots of money, but they give you a wee piddle-bit back. The money is often locked in, meaning you can't withdraw it until the term is up or perhaps there will be a penalty if you can. Be sure to get all the fine print from your financial institution before you invest in a GIC. You wouldn't invest this money to get rich, but you would invest it in a GIC if you wanted to avoid spending it or to keep the money fairly safe.

ISA or Individual Savings Account (UK): a tax efficient way to save and invest. Any investments you hold in your ISA that grow or earn interest are not taxed. Check your personal limit as the amount you can hold in an ISA is restricted. (But max that sucker out, friend!)

High-Interest Savings Account: it is kind of a slap in the face when the bank says they will pay you 2 percent interest on your money and they call it a 'high-interest' savings account. Perhaps a better name would be "higher-interest savings account" because it's better than the 0 percent you typically earn when your money is sitting in a regular bank account.

HMRC: this is the UK's tax, payment, and customs authority. It stands for "Her Majesty's Revenue and Customs," which I cannot help saying in a very terrible British accent, for which I ought to apologize.

Insolvent/Insolvency: when you've taken on more debt than you can possibly ever pay, we say you are insolvent. There's a formal proceeding to relieve you of this debt that is mandated by your government. If you are insolvent, you will still need to learn all the things in the *Get the Hell Out of Debt* book or program to ensure you stay the hell out of debt! In most areas, your insolvency becomes searchable on public databases so potential lenders can look this up, but so can your neighbors.

Individual Insolvency Register: this is the permanent searchable database where your name will appear if you have ever become insolvent in England or Wales.

IRA: this is an "Individual Retirement Account" in the USA. It's a personal account that you open at a financial institution to save for retirement. There are a bunch of different IRAs...and here is the gist:

Traditional IRA: these are taxed similar to 401(k)s meaning you put money in the investment (but not through your employer, you do this yourself) and you pay tax at the time of withdrawal when you are retired.

ROTH IRA: this is a retirement account that you contribute "after tax" dollars to, or money you've already paid tax on, and you are not taxed any further on it. So when your money mates and spawns new money, you don't have to pay extra tax on those new money babies.

SEP IRA: this means "simplified employee pension," and it's set up by employers for their employees. This can be set up as a sole proprietor, partnership or corporation, so talk to your accountant if you own your own business.

Self-directed IRA: this is designed for sophisticated investors who want to invest in non-traditional investments; for example, you can hold real estate in your Self-Directed IRA.

SIMPLE IRA: SIMPLE stands for Savings Incentive Match PLan for Employees (seriously what is it with Americans and acronyms). This is similar to a 401(k) and it's tax-deferred, meaning you pay income tax on that money when you withdraw it. This is typically for small businesses with less than one hundred employees.

Spousal IRA: if you file a joint tax return and one of you earns significantly less than the other (or earns no income), then the non-or-low-income earner can use this account for retirement, and either spouse can contribute.

Non-deductible IRA: contributions are made with after-tax dollars, but they are not deductible. But, the good news is, you are not taxed on the growth. You would likely have one of these if you exceeded the income limits in your other retirement plans.

As with anything, please review all the current guidelines in your area and for your specific financial circumstances and consider hiring a local professional before making any decisions.

Line of credit (secured): this is a loan against what a bank considers to be an asset. Something that they could essentially sell off to pay the loan off if you defaulted. Like a car, or a house. Secured lines of credit or loans usually have a lower interest rate because the lender considers them less risky because of the collateral.

Line of credit (unsecured): this is a loan that is not "secured" against an asset; most often it's a credit card or a general loan where the bank can't sell something of yours to pay off what you owe them. (They aren't going to come into your house to sell the Sephora purchases you made on your credit card if you default on your payment, but with a secured loan, they might repossess the car to pay off the car loan.) Unsecured loans or lines of credit typically have a higher interest rate than secured lines of credit or secured loans.

Mutual funds: are groups of stocks or bonds or other investments. Think of them like a mix tape of investments that diversify your risk. Mutual funds usually have higher fees so be sure to understand the cost of investing in them.

Next-of-kin: this refers to a person's closest living relatives. In some countries, this is defined by the legal system and must be a blood relative.

Non-registered money/funds: these are investments that are entirely taxable and there is no tax-deferred or tax-free/sheltered status by the government. The good news is that in some jurisdictions, these are taxed favorably compared to income, and you're usually only taxed on the growth portion of the investment when you make withdrawals, not on the whole dollar (the portion you put in), as you typically are with some registered investments.

NPII or National Personal Insolvency Index: the NPII is a searchable database that details insolvency proceedings in Australia, including bankruptcy. This is where your name and deets will appear on public record if you've ever been insolvent.

Options: when referring to stocks, this gives the buyer the right to purchase something at a specific price by a specific date. It's a contract of sorts, and it is a security, and the contract itself is the investment.

Phase One: the foundations of money management and understanding the flow of cash in and out of your life.

Phase Two: creating a structure to pay off your debt and manage the flow of cash in and out of your life.

Phase Three: using the principals and skills you've practiced to continue managing the flow of cash in and out of your life. You'll take the money you were using to pay down debt and apply (most of) it to buying assets.

Power of attorney: the legal authority to act on behalf of someone else when it comes to personal, business, legal, or financial matters.

Quick and Dirty: this is the equivalent of one paycheck that lives in your Safe Zone (no-fee) Account. This money is to be "found" money wherever possible so as to not disrupt the budget but must be accumulated quickly so you can get back to paying off debt.

Registered money/funds: a registered account is an investment account given tax-deferred or tax-free/sheltered status by the government.

Roth: everyone asks, "Why are these investment accounts called Roth?" and the answer is not very romantic. A dude named William Roth was a senator from Delaware who led the creation and implementation of retirement accounts for all Americans, not just the wealthy ones, and so these accounts were named after him. As a side note, he seems like one of the few senators who lived and died without a major scandal to his name, so maybe the fact that he didn't send unsolicited dick pics to underage women and remained married to his wife for nearly forty years is romantic after all.

Safe Zone: this is the nickname I give an account that has no fees and that is primarily used to hold cash reserves you've accumulated for emergencies. It needs to be at an institution you don't typically bank with so that it is not too easy to access.

Second or third mortgages: I see you. You likely got these as a way to consolidate debt, or pay for an expense that you couldn't afford, but you were maxed out on other options. These are mortgages that are on top of your existing mortgage, and usually at a higher interest rate because they are higher risk to the lender. I want you to tackle these in Phase Two.

Stock: a company is divided into shares, and individuals like you and I are allowed to purchase these shares when the company is publicly traded. In North America, we often refer to these as "stocks."

Superannuation/Super: superannuation is designed to help Australians become self-sufficient when they retire, and it is sometimes referred to as a "Super." You can supplement compulsory superannuation contributions with voluntary contributions, even by diverting your wages or salary income into your investment, and the tax is not payable until retirement or withdrawal.

Tax-deferred growth: this refers to accounts that are registered with your government that allow you to invest and grow money, but not pay tax on the growth of the money you've invested. For example, a 401(k) in the US, an RRSP in Canada, and a superannuation in Australia.

Tax-free growth: this refers to accounts that are registered with your government that allow you to invest and grow money but not pay tax on the growth of the money you've invested. Examples include the TFSA (tax-free savings account) in Canada, some IRAs in the USA, and an ISA in the UK.

Term deposit: you give the bank some money for a contracted amount of time where you will not access it, and they give you a bit of interest for the privilege of turning around and spending your money while you aren't looking. They'll give it back to you at the end of the term, but not after they've made a bunch more interest on it than they are sharing with you.

Traditional 401(k): this is an employer sponsored plan in the USA where the employee generally picks the investments, but the plan is administered by the employer. The contributions and the growth on the investment is not taxed until it is withdrawn. Some employers offer a "match" as a benefit to their employees, which means the employer also contributes to the employee's retirement.

TFSA or Tax-Free Savings Account: this is an account in Canada that allows your investments to grow tax-free. You will have paid income tax already when you deposit the money you've earned, but you won't have to pay more income tax on the growth of this money when it makes money bunnies.

Trade lines: this is in reference to your credit report. Every debt you've had forms a "tradeline" that is tracked with your credit bureau and helps to form a score.

Recommended Reading

W. Brett Wilson, *Redefining Success: Still Making Mistakes*

This book is absolutely critical reading so you can clearly define success on your own terms. You'll be inspired to radically improve your financial circumstances, not only so you can get the hell out of debt, but then make meaningful contributions in the world that will leave a legacy for the people and causes that matter to you. Brett is one of the most authentic humans I have ever met, and regardless of your politics, your religion, or your personal views, there is no denying that he has and will continue to positively impact millions of lives every day through his financial generosity.

Peter Mallouk and Tony Robbins, *The Path: Accelerating Your Journey to Financial Freedom*

When you have mastered the basics of money management in this book, you'll be ready to tackle investing. You must start with the practical and tactical strategies that Peter Mallouk so brilliantly outlines in *The Path.* He's also written a number of other bestsellers, including *The 5 Mistakes Every Investor Makes and How to Avoid Them* and *Unshakeable, Your Financial Freedom Playbook.*

Tony Robbins, *Awaken the Giant Within*

This is not exactly a financial book, and it was written decades ago, but it stands. I was a young pup, living and working in London and in the middle of a tube strike, popped into WHSmith to find something to pass the time. This book radically and instantly changed the trajectory of my life. If you would have told me back then that one day I'd be working with and for the author I would have had an accident right there in the London Underground. If you have ever met a life coach, a motivational speaker, a successful business owner, a non-fiction author or a highly developed human, they have either directly or indirectly been influenced by Anthony Robbins' work, so you might as well go directly to the source. Read this book, and come to a live event like UPW (Unleash the Power Within).

Jamie Kern Lima, *Believe IT: How to go from Underestimated to Unstoppable*

Often when you hear about people with massive success, you get a highlight reel of their lives. Jamie Kern Lima takes you behind all the layers of being a self-made entrepreneur, philanthropist, keynote speaker, and co-founder of IT Cosmetics and bares her soul in this book so you can truly see the inner work she did when things were hard. You won't be able to put this book down so make sure you have tissues and water handy to help with all the laughing and crying you'll do. Buy two copies and give one to a friend so you can be fearless squirrels together! In addition to being an incredible author, Jamie is a champion of women, and a believer in all things possible, and you'll fall in love with her by the end of Chapter One.

Jesse Mecham, *You Need A Budget*

This book is a deep dive into budgeting with really practical strategies for living (including how to teach your children about budgeting!) Jesse and his wife Julie navigated financial uncertainty and everything they did in order to find huge success is in this book. Jesse is the founder of the app I recommend which is YNAB (pronounced "Why-Nab") which is by far the best budgeting app on the planet.

OTHER GREAT BOOKS TO EXPAND YOUR MONEY OR MINDSET:

Brendon Burchard, *High Performance Habits*

Bola Sokunbi, *Clever Girl Finance: Learn How Investing Works, Grow Your Money*

Dallas Hartwig, *The 4 Season Solution*

Danielle Town, *Invested*

Darren Hardy, *The Compound Effect*

David Bach, *Smart Women Finish Rich*

Gary John Bishop, *Unfu*k Yourself*

Glennon Doyle, *Untamed*

James Clear, *Atomic Habits*

Jen Hatmaker, *Fierce, Free, and Full of Fire: The Guide to Being Glorious You*

Jesse Itzler, *Living with a SEAL*

Mel Robbins, *The 5 Second Rule*

Phil Town, *Rule #1* and *Payback Time*

Order of Operations For Paying Off Debt

PHASE ONE

- Commit to ten minutes a day of self-study, learning, doing your money work.
- Commit to thirty minutes a day of exercise. This is crucial for your long-term financial wellness.
- Complete your net worth calculations and commit to updating your net worth as a new habit.
- Complete your budget and commit to updating it as a habit.
- Open a Safe Zone Account.
- Gather your Quick and Dirty and deposit it in the Safe Zone.
- Commit to not using credit while you complete the phases—especially Phases One and Two!
- All of these need to be complete before you go on to Phase Two. If you are in Phase Two and one of the above becomes undone, pause Phase Two and return to Phase One to ensure all your boxes are re-checked, then continue forward to Phase Two.

PHASE TWO

- Choose your debt payoff method.
  - Highest interest rate
  - Smallest balance
  - Highest payment
  - Emotional mastery/spicy method

    - Make a list of the order you will pay your debts off.
    - Add the minimum payments to your budget if they are not there yet.
    - Now focus solely on the debt at the top of your list. Pay it down until it is annihilated completely. Then go to your second debt. And so on.
    - While you are working on that, make a list of your Class Two experiences and commit to doing them regularly in spite of how you feel.
    - Squeeze extra money out of your budget and where possible, produce extra income to throw on the debt you are currently annihilating.
    - Create and master your financial boundaries while you pay off debt.
    - As you pay off debt, have a debt completion ceremony.
    - Make a list of your directional activities and supporting activities to keep you focused to avoid debt burnout.

PHASE THREE

- Create your new identity around living a debt-free life.
- Your Safe Zone now becomes your new credit card—your emergency fund. Fill it up using the same strategies you used in Phase Two.
- Once that's full, begin investing using the same budget and squeeze strategy you used to pay off debt, except you will now start building your investments. You focus just as you did before. You allocate the funds you were putting toward debt on investing (and paying down the mortgage, if that's a goal of yours), and continue to update your net worth frequently to stay on track and monitor your wealth-building progress.

Acknowledgments

This book would not be possible without the people who showed up for a class or event and gave themselves fully to the process I teach. For being a steadfast and tireless volunteer. For arriving early and staying late. For committing to a should-less life. For participating. For telling your friends. For sharing the messages of transformation and freedom on social media. For coaching others to excellence. But most of all, for giving me the most precious gift a human can give another human: your time.

Aaron, Adam, Adele, Agata, Agatha, Agnieszka, Alaura, Alba, Albina, Aleasha, Alec, Alex, Alexandra, Alexia, Alexis, Alisha, Alison, Allison, Allissa, Allyson, Alycia, Alyssa, Amanda, Amber, Amélie, Amy, Ana, Anada, Ana Maria, Anastasia, Andrea, Andrew, Angela, Angelo, Angie, Anita, Anna, Annalisa, Annette, Anne, Annie, Athena, Anthony, Arlene, Art, Artur, Ashlee, Ashleigh, Ashley, Ashly, Avery, Bailey, Bani, Barb, Barbara, Beate, Becky, Benita, Berna Lee, Bethany, Beverly, Biana, Billie Rae, Blair, Blanche, Bobby-Jo, Boni, Bonnie, Brad, Brandie, Brandi-Lee, Brandon, Brenda, Brett, Brent, Brieanne, Brigette, Brittney, Bronwyn, Bryce, Bryna, Brynna, Caitlyn, Camille, Cara, Caran, Carey, Carla, Carley, Carmen, Carol, Carole, Carole-Anne, Carolina, Carolyn, Carrie, Carrie-Lynn, Cassandra, Cassidy, Cate, Catherine, Cathleen, Cathy, Cecelia, Celeste, Celina, Chad, Chanelle, Chantel, Charlene, Charmaine, Chase, Chella, Chelsea, Chelsey, Chelsi, Cherie, Cheryl, Chloe, Chris, Chrissy, Christa, Christie, Christina,

Christine, Christoph, Christopher, Christy, Cindy, Claire, Colin, Colleen, Connie, Cordelia, Corie, Corinna, Courtney, Craig, Cristie, Cristian, Crystal, Curtis, Cyndi, Cyndy, Cynthia, Czarlyn, Dale, Dallas, Dan, Dana, Danelle, Danica, Daniel, Daniella, Danielle, Dara, Dara-Lee, Darci, Darcie, Dare, Darko, Darlene, Darrell, Darren, Darylann, Dave, David, Dawn, David, Deanna, Deanne, Deb, Debbi, Debbie, Debbra, Deborah, Dennel, Dennis, Derek, Desiree, Destiny, Deveney, Diane, Dianna, Dianne, Dionne, Don, Dónal, Donna, Donny, Dorothy, Drew, Dustin, Elanda, Elena, Elesa, Elise, Eliza, Elizabeth, Ellen, Ellie, Emile, Emily, Eric, Erich, Erica, Erika, Erin, Erinn, Erynn, Eve, Farrah, Faye, Fillitse, Francesca, Furkhan, Gabriela, Gabriella, Gary, Gemma, George, Georgette, Gerald, Geraldine, Germaline, Gerri, Gina, Glen, Gloria, Gordon, Grace, Grant, Greg, Gregory, Greta, Guriqbal, Gurmeet, Hadija, Halle Bee, Harmony, Haylie, Haz, Hazel, Heather, Heidi, Helen, Hèlène, Holly, Huy, Ian, Ida, Ilona, Ingrid, Irene, Irlene, Isadora, Jacinda, Jack, Jackie, Jaclyn, Jacqueline, Jacquelyn, Jacquie, Jade, Jaime, Jaimy, Jaleesa, James, Jami, Jamie, Jan, Janel, Janelle, Janessa, Janet, Janice, Janine, Janna, Jarad, Jared, Jas, Jason, Jayme, Jean, Jeanette, Jeanine, Jeff, Jen, Jenn, Jenna, Jennifer, Jennine, Jenny, Jeremy, Jesse, Jessica, Jessie, Jill, Jillian, Jim, Jina, Jo-Ann, Joanne, Jocelynne, Jodi, Jody, Joel, Johnson, Jolene, Jon, Jonathan, Joni, Jordan, Josh, Joshua, Josie, Joy, JP, Juanita, Julia, Julian, Julie, Julieann, Julie Ann, Justin, Kaajal, Kacey, Kaila, Kaitlyn, Kara, Karen, Kari, Karla, Karlen, Karlene, Karly, Karrie-Anne, Karyn, Kasia, Kassondra, Katarina, Kate, Katherine, Kathleen, Kathryn, Kathy, Katie, Katrein, Katrina, Kattie, Kayla, Keely, Kelley, Kelly, Kelsey, Kelsy, Ken, Kendall, Kenddy, Kendra, Kenna, Kennedy, Keri, Kerri, Kerri Ann, KerriRae, Kerry, Kevin, Kiara, Kim, Kimber, Kimberley, Kimberly, Kirsten, Kit, Korina, Kris, Krista, Kristeen, Kristen, Kristi, Kristin, Kristine, Kristy, Krystle, Kyla, Kyle, Kyra, Lacey, Lana, Lance, Lara, Launa, Laura, Lauralyn, Lauree, Lauren, Laurel, Laurie, Lea, Leah, Leanna, Leanne, Lee, Lei, Leia, Leigh, Leila, Leslie, Levi, Lex, Lexi, Ley-Anne, Lily, Linda, Lindsay, Lindsey, Lindy, Lisa, Liz, Lonni, Lorelei, Loretta, Lori, Lorissa, Lorraine, Lou-Ann, Louise, Luke, Lynda,

Lyndell, Lynn, Mac, Machelle, Macy, Madison, Magdalena, Maggi, Maggie, Malcolm, Mandy, Manny, Marcy, Maren, Margaret, Margie, Margo, Maria, Mariana, Mariangela, Marie, Marie-Noel, Marilyn, Marina, Mark, Marla-Lee, Marle, Marlene, Marnie, Martha, Martin, Mary, Mary Beth, Mary-Jean, Mary-Sue, Marzena, Matt, Matthew, Meagan, Megan, Meghan, Meighan, Melanie, Melissa, Mellisha, Meredith, Micalah, Michael, Michele, Michelle, Mike, Mila, Minda, Miranda, Miriam, Mona, Monica, Monsy, Morag, Moreen, Morgan, Nadine, Nancy, Naomi, Natalie, Natasha, Nate, Nathan, Naticia, Navneet, Neena, Neil, Nick, Nicki, Nicole, Nivia, Nola, Noel, Noelle, Olga, Oluyomi, Owen, Pam, Pamela, Pamie, Pascale, Pat, Patricia, Patrick, Patty, Paul, Paula, Paulina, Pauline, Penny, Peter, Phil, Pieter, Poppy, Pouran, Priscilla, Rachel, Rachelle, Ramona, Randi, Randi-Lea, Ray, Rayline, Rebekah, Reg, Renee, Rhea, Rhoda, Richelle, Rick, Rita, Rob, Robert, Robin, Robyn, Rodolfo, Roger, Rory, Rosalie, Roxanna, Roxanne, Ruth, Ryan, Sabrina, Sadia, Salim, Samantha, Sammee, Sandi, Sandra, Sara, Sarah, Sasha, Sayla, Scott, Sea, Selina, Serena, Shalene, Shallen, Shandra, Shane, Shannon, Sharleen, Sharlyn, Sharon, Shawna, Shay, Shaylene, Sheebee, Sheel, Sheena, Sheila, Shelley, Shelley Mae, Shelly, Sheri, Sherri, Sherry, Sheryl, Sheryl-Ann, Shirley, Shona, Silvy, Simen, Stacey, Stacie, Stefanie, Stephanie, Steve, Stewart, Summer, Susan, Susanne, Suzanne, Sydney, Syrina, Tabitha, Tamara, Tami, Tammie-Lynn, Tammy, Tannelle, Tannis, Tanya, Tara, Tarra, Taryn, Tasmin, Tatiana, Taylor, Ted, Telesa, Tera, Teresa, Terri-Lynn, Terry, Theresa, Tiffany, Tim, Tina, Tish, Todd, Tomi, Toni, Torrie, Toy, Tova, Tracey, Tracie, Tracy, Tricia, Trish, Trisha, Troi, Twila, Tyler, Val, Valerey, Vanessa, Venesa, Vern, Veronica, Veronika, Veronique, Victoria, Vince, Vivian, Wade, Wanda, Wendy, Wesley, Yarina, Yegana, Yeshwanth, Yvette, Yvonne, and Zach.

To all the members of my one-on-one or group coaching programs, I love working with you. I love the fire and laughter and love you bring to everything you do. Thank you for giving me the encouragement to go after my goals as I cheer you on with yours. I celebrate you daily!

Allie Woodlee—the fine-tooth comb with which you went over this manuscript must have no teeth left! Thank you for your impeccable attention to detail. Thank you for your incredible feedback, and for leaving your editorial wisdom on every page. I still have no idea when to use "laying down" or "lying down," but every time I strain my brain thinking about it I do want to take a nap, so there's that.

To Anderson. It is such an honor being your mama. I love that you remember nearly everything, that you ask curious questions, that you believe the best in people, and that you fight for what's right. I hope you always continue to self-lead, because trusting yourself has never led you astray. You are a man of integrity, character, wisdom, and kindness. When things get hard, remember to unplug and spend time in nature…it makes your soul sing. Promise me you'll always update that net worth spreadsheet and stay away from the red column. I'm proud of all the things you do, but mostly I am proud of who you are. I love you.

Aidan. One of your greatest superpowers is your ability to navigate very complicated situations with simplicity and ease. I appreciate how your calm, kind presence shows up in leadership for you and for those you interact with. You make great decisions, bud. I hope you will forever continue to trust your own instincts and see the good in people even when they can't see it in themselves. In a world where it is so easy to be a critic, I love that you choose to be a source of encouragement. I loved you before I met you, but when I met you, I loved you beyond comprehension.

Art and Salim. I miss you and I wish you all the success in the world.

Avery. At times I want to protect you in a giant bubble because you are just too good for this world. You are one of the funniest young women I know but that is because you are deeply intellectual. Clever funny is the most brilliant kind of funny, and your creative designer brain does the most magical things with words and timing. It feels like the deepest honor to be involved in the very important job of creating the right-sized container to raise you: something big enough that will allow you to grow to your full potential and something small enough to keep you safe. I love you to pieces.

Coaches, Teachers, Experts—to all the coaches and financial experts out there teaching people to budget and providing all levels of money education and service, I honor and respect you. We only get so much time on this earth and the work you do from a place of integrity absolutely improves the quality of people's lives. Let's continue to work together to change the system. If I can be of service, let me know.

Debby Englander. I adored you from our very first phone call. You are the most efficient straight shooter in the business and I love your candor. Thank you for whole-heartedly honoring my request for sensitivity readers, and for providing me with the very best team. If this book has any impact in the world, it is because you took a chance on it.

Derek Loose. I am forever grateful you shared the first writing project with me. Thank you for being a role model friend who sets *big* goals and lives a beautiful life. I have admired your tenacity over the last decade; I know it wasn't always easy, but we grew the most wonderful possible outcomes out of a pile of someone else's compost. Thank you for your loyalty, your respect, your kindness, and your humor…and for sharing the first firewalk experience!

To God. Thank you for all of the obstacles and all of the grace. In all of the pain, I knew you were there. I don't often know what you think about this life of mine, but I know for sure that you do not want your people burdened by debt. Let my life be a love letter to you.

Gord Appel for being both eternally wise and full of more grace than my five-foot-one-and-three-quarters human body can handle.

Heather King. Thank you for your unwavering support and guidance. Thank you for your warm welcome, and always meeting me with kindness. Thank you for never saying "as per my last email" and making me feel like the most important author, even though you magically do that with each one of us. You have blessed this experience for me.

Jacqueline Kademian. There is no soul as positive as you. Your work breathes life, and the gift you give by your presence is legacy-making. I'm so grateful for where our lives have intersected and I am cheering you on as you continue to have beautiful impact.

Jenny McKinney for asking the right question ("What is the lesson in this?") on the day that twatwaffle with the shattitude was doing you-know-what backstage. Thank you for seeing the child and the hurt inside every human and for making everyone more beautiful and whole by your presence.

Jerde. I love you. There is a teal envelope taped to the underside of your bedside table. Follow the clues. Thank you for the countless hours you poured into this book all while writing *Of Dreams and Angels.* Thank you for your unwavering faith in me, and for loving the people I serve the way I love them: wholly and completely. I will love you until I die, Jared Morrison. (Or until you die, and then I will send you adrift on your flaming funeral pyre as Darth intended.)

Jeremy Goldberg. Thank you for reaching out for that first Zoom call that started what I am certain is a lifelong friendship. Doing this work is so much easier with friends in this space to laugh with, support, cheer on, and celebrate. Thank you for taking that brave risk all those years ago not to suck coral sperm through a straw and instead create long distance love bombs that change the world. I'm sure you would have excelled at marine biology, but the humans on the planet needed you more.

Jesse and Julie Mecham. Thank you for creating the very best budgeting app, YNAB. Thank you for making financial management accessible for so many and thank you for educating as you do.

Julie Gwinn and the Seymour Agency. Thank you for your expertise, your wisdom, and your guidance. How you've managed this year and all its challenges is a lesson to all of us in love and grace. I am so grateful for everything you have done for me, but mostly I am just grateful for who you are and how you show up. It's an honor to be represented by you.

Kiera Baron. Shorties unite! Thank you for treating these silly words with a reverence far beyond what they deserve. Your careful attention to proofreading shows that you love and respect my readers as I do, and that means the world to me.

Kelsey Grant. Thank you for using your voice. For words. For music. For blessing others with radical self-love and grace. If empowerment and spiciness was baked into a human cake-of-awesomeness, it would be your deliciousness that feeds the world. The way you've carried yourself through some tough times has inspired me through all of mine. Forever grateful to you, and for you.

Keri Blakeney. I am grateful every day that I've had you in my life for all these years. I barely remember what our friendship looked like in those early days before marriage and kids, but I know it involved insane amounts of alcohol and laughter, and it set the foundation for a lifelong friendship I still have no idea how I deserve. I'm so glad we kept the laughter. Thank you for being the kind of friend who remembers the details, who loves other people's children as fiercely as her own, who does the right thing even when no one is looking, who makes hospitality look easy because it comes straight from your beautiful heart, and who has the best damn laugh this side of heaven. You are the most funny, brilliant, creative, gorgeous, intelligent woman I have ever met, and I get better every day because of the example of awesomeness you set.

Lynn Hemming. (It feels weird not calling you Mrs. Hemming.) As my high school English teacher, you are probably just as surprised as I am that I turned out to be a writer. Thank you for encouraging us to journal, to express, to write "for fun." Thank you for reading our teenage nonsense and treating it as though it mattered. Whenever I see anyone playing with their dangly earrings, I think of you and say a silent prayer of thanks for my life's most important lesson: words have the power to heal, and words have the power to destroy. We each get to choose the words we use, and the words we surround ourselves with, and the words we give to others. Thank you for always choosing the life-giving ones.

Lily Miller for your brilliant edits and developmental guidance. Thanks to your tireless work, the sentence *"Other than your d*ck, what are you bringing to the party, bro?"* did not make it into the book. Whoops.

Marilyn Kirkby for producing the "Get the Hell Out of Debt" podcast. I loved you the minute I met you all those years ago when we worked in radio together, and I'm so grateful to be connected to someone as talented as you.

Mark Groves. I have tried many hours to write a simple sentence and I continue to fail. Thanks to Julie for introducing us long ago, but thanks to you for showing up. Consistently. With love. Thank you for Mark Grovesing, my friends, and my community. Thank you for doing your incredibly profound work in the world, even when it's hard. Especially when it's hard. You are one of the most important people in my life, and yet I love that I get to share you with millions of others, because the love you've created cannot be contained.

To my Master Trainers. *Thank you.* Thank you for being the kind of people who take action toward your dreams. Thank you for inspiring others to do the same. Thank you for believing in Transformation Weekend and training so hard to be able to teach it. Thank you for walking the walk and playing full out. I am cheering you on, always. I am here for you.

Mike. Thank you for being a most wonderful father and friend all these years. I appreciate every sacrifice you've made to create a loving, peaceful home.

Monica Schultz. Thank you for being a faithful friend all these years. I am so glad we met back when we were young and we thought we were less than awesome. We were wrong. I would give anything to go back in time and give those two young women a talking to.

Peter Mallouk. Your exemplary work has been an inspiration to me, not only because of the clear and concise way you educate people on financial matters but because you truly care. In a world that often preys on the financially vulnerable, you are a shining light of goodness and a beacon for financial transformation.

Post Hill Press, to my entire team: I do not have the words to adequately thank you. Special thanks to Devon Brown and Katie Reid for handling publicity, to my associate publisher Megan Wheeler, and to Anthony

Ziccardi for leading this exceptional team. The care and attention you put into this work shows up in every detail.

Rael Kalley for being awesome even though I am terrible at returning your phone calls. I love you to pieces.

Rob Kealy for producing my audiobooks and much of the audio in my online courses. Thank you for your guidance, your professionalism, and your clever wit. My favorite characteristic in a human is humor and I love that you take both everything seriously and nothing seriously. Grateful for you.

Sarah and Cait and Jade and Keri for supporting the people in our community while I was writing this book, and for being the kind of women who leave a trail of sunshine everywhere you go. Sarah, I only have inadequate words compared to the amount of love and respect I have for you and your genius brain. I will forever cheer you all on!

Silvy Khoucasian. You are probably the greatest listener on the planet. You hear the things that people don't even say! You are changing the world with your work and I am so honored I've shared space and time with you. Thank you for teaching the masses about the importance of boundaries and doing it in such a loving way.

Sonja and Les. Sometimes I forget to be excited about the little milestones until you bring your unbridled parental enthusiasm to the table. (And also your famous mashed potatoes to the table.) I am overcome with gratitude when I think about the timing with which you entered my life, and I'm tremendously thankful for the love, the recipes and the ongoing awesome fiction book recommendations. You are the best.

To all the amazing students through www.GetTheHellOutofDebt.com, and to the ones we have yet to meet: I'm so proud of you!

Taz Rajan and Shawn Stack and the entire team, thank you for doing the love-led work on the front lines of helping people rebuild their worth. The work you do goes far beyond the numbers, and I'm so proud to know you.

To Mr. and Mrs. Robbins for the opportunity to use all my life experiences for one massive heart-led mission. Working with you and for you, Tony, has been a dream come true. Working for you, Mrs. Robbins, has been a true honor and gift. I'm so grateful I accidentally picked up *Awaken the Giant Within* in the late '90s because it led to all the best miracles. What you imprinted on my heart through that book has impacted nearly every person I've met over the last twenty years. Thank you to Jonathan Cardozo for picking me out of you-know-where. To the entire RRI Live Events Team, it is an honor to serve alongside you. To Jessie and Emily for consistent commitment to CANI and for the random spontaneous eighteen-second dance parties. To all the Sr. Leaders and Trainers, thank you for pouring love and attention into every attendee. I can see your love from the riser. To the Crew, thank you for the unstoppable energy you bring and the way you continually step up. To Creative for your outstanding communication. To Tech for producing the most innovative events in the world and for sometimes letting me push the shiny buttons. Eberts, I will get you back. I love and respect you all. I picked up that book by accident in the late '90s, but it turns out there are no accidents.

W. Brett Wilson. Thank you for saying yes to strange talk-show topics and being willing to share your wisdom and opinions, even when they are polarizing. Thank you for leading by example when it comes to living generously. Thank you for consistently seeking out opportunities to make the world better: through discourse, through philanthropy, through both quiet acts of random kindness and loud bold gestures that encourage communities to do more, dig deeper, and work together. Thank you for including me in your world, and inspiring me to make mine better.

Weston. I am so grateful you burst into the world, and through every doorway like Kramer. You are my Wild West and my fun compass. I love that you live life to the highest standards, full of color and music and words. When things get hard, remember to give yourself grace. The very best parts of life are messy and imperfect, and even though I'm proud of you every day, you don't have to accomplish anything for me to feel that way. Promise me you'll keep on top of your numbers, not for me but for you, and that you'll always feel the way about debt as you did when you were four. You are a man of excellence, focus, determination, and thoughtfulness. I love you. Thank you for all that you do and all that you are.

You. The reader. Thank you for sticking with this book. One of the most common questions I get asked is, "Why is there a bike on the cover?" Frankly, it's because the awesome Cody Corcoran, my cover designer decided there ought to be. But I want you to think back to the first time you learned to ride a bike. Did you master it on the first try? If you are human, you probably had a few wipeouts or if you are anything like me, you banged your crotch on the bar and skinned your knees a few times before you got the hang of it. But once you started to pedal, you found total freedom. Getting out of debt might require a few crotch bangs along the way, but I promise you if you stick with it, you can be financially free. I'm proud of you for taking control of your life. I will forever be cheering you on.

About the Author

Photo by Nicole Dypolt

Erin Skye Kelly is an award-winning and bestselling author who has helped thousands of people pay off millions of dollars in consumer debt and ultimately change their lives.

In spite of her terrible stage fright and general Canadian awkwardness, she has shared the stage with legendary motivational speakers such as Tony Robbins, Phil Town, and Gary John Bishop.

She wrote *Get the Hell Out of Debt* after her own struggle to become free from consumer debt. She was tired of listening to middle-aged men in suits tell her to consolidate and refinance her debt when all that seemed to happen was she'd end up in more of it while they profited.

Her seminars and workshops are judgement-free zones made up of equal parts personal growth, rock concert, and love. She is hired to work with ordinary humans who want to achieve extraordinary things, and because of her track record helping people create a trajectory of success, the phrase she most often hears when people meet her for the first time is, "Wow. I thought you'd be taller."